Brakhage Scrapbook

Stan Brakhage

Collected Writings 1964-1980

Edited by Robert A. Haller

Documentext

Preparation and publication of this book have been assisted by grants from the National Endowment for the Arts, a federal agency; and the New York State Council on the Arts. Manufactured in the United States of America. First Edition.

Library of Congress Cataloging in Publication Data

Brakhage, Stan.
  Brakhage scrapbook.

  Filmography: p.
  Bibliography: p.
  Includes index.
  1. Moving-pictures—Philosophy—Collected works.
I. Haller, Robert A. II. Title.
PN 1995.B715   791.43'01   82-1960
ISBN 0-914232-46-0
ISBN 0-914232-47-9 (deluxe)
ISBN 0-914232-45-2 (pbk.)

Paperback cover, frontispiece of clothbound edition, and photo insert printed by Open Studio Ltd., which also provided substantial typesetting. Open Studio, in Rhinebeck, NY, is a non-profit production facility for writers, artists, and independent publishers, supported in part by grants from the National Endowment for the Arts and the New York State Council on the Arts. Text printing and paperback binding by Capital City Press, Montpelier, VT. Clothbinding by Riverside Bindery, Rochester, NY.

The paperback cover and the frontispiece to the clothbound editions reproduce all 190 frames of the film *Eye Myth*.

Photographs and frame enlargements appear courtesy of Anthology Film Archives and Stan Brakhage. The photograph opposite the title page is by Robert A. Haller, 1971.

Grateful acknowledgement is made to the editors and publishers of the following journals and magazines in which some of the material in this volume previously appeared, occasionally in slightly different form or under another title: *Dartmouth, Jogulars, Film Comment, The Yale Literary Magazine, Film Culture, Newsletter of 8mm in Education, Guerrilla, Filmwise, Los Angeles Free Press, Mile High Underground, Dance Perspectives, NY Film-Makers' Newsletter, Harbinger, Io, Los Angeles Institute of Contemporary Art (LAICA) Journal, Credences, Cinemanews, Criss-Cross Communications, Cinema Now, Downtown Review.* "Stan and Jane Brakhage (and Hollis Frampton) Talking" first appeared in *Artforum*, © 1972 by *Artforum*, and is reprinted by permission of the publisher and Mr. Frampton. *A Moving Picture Giving and Taking Book* was originally published by Frontier Press, copyright © 1971 by Stan Brakhage. *The Seen* was originally published by Pasteurize Press (Zephyrus Image), copyright © 1975 by Stan Brakhage. The poem "R" and line excerpts from other poems by Robert Kelly are reprinted by permission of the author. Quotations from "Proprioception" and line excerpts from poems by Charles Olson reprinted by permission of the Estate of Charles Olson. Quotations from poems by Michael McClure are reprinted by permission of the author. Line excerpts from "Canto XXV" from *The Cantos of Ezra Pound*, copyright 1937 by Ezra Pound, reprinted by permission of New Directions Publishing Corp. Line excerpts from *Hermetic Definition* by H.D., copyright © 1972 by Norman Holmes Pearson, reprinted by permission of New Directions Publishing Corp. The books paraphrased in "Film:Dance" are *Lectures in America, A Geographical History of America,* and *Four in America* by Gertrude Stein; *Studies in Classical American Literature* by D.H. Lawrence; *In the American Grain* by William Carlos Williams; *Call Me Ishmael* by Charles Olson; and *Nine Chains to the Moon* by Buckminster Fuller.

Two hundred copies of *Brakhage Scrapbook* are bound in buckram, numbered, and signed by the author.

INTRODUCTION

This book passed through several editorial hands on its way to publication, but from the first *Brakhage Scrapbook* was designed to be a collection of published essays and selected letters by a prolific film-maker who is as capable as a writer and nearly as influential. P. Adams Sitney, the critic who edited Brakhage's first book, *Metaphors on Vision* (1963), made the first selection of texts in the mid-sixties until Brakhage concluded that the material was insufficient. After Frontier Press published *A Moving Picture Giving and Taking Book* in 1971, Brakhage urged its publisher, Harvey Brown, to take up the *Scrapbook* project. Brown went so far as to set an enlarged manuscript and to proceed to galley proofs before he was forced by other circumstances to close his press.

At that time—1972—the collection consisted almost entirely of writings composed between 1964 and 1970. By the late seventies the anthology came into my hands; when Documentext agreed to issue it the scope was expanded to include the writings of the seventies, a section of photographs, and to make available again the out-of-print *Giving and Taking Book*.

In the most fundamental ways, however, the nature of this volume has not changed. It is not an explanation of what Brakhage has sought to achieve or has accomplished in his films (he does not feel the latter can be appropriately described in words) but rather a parallel musing (tempting one to say *music*) with another instrument about the same themes: the experience of apprehending, the adventure of seeing, the "wondering" vision.

A much-discussed and controversial film-maker since the mid-fifties, Brakhage has been involved and sometimes identified with many of the most interesting aesthetic developments of avant garde cinema, quite a few of which are discussed, and disputed, in this book: the growth of 8mm film-making and the place of "amateur" film-making; the work of such contemporaries as Bruce Baillie and such predecessors as Willard Maas and Marie Menken; the role of music in cinema; the politics of film-makers' associations. Particular formative situations of various of his films, including *The Text of Light* and "The Pittsburgh Trilogy," are described. The interview with Hollis Frampton and Jane Brakhage is perhaps the most memorable Stan Brakhage has ever given.

The letters often contain brief articulations of his creative process. To Manis Pinkwater he writes that "an artist MUST act on dream instruction." To Ed Dorn he says "the urge to write threads thought impulses to the fingers along a line of melody...." Succinctly, and then less so, he has described the uncalculated, unpremeditated, open-ended character of both filming and writing. The Dorn letter illustrates this by eccentric use of parentheses—again and again opening parenthetical statements and asides, never closing them, piling tangent upon digression, and then ending with the word, "end-parenthesis." In addition to these formal methods, Brakhage's writing glows in the collisions and couplings and rhymings of his words. The method is a way of dealing with experience—not just a manner of speaking. Capitalization, puns and word play are used fully (his letter to Yves Kovacs begins with an apology for a double pun) in the same way that grain and visible splices appear in his films.

For Brakhage, cinema is a process, a continuous personal encounter, a determination to escape the habitual shuttered sight that limits and conventionalizes the sensations that travel from the eye to the mind. One of his pivotal films bears the title *The Wonder Ring*. Given his professed love for word play it may not be inappropriate to take that image as a kind of epithet for Brakhage himself—a wondering eye. Just as he embraces and reduces his filmic images, he presses against the structures of language in these writings. Writing—especially poetry—was Brakhage's earliest aspiration. Had he, by his own standards, succeeded as a poet, he might never have turned to cinema. Many of his earliest and continuing friends have been poets, and various letters to Robert Kelly, Ed Dorn, Michael McClure and Guy Davenport are in this collection. Gertrude Stein, Ezra Pound, and Charles Olson are enduring influences on his work in film and his appreciation of poetry. He is often associated with film-makers who are also poets or writers: James Broughton, Sidney Peterson, Gregory Markopoulos, Maya Deren, Jonas Mekas, Willard Maas. While his films can hardly be described as literary, he has "worked from" certain texts in making films, such as Jean-Paul Sartre's *Nausea* in the making of *Black Vision* (1965) and the poetry of Osip Mandelstam in making *Short Films 1975*. The brief narrative text to *The Stars are Beautiful,* published here for the first time, highlights one of the tensions between Brakhage's perceptions of language versus image—it is, in effect, a species of ethnopoetics, of creation mythology, and it reminds us that by far the greater number of his films are silent.

For Brakhage, the physical act of writing is also filmic: since 1955 the titles of his films have been scratched out across a hundred or so frames, words jaggedly growing before our eyes. But only in these titles does he make an equation between word and image, which in the rest of his work are essential but different mechanisms of insight.

To watch a Brakhage film is to be forced to watch attentively: images flash onto the screen and disappear in the duration of a few frames. His camera will dart across a shallow focus space so swiftly that identification of the background can be utterly elusive. Context, situation, familiarization: all these are undermined by the fragmenting close-up, the briefest of cinematic glances, the differentiation of colors when rigorously presented in spatial isolation. Brakhage epitomizes this in *Metaphors on Vision:* "Imagine an eye unruled by man-made laws of perspective, an eye unprejudiced by compositional logic, an eye which does not respond to the name of everything but which must know each object encountered in life through an adventure of perception...."

Brakhage's cinema is unusual for his extraordinary rendering of vision and for his very ordinary subject matter: his wife, their children, their mountaintop home, himself. By shifting his focus in the late-fifties to domestic landscape, he stepped away from a tradition of alienation and anguish which marked the psychodramatic forms of his earliest films. There is no single year or film which signals absolutely this change, and I am not suggesting that there is no anxiety or pain in subsequent films, but a certain obsession faded which allowed Brakhage to grow as an artist beginning with *The Wonder Ring* in 1955. During these years Brakhage was influenced particularly by his contacts with Joseph Cornell, Marie Menken, and Jane Collom. All three broke through different kinds of isolation he faced. Cornell commissioned *The Wonder Ring,* which in a sense is about personal vision accepting and moulding but not rejecting the world. Menken's cinema celebrated the minutia of common experience, the implications of detail—a secret everyday world. Collom married him; at the time they met, she remembers,

> he was fresh out of the hospital...from a bout with double pneumonia mixed with bronchitas and asthma. A year before, he'd been dying of acute appendicitis. He was frightfully sickly. His eyelids were puffy, making his eyes burning slits. His skin was a sort of a pale chartreuse....
>
> When we were married three days after Christmas in '57, I was 21, Stan was 24. He was walking on a cane at the time because of arthritis in his left knee. He also had it in his right hand, making it more and more difficult to edit.
>
> He was working on Anticipation of the Night when I met him. He said later that he'd never have had the nerve to marry if he wasn't positive he was going to die in a few weeks or so.

Brakhage has written about his personal and often difficult transformations, and of the importance of his marriage and formation of a family to his identity. At the age of two weeks he had been adopted in Kansas City, the son of parents never officially identified. (In 1976 he learned that his mother's name was Mirabell Sanders, and his given name, at birth, was Robert.) Not knowing their identity, and so not his own, was a consciously disturbing factor. He was told he was an orphan early on, and as a child he was haunted by the question of his origin, which was aggravated by the unstable family that adopted him. A prodigy in high school, he joined the Gadflys, a small circle of fledgling artists and writers united against the athletics-centered social system of his fellow students. Earlier, he says, he led a gang of small-time thieves. Later he became associated with the Experimental Cinema Group in Boulder, Gryphon Films, the Film-Makers Cooperative, the New American Cinema group, Anthology Film Archives. It would seem that in all of these associations Brakhage has been motivated by ambivalent impulses: to make contact with others like himself, and to sever that contact whenever it seemed to undermine his sense of integrity. For Brakhage would never become just a member: he *belonged* to the group, and it too, in a way, would belong to him. The forces he accepted as self-transforming in his life have reinforced the identity or persona established in the films, culminating in what Sitney has called the "lyrical film."

> *The lyrical film postulates the film-maker behind the camera as the first-person protagonist of the film. The images of the film are what he sees, filmed in such a way that we never forget his presence and we know how he is reacting to his vision.*

In his writings Brakhage does not so much tell what he had learned—which he shares again and again in the active process of his films—but how he has come to it. A letter he wrote to Harvey Brown in 1970 sums up the intention of this collection:

> *The films exist for themselves and can, like anything else on earth, be either a pleasure or a bother or neither: the writings exist as the best defense I've been able to truthfully fashion against all that which, in the name of Truth, would destroy those works and myself as source thereof. I have truthfully told what I have learned from the works and my working of them: but there is no end to that telling because it is not an art: thus each statement of mine in itself is a lie. I've lied each time I've capitalized Art: and I've done so to joust with the greater lie that Historical Art can be meaningfully more than Antique when considered in historical context. An art is alive to us now as we are alive, or it is not as we are not: it is always alive, and simply that, to any 'I' that attends it.*

Robert A. Haller   New York, 1981

CONTENTS

MAKE PLACE FOR THE ARTIST

This is to introduce myself. I am young and I believe in magic. I am learning how to cast spells. My profession is transforming. I am what is known as "an artist." Three years ago I made a discovery which caused me dis-ease at the time: neither the society in which I had grown up nor my society of that moment, my college, knew what to do with me. They were wary of me.

I, suddenly without inheritance, began a three year adventure to seek the fortune of myself. This information is for professors wondering over an age of introspective art. Some say that no one has ever known what to do with the artist until after he is dead. Then his body is disposed of and his life works are buried in museums and libraries and, sometimes, in men's minds.

As over half of the culture professors of this and every other college campus earn their living from picking the bones of the dead, it is hoped they will be interested in the flesh of their future. This is a living artist speaking. It is a re-quest which brings me back to Dartmouth at this time. This is a state meant.

I am presenting it in writing for someone else's future. Someone may someday realize that the living artist has the eyes of the age he lives in. They may understand that he makes his magic for the moment. Who knows? Here's what to do:

Make place for the artist. Do it now. For you, as well as him, tomorrow is too late. First must come understanding, not of the work but of the worker. Give him the right conditions. Here are the conditions. This breed requires freedom. Cages kill him. Restrictions constrict. This animal is forever at war with his own limitations by nature. The rules others try to impose usually only baffle and, finally, either destroy or else disinherit him.

The artist must be given more than enough rope. He often hangs. himself for the experience, however this creature has a tough neck, give him time! He is perhaps more aware of time than any other type of individual. He is an explorer of his own dualities. He embarks on as many adventures as there are in a day. These are the components of his witch brew.

It takes time, also, to stir up a magic potion. Information for opportunists—the best way to get something from an artist is to leave him alone. Contradiction is part of the honesty he exercises. It is impossible for any man to express without contradicting himself every other statement and be anything but a liar, unless he is playing a part. The artist plays his part best apart.

It is because this college has a tradition of individuality that I speak so frankly. I have, during the last three years, uncovered many radical art schools with much display of individuality but no foundation for keeping it alive. Their fires are explosive but they frizzle quickly. I believe that Dartmouth has coals unturned.

Perhaps I'm no match for it. I am a match that would like to ignite without being consumed. My words have turned up a circle, and I'm back to ideas I had when I first arrived in Hanover three and a half years ago.

It was a liberal education I wanted. I was, and am, alive with more curiosity than it would be possible for any man to satisfy in a lifetime. A college was expected to save me time in my investigations, but it was not dreamed of that time would be saved by pre-digesting those investigations.

I was barraged with a tangle of facts and given no time to unite them. The explorer will never be satisfied by the motion pictures of the expedition. I had assumed that a liberal education would be taught liberally to everyone according to his individual inclination.

I had exepected there would be time for keeping the fires burning under the magic potion. Instead there was only an endless series of pot-boilers to be warmed over. The smoke dreams of the artist are as necessary to his well being as the air he breathes.

Make place for the artist, Dartmouth, for he is the most demanding but at the same time the most generous of all the individuals your tradition might speak for. He is the fire for a living theater under the hands of your great drama professors. He is the dream of your inspiring professors of literature.

He can make use of their inspiration. He can give you a literary quarterly worth keeping. He is the unheard sound of your musical department. He can give your instruments new notes to play. He is what your artists in residence are residing for. He can make your screens alive with your own cinema images. He must never be used as material. Those who try to hold fire either burn their hands or put the fire out.

This is a hair of the dog, given with love and expectation.

THE ROBERT LETTER (TO ROBERT LEE TIPPS)

Near end July, 1964

Dear Bob,

I hasten to answer your letter, your beautiful letter, "The most clear letter," Jane says, "we've ever received from Bob"; BUT I am also somewhat saddened that I haven't any capital "A"-Answers to some of your worries, I have no place in mind where human flowers are permitted to bloom openly . . . God, all my Roberts, my dear Roberts: Bob Benson, for instance, permitting himself to be destroyed in the no-man's land somewhere between the New York Stage and Taggart's Basement, that is: The San Francisco Workshop which has degenerated into a sort of Pee-Wee Golf Course, a narrow way directed the same as Broadway, same ultimate dis-stinct— to be shunned by all but those who seek destruction the slooooooooow, rather than speedy B', way; but how was I ever to say to Benson that what drama needs more than anything else is an actor who disciplines himself privately as purely as creative painter, say, thoughtless of attention, shunning even all but whatever audience angels bring his way at moment *when it is given to him to create,* accepting whatever circumstances so long as they are free of even the anarchic commissioning in Taggart's Basement?—how was I to say this to him who cannot stack up his creative moments in a closet or send them out from himself intact for a usage he's free-of once performance is completed? . . . except to demonstrate as much of that process as was possible in the making of "Blue Moses"? . . . AND SUDDENLY I *DO* SEE that THAT *WAS* enough: I suddenly realize in writing this to you that those same recording means, film and tape, are as available to a *performing* artist as they are to so-called *creative* artist—"so-called" because all superficial distinctions between those terms "performing" and "creative" melt, indeed "resolve themselves into a dew," i.e., make perfect *natural* form for whoever has the strength to take *means* at his hand as *medium* in hand—Benson could carry around a tape recorder, a camera, as easily as I, and carry this equipment, as he does all his training, as preparation for coming moments of inspiration and in homage to what was given him, his sensibilities, his gift for acting; and he could also carry all this equipage, as I must, with due homage and humility with respect to forces beyond his control, striving always for the perfection of *White Magician* as defined by Graves in the sense of *He-Who* prepares himself all his life so that he-whom the angels intend to move the mountain may do so without debt, Black Magic, when the moment for moving the mountain comes to pass, as it may not within any particular man's lifetime—but that latter part is an over-emphasized pessimism of Graves, perhaps himself too concerned with mountains, because, as it has at least been my experience, the angels, angels being my name for forces moving thru me beyond my knowledge, my sensing of multiplicity of forces rather than sensing what may be a most singular force, these angels do seem to find plenty of work for all so disciplined, all White Magicians, that is: I know no idle good men—tho' plenty distracted by work-work, a kind of double positive making negative in this field as any other regarding magic of grammar . . . and have heard of some who seem to me to have misunderstood various Eastern teachings, etcetera . . .

Well, WOW, what a simple thing for me to have overlooked all these years; and I can no longer excuse, that is pity, the so-called performing artist in this, God knows, that is as is singularly known, difficult time for all of us; and I realize that pity was with regard to myself as performing artist as I once was singer, actor, rhetorician, etceterician, did even once want, as still somewhere in the pity of me want, people to look over my shoulder as I was editing, do still pull on Jane for that double distraction, non-traction in the working process, still want to teach, lec-tour, even tho' I know all admiration and/or hatred for me distracts from the images on the screen as surely as if I took a pointer during any film showing and created shadow lines and the form of my body to partially block the light, the creative intention—*that's IT,* do then at best refer to *intent* in a shun of the creative realiza-tion, do tattoo mySELF all over, in such action, with dislocated pieces of my own— ah, notice how "own" slips in—images, do indeed then make them my own at the expense of any freedom, vulgarly, rub them off on myself, a showing off for sure, an exhibitionism not even courageous to go naked, a flaunt of what can only be moving designs patterned for dress when thus, by lecture, singled out of creation and superimposed upon myself as teach-preach-err reaching for an each which would make a kind of stifled scream of me, to draw attention to the anti-poetic "I," or to those who hate me then an Ass, a capital "A," and to the neutral an "Exhibit A" at best. And I remember so clearly now Robert Duncan's warning:

> If I've tried to get one idea across in the art it is that
> the poet must have *no* deep and complex feelings, no 'I'
> at all, that does not belong to, arise in the orders of, the
> poem itself.

and the passages where those concerns take form in his Day Book:

> Liberty too is a demand of the anti-poetic. The poet
> cannot take liberties in the poem. For just there, where
> the arbitrary, self-expressive or self-saving, where the
> self-conscious voice comes, the ιδιόνης, idiot howl or moan
> or the urbane sophistication breaks or takes over from
> the communal voice. In the communal consciousness,
> the idiot is a member. But the difficulty of self-expression
> or of accomplished performance (self-possession) in verse
> is that this false "I" usurps the place of the 'I' that we
> all are.

A long time ago, after you had performed the piano background music to James Broughton's reading, you confided to me that you and he could share a "performer's sense" which, as you said, I lacked. The ambition in me which drove me to San Francisco in search of *A* Round Table, and that which drove me of late to New York in search of even a square one, all prompted by fat of my youth which had kept me from getting under the brother-hood, which I never till lately thought of as my being too BIG (God, how singularly poet Robert Kelly has redeemed much of my childhood—as you too, my musical Robert, when the SIZE of you took shape in your play as the beauty of your playing), this statement of yours did make me feel excluded from a kind of Three Musketeership at the time, did prove troublesome, as any lack, to "A small boy's notion of doing good," as another Robert, Creeley, puts it in a poem. I NOW, as of the spelling of this lettering, acknowledging faults as cracks of mis-spells, must run through my ignorance in these several pages, an acknowledgement to save me from some statute of myself, DO, from break-through of feeling that I wish it would have been so, RECOGNIZE A WOULD IT WERE TRUE, a becoming present, AND WILL IT TO BE TRUE that I lack sense of performance, HEREBY SWEAR AN OATH in homage to the forces beyond my knowledge, my angels, THAT I WILL TALK NO MORE ABOUT MY FILMS, NOR WRITE OF THEM EITHER, TILL IT IS GIVEN TO ME, a sense of need shaped to sign, THAT I MAY SPEAK, OR WRITE, WHITE WORDS ONLY IN WHITE RELATION, or at least as of the same impulse felt in the act of creating.

As you have met, known or know something of all the other Roberts of this letter, but Robert Kelly, I will send you a poem just received from him, from his alphabet book named AT THE FOOT OF THE LETTER; and as you may wonder what I mean by "a sense of need shaped to sign" I will send you "R" which *may* be *taken* as a sign if there be need enough in you to read carefully:

R

Robert, *Robertus sum.* Bright fame. Son or
daughter of all that made me. Don't you know.
Yes I know. Robert. The name taught me
to steal, & expect to be punished. Anybody
can steal but only rob•bers are punished.
I am the Queen's poet & know no names.
The Kings poet. Yes. Once I have made
my music I will not write *I* again.
Robertus sum.
        Not robber. It is easy to be im-
mortal but where is the song? Song/after
death, who needs it? No more questions.
The song. Above all gardens & in dirt.
Whence grows.
           In one rush:
           matter & song, triumphant, thru the tree's
           body. Robert's
concerns, cocks, houses, oak for upright,
           the house stands strong.
But what what given is a flower or a country,
           & he could not live on it. Love
loving anything it can. Maple for shade. O
tall house air lives in, to stand up therein.
Is song. Oneself, River, or shore of a lake,
wind, who, from the south, the drab water

Whatever is sung
is for the republic
& that is where
houses live & how.
The water, the words
are never our own,
are not ours
but to make over

& rob the princess from hell. Flecked black
& white with music, he drives to his baptism
in the same cart. No one can see him.
Return
    at length
        to your land
& raise
    the living
        from the dead.

Robert is strong enough to bear all burdens
Robert will live forever
Robert can make cities from flowers & love from a house
Robert flows his waters all over you
The apples he steals are his own.

Very personally I could wish nothing more than that you would find that "your land" was near to us in every respect. You do write out of your nostalgia for things that are no more: Boulder is no more a place where even beauty of performance flows, no one of interest to me performs there. I no longer perform there either: most of your friends are scattered, all those names, Bill and Mary travelers, it may have been The Meader's film sign you saw in Maine, as that is where they are, etcetera, and even Jane and I can no longer be considered of-Boulder: As for Denver, it fares no better, except that perhaps it might in Jane's ironic sense that "Now that Taggart has at last left Denver art may flourish there just to spite him": and we have very much changed, even the children you speak of playing with (our girls who came to call all welcome visitors "Bobs" as if it were natural English usage) are older and more various in their ways; but we have none of us changed with respect to what we love, "Bobs" and the particular Bob you are.

QUEST: SHUN-AIRE

When I first received your Quest: shun-aire: I tossed it out because, because-because—ah well, I thought it unappropriate to dwell on such *matters* wherein *means* were what was needed— and then did balk at Cat. II: "GIVE A SKETCH OF YOUR PROFESSIONAL WORK IN FILM": to which I could only, with specific regard, have replied with a list of some of those jobs I've taken upon myself, the burdens of T.V. commercials, educational films, etc., wherewith I've earned enough to feed my family and continue my non-professional work wherein I find myself amateur, lover, enough to permit the passage into being of the medium of film into form which, at most, can only be said to have been permitted, rather than created, by my being, and perfect in its being only to the extent I have been care full, i.e.: working out of the *full* necessity, and necessity only, of my being: and of the clarity Zukofsky spells, in "Bottom On Shakespeare": "when reason judges with eyes, love and mind are one.": and am, thereby careful to know I "cannot take liberties with the poem," as Robert Duncan puts it, or with the film as I transcribe it across script to the light of the visual medium wherein I find the taking of liberties in any departure from sense of light as source of the medium, move of fire prime movemeant, etc., but growing away from limitations thereby, such as Christian artist's limit of only pain's: taking-care wherefrom we can now grow into consciousness of joy: taking-care and/or move among all emotions to a care *full* taking shape of all, a form ALL without as much RE-guard as in BE-fór, etc.

BUT, you see why I balked at a-gory II: for the real distinction between Professional & Amateur does bogg down in description wherefrom any lover would flee unless, and my only hope in spell of above, he used of-script FOR shun, took intricate tools of above to spring therefrom; but lovers shun "use" first, usually, and thus find most individual way to escape any circling, only their robber nature burdening them with a lute, an instru-ment, a boot, too big for the foot if poet, or a camera if film maker and/or rolls rollls, and so a being FOR-the: materials replacing matter; money, means; etc., engendering a lack of fay-the, a lack of daisyc-all: sense of how the flowers flower: an Et-Set-Era of "woe, woe, etcetera" . . . and/or a *"hangup"* which does bring us naturally to considerations of the need for "VARIOUS *FOUNDA-TION* GRANTS TO THE ARTS" (my italics).

One 20-degree-below-zero day in a phone booth on the streets of Custer, South Dakota, I returned a long-distance call from Film-Maker's Cooperative and was informed that I had won no awards at the Brussels' 1964 Exhibition. As I had entered none of my films there (they had all been entered for me by friends) and as I had several days before sent a telegram giving permission to withdraw them (in reply to request from Jonas Mekas making protest over exclusion of FLAMING CREATURES, which I had not even seen at that time) and as I thought no expectations of awards from Brussels existed within me (particularly since my experience at Brussels in 1958), I was much surprised to find myself doubling-over with nausea in that phone booth and barely able to catch enough breath to finish the conversation. My needs were great at the time, food low, Custer job becoming daily more impossible for me, DOG STAR MAN expenses impossible, etc.; and some-such desire for Brussels Salvation had assumed subconscious proportions of comparable greatness to balance needfulness I wasn't permitting myself to consciously think-of-on-about; and

all this sub-blossoming, mad-dream, world aborted in phone booth leaving me utterly hollowed in feeling and stumbling down the streets of Custer. As it happened, as it was Saturday, there was a kiddies afternoon movie beginning in the one local theatre there; and I gravitated naturally into that atmosphere, that which has been to me most church of my time, most unchanging ceremony of my childhood, most rite to me. I had no sooner taken my seat than the lights dimmed and the semi-darkness enclosed me in this children's world wherein all social barriers, age or otherwise, vanish at the first illumination of the screen. The service began with a Woody-Woodpecker Cartoon; and I will describe it to you briefly:

An artist, complete with beret and mustache, palette and brush, is seen painting. It is soon revealed that he is painting a semi-nude on a necktie. Then we see the outside of his house: an appropriate shack. Beside this is a tree: the home of our Woody hero. A magazine is thrown upon the porch by postman; and Woodpecker runs down his tree to read the news, which does turn out to be Art News advertising a painting competition, award of $5,000 First Prize to be given to the best painting of a desert flower. The artist emerges from his wooden house; and a fight begins over the magazine, over who is to paint the best flower, over transportation means to get to it, etc. Finally, both Woody and the artist, both now in berets, with palettes, brushes, etc., converge across a vast expanse of desert upon a single blooming desert flower. From here on, for awhile, the Hollywood animators take their cues from McLaren's NEIGHBORS, as the flower is fought over, ground under, etc.; but then Woodpecker remembers who he is, returns in stride and feathered style to triumph in the following manners: first, he paints a mirage of water and oasis scene upon a rock, jumps into and swims about in his painting (reminding me of the ancient legend of the Chinese master who adds one stroke a day to his masterpiece and finally bids the impatient emperor goodbye and walks off into it); but, of course, of a course so natural as to be anticipated by the laughing children around me, when The Artist (who should have been capped throughout this description to signify his beret, etc.) tries to follow suit he smashes against solid rock and the oasis vanishes: then Woody draws a bulldog, the inevitable Tom-&-Jerry-type bull (but taking on significance of "Beware The Dog" which latin poet once posted on his house), which bites

The Artist in his unwatched behind (reminding of Olson's statement on the creative process: "You follow it. With a dog at your heels, a crocodile about to eat you at the end, and you with your pack on your back trying to catch a butterfly.") : then, as The Artist goes on trying to paint the, by now, dishevelled flower, Woody draws ties on the sand under and, of course, two neat rails on either side of him; and a train (locomotive) obligingly rushes over the tracks leaving The Artist all battered and entangled in ties and twisted rails with a desert flower drooping over his nose: then a frame is formed around this, and it is seen to be exhibited, as a painting, in an art gallery; and the announcement is being made that Woody Woodpecker is to receive the first prize for his "abstract" painting of a desert flower, after which, and after The Artist in the painting blinks twice (WOW what a world of thoughts about "Abstract" and "Realism" fluttered thru my laughing mind) the fat, cigar-chewing, master of ceremonies hands our feathered friend a painting of a money bag with $5,000 lettered upon it, at which in answer, and of expectancy's course, Woody Woodpecker smashes the painting over patron's head and laughs his most individual laugh in midst of laughter all around.

The above came to me, in cartoon form, as religious experience under child-hood. It, naturally, suffers in translation; but I hope hereby to give some sense of the restorative values of the experience to me.. Some I've told the story to have insisted I made the whole thing up, have insisted I took material of other cartoon and created, in mind's eye, a miracle cartoon of no Hollywood origin—they thereby credit a non-god with a sense of timing, forgetting that miracles are ever present and that humans create The Time, can therefore create the most continual clock of miracles they want if they but see to it . . . I, as is my usual, had necessity to help me SEE to IT: any appropriately passing miracle which could take shape therefrom my need, could have taken shape clear thru to form of itself had I been PRESENT, gift of myself, enough in the moment to go to work, contemporary source, rather than source in childhood . . . but I had not been aware enough of "crocodile" at "end," aware enough of my tail, sub-conscious, in discipline of myself those Custer days, to make the most of the bite of experience then.

When the rejection from the Ford Foundation arrived, I was not much surprised by either it or myself: my own reactions: which is not to imply that I received it painlessly but that I was full of care rather than consciousness care-lessness. These areas of self-discipline are the grants foundations have given me. They have given me also lessons in jealousy and the eventual joy that contemporaries of mine, among them many close friends, have so disciplined themselves as to receive the means in the form of large sums of money which, apparently, do not abstract them: batter them into blinking monuments in galleries. I rather fear, to judge from my sick reaction in Custer, that a money award at that time might have been the worst possible Fate-all. Anyway, it seems to be my fate to receive the means in small amounts from many individuals and of an irregular, but always miraculous, timing so that economics does come to me in daily relationship physically specified by stomach, abstracted only as regards my children's stomachs, etc., and with respect to THAT particular roll of out-dated film given by that particular person, etc., which takes the form of making a living in the creative sense of permitting it to pass through me into a being of its own, having it only in the sense of gift, an exchange possible in the sense of myself as present, etc. For instance: when we had our first child I worried as to whether or not the salary I then had from a commercial film company was enough to meet family needs—I now have no job, am indeed increasingly incapable of holding one at all; and we have five children. Obviously a miracle has shaped itself in relation to our family needs; and I must, of 5-times greater necessity than then, believe in the form of that miracle. Also, when I submitted my request to the Ford Foundation, I wrote what I then thought the truth of the matter, that I couldn't possibly complete my 4½ hour epic film DOG STAR MAN without a foundation grant—I am now nearly finished with it, about 2 weeks editing to go on Part $ (interesting Freudslip for Part 4, which I interpret hopefully as indicating I am about finished money-worry-work, that that sign is taking shape for new considerations, deeper thought, etc., as in this statement your questionaire has prompted from me in need, as I now am and am now realizing, writing this, that the means and the matter have relationship as have I, as means, and the matter, as film, coming into being, that "the need" is given, as "the work" is in terms of "necessity" for me but taking shape through instrument of my total being, need only prompting unless feeding back on itself, whereas "the matter" is, as the creation, the film, say, coming

into being, feeding back on itself only in the sense *of*, or senseless,: "What's the matter?": senseless unless asked after, after its coming into being; but miracle can move through all of it: the need of miracle, if taken as gift of "inspiration," as they used to say; the means, if miracle, always available in some form if matter is permitted to take shape of itself; and, if so, matter, of course, is a miracle, the specific miracle of art if in coming into being it passed through the being of an artist, and fine as such as he was sharp, and new as such as he was creative in the sense of his permitting its taking shape within his individual being, and perfect as such in the extent he permitted it to come through him into its individual being, and traditional as such to the extent of his knowledge of art tradition, and so forth . . . Ah, well, Olson was right: there's no end to a parathesis . . .

Your questionaire has been of help to me, especially in coming to new terms under Dollar Part; and I hope in this exchange (Ah, there's a lovely money word: change) my replying of old concerns will be of some help to others in like circumstances, in kind, a' kin and will be of amusement to those who have otherwise come to terms with grants, foundations; means, matters.

TO YVES KOVACS

Near mid-Sept. 1964

Dear Yves KOVACS,

I must admit I'm finding it difficult to either fulfill your request or reject it. You see, I simply do NOT write "On Subject," as it's termed, nor work: film-or-write-wise "Under Commission"; but then your letters are either turning my mind to Surrealistic considerations and/or are arriving at the opportune time when these considerations are arising within me again in a form where they might loosely be clustered under the term "Surrealism." I have, as you know, been corresponding with poet Kelly about what we term "The Dream Work." But then, I feel especially hampered in my writing to/for you/your magazine in that whatever is to be of use to you must be translated into French which restricts my sense of pun—as, for instance, my thoughts turn to the phrase: "Sir Real & The Drag" . . . ah, well, if you'll forgive me that one & two pun, I'll try to be gracious enough to give you a couple paragraphs of straight thoughts in the subject specified without becoming too school-boyish about it, viz:

Max Ernst, on the subject WHAT IS SURREALISM (from Ausstellungskatalog Kunsthaus Zurich, 1934) says: " 'The accidental encounter of a sewing machine and an umbrella on a dissecting table' (Lautreamont) is today a universally known, almost classic example for the phenomenon discovered by the Surrealists that the juxtaposition of two (or more) apparently alien elements on an alien plane promotes the most potent poetic combustion." With this I would juxtapose some sense of William Carlos Williams' "No ideas but in things" (from "A Sort of a Song"); and I might even underline the "in" therein. Then I would direct you to the accidental appearance of whatever page you're reading this off OF, and make "OF" here signify SOURCE or/and/or/in this encounter. I would deepen this experience with Robert Duncan's take-off ON a quote: "The physical world is a light world. The real world, Thomas Vaughan wrote, is invisible. Thus, in the physical or spiritual or light world all forms or beings—stones, trees, stars, streams, men, flames and turds—are really facts of invisible presence. Mineral, wood, fire, water, flesh are terms of dense soul-full sense." And I would re-direct the reader "Whomsoever" to specifics such as the metal of a sewing machine, the wood handle of a remembered umbrella, this page as imagined dissected by flames, the thought-full struggle of imagining a water-thing (without recourse to word-sense "body of water" and/or imagined container) and the flesh of the eye reading this. Then I'd take Jack Spicer's command (from "A Textbook of Poetry") "See through into" and dissect that, as he does, with his: "like it is not possible with flesh only by beginning not to be a human being. Only by beginning not to be a soul." (Both Duncan & Spicer quotes are from Duncan's "Properties And Our REAL Estate" from "Journal For The Protection of all Beings—No. 1".)

Taking the above quotes as axiomatic in inter-action of the trace from France (1) to Germany (E) to East Coast U.S. (W) and thru filter of American continent to West Coast (D & S) of consideration's change from OF things to ON things to THRU INTO (the eye of the reader taking place of "things"), that is: taking the above as international law (of Surreal manifestation) and conditioning sub-laws pertaining finally to properties of thingness, I find foremost FORce of Surrealism TO BE a directing OF itself (History) ON object ("object" replacing "things" in this light) rather than on position of things ("juxta" or otherwise) for a going THRU INTO ("IN": The Present) in celebration of (Future: Imaged) sense of Being; but, having come full circle (to: ". . . of . . . of") following a thread of paper thru the things words are to the needle in the eye of the imagined-future reader, let us (as imagined) celebrate (rather than consider) the Surrealism created (originated) on the thread between things; and let us remember (piece together) the ashes of it, FOR (if we remember correctly) it was a burning thread; and then let us wonder if we have (with/in all these considerations) but put out the fire (perhaps to prevent it from consuming the things).

An Alexander (such as Burroughs or Byron Gyson) would at this point simply cut the things (as Alexander did the Gordian Knot when it was of prime consideration); but I do find *that* a killing of the goose that lays the golden egg. We can deepen our considerations of this matter by a Western faith in the eternity of the thread and/or an Eastern Zen resignation: sense of the burning of the page this is printed upon, all print evaporating in a slow smoke; but I will leave those processes, thankfully, to the whomEVER (theologian and academician) reader and pass, gratefully, on to my sense of eye as visible brain matter, as surface sense of brain; and I will continue, thereby, in consideration, viz:

A careful re-reading of the first paragraph, taking quotes as Law and conditioning sub-laws, gives sense that it was the light of the "combustion" which was most permanent in the course of our following from BETWEEN to THRU INTO things ("BETWEEN" now standing for OF-((SOURCE))-ON); but "things resist the light, reflect it, to block our seeing THRU INTO, yielding us only a surface-tension." But if we begin "not to be a soul," give up the drama of perception, and all other adventure-senses easily prefaced with "self," do we not ourselves become reflective OF the light? and can we not think ON the surface as beginning? as a gain; and have we not thereIN ignited the fire of the thread of imagination? (our double "of" telling us where we are again: Present to these past considerations). The things, as these words are things, will now put forth threads OF illumination entangling viewer, reader, and eachother. None will seem "alien" to eachother or on an alien plane either; but neither can they engender an INTERnational Surrealism, as each word hereIN must transform TO French word-clusters for the imagined-future reader. At the point where a relationship between things includes the imagined viewer-reader-etceterer, all communication becomes imaginary. But all communication IS imaginary in any given PRESENT. Even the Kinesics (such as Ray L. Birdwhistell) are scientifically informing us: "We do not communicate. We participate in communication." And I would again, underline the "in." Or, as poet Charles Olson says: "Landscape is what you see from where you are standing." Or, as Gertrude Stein put it (in "Four In America"): "Now what we know is formed in our head by thousands of small occasions in the daily life. By 'what we know' I do not mean, of course, what we learn from books, because that is of no importance at all. I mean what we really know, like our assurance about how we know anything, and what we know about the validity of the sentiments, and things like that. All the thousands of occasions in the daily life go into our head to form our ideas about these things." I would, of course, underline "things." I include these last two quotes to make it clear that if I sent you objects, other than words, or pictures, moving or otherwise, it would in no sense alter the individuality of the gesture other than as I re-considered the imaginary viewer (as of "rather than reader") and made "re" otherwise referential in my considerations. Thus, Surrealism has become an individual matter, as it was at beginning, as was all-ways in consideration.

But then, what do we share (under title of "Surrealism" or other, such as "Nation," etcetera) in these exchanges? It is, of course, The Light (which I now capitalize to signify its signification). Surrealism (a capitalization signifying several seemingly related combustions which, occurring at a time, or The Time, made many men aware of the light, simultaneously aware, did engender a dance thereby, which has now become The Dance), takes its shape there *by*: "Who shall most advance the light—call it what you may," as William Carlos Williams wrote (in "Asphodel"), and as it would, as a Thing, search THRU INTO does depend upon past tensions such as outlined by Olson (in "Pieces of Time"—"1. Proprioception"):

"Physiology: The surface (senses—the 'skin' of 'Human
                  Universe') the body itself—proper—one's own
                  'corpus': PROPRIOCEPTION the cavity of
                  the body, in which the organs are slung: the
                  viscera, or interoceptive, the old 'psychology'
                  of feeling, the heart; of desire, the liver; of
                  sympathy, the 'bowels'; of courage—kidney etc.
                  —gall, (Stasis—or as in Chaucer only, spoofed)":

does take its directive ON, as Olson continues:

        Today:
                  movement, at any cost. Kinesthesia: beat (nik)
                  the sense whose end organs lie in the muscles,
                  tendons, joints, and are stimulated by bodily
                  tensions (—or relaxations of same).
                  Violence: knives/anything, to get the body in":

THRU INTO you, WHOMever. But, for example, if the word-thing "Surrealism" sees thru into you as you see thru into it; the "it" being an other word-thing will disperse the vision (except, for instance, as you "read-into" Surrealism—for in-stance read "it" into "Surrealism") unless you participate in SEEING THRU INTO, in the sense of participating in communication. Such participation resists a reading-into, or any other form of Projection, resists your imposing upon a thing, and/or Super-imposition, as the surface of a thing resists light for reflection. Thus the individual surreal encounter (uncapitalized surrealism, original of Surrealism) is created as an imagined you (or as I imagine myself) imagines a thing seeing thru into you seeing thru into, etcetera. Olson suggests this with:

The gain :   to have a third term, so that *movement* or *action*
                    is 'home,' Neither the Unconscious nor
                    Projection (here used to remove the false
                    opposition of 'Conscious': 'consciousness' is
                    self) have a home unless the DEPTH implicit
                    in physical being—built-in space-time specifics,
                    and moving (by movement of 'its own')—is
                    asserted, or found-out as such. Thus the
                    advantage of the value 'proprioception.' As such.

The dream-work of Surrealism seems to me to formulate itself
(historically) thus: "I see thru into myself seeing thru into you
seeing thru into yourself seeing thru into me seeing me see you seeing
you see me." Poet Robert Kelly (in "THE DREAM WORK/2," in
"matter/2") strings names along a line, thus:

"Europe) Gilgamesh Aristotle Cicero Chaucer Colonna . . .
Freud Jung":

and, in earlier writing confined to "dream as psychic event in the
life of the dreamer," writes: "My premise is that the dreamworld
in us is (like our lives, Q. E. D.) a complex solid of such a nature
that 'crystalline structure' is a more useful analogy than 'line,' chem-
istry a better ancilla than history." ("THE DREAM WORK,"
"matter.") This is a strong *prime* envisionment; but as I imagine
myself crystalline in my seeing thru anything seeing thru into me,
I am blocked from seeing thru into me seeing thru into anything
seeing thru into me seeing thru into . . . the "I" cut off from secondary exchanges. Thus I am inclined to string "myself" along a line
of terms like "I" and "me"—a dream becomes a thing, again, to be
told-OF or to be visually represented as, say, picture OF crystal OF,
etcetera. In following these considerations I would soon find myself
as dependent ON three-dimensional perspective and sense of immo-
bility as most Surrealistic painting; and words would become as
specifically referential, immobile as symbol, as in most Surrealistic
poetry; and my film work would soon restrict the "motion" of
"motion pictures," as Surrealistic films have never shown themselves
in complexities of movement, have rather tendered to "slow motion";
and the sense of seeing would reduce to scenes referential drama, as
Surrealistic dramas, in films or even improvizations, present themselves primarily as staged events.

I cannot, at this time, suggest a more useful analogy than 'crystal-line structure,' turn Kelly's crystal around and around in my head, letting it dissolve like snow "settling crystals locking and unlocking with crystals" as he suggests, re-freezing it again and again. It took the Zen masters time to come from "Dust is misplaced matter" to "the dust is in the mind." I feel sure it is The Time in which we are related THRU reflection, rather than combustion, IN small "s" rather than capped surrealism TO SEEING THRU INTO.

TO ED DORN

September 30, 1964

Dear Ed,

Some Bach Pedal Harpsichord music playing here beside me; and I've an irresistible urge to write you—yet music pulling me strongly (making long pauses in the typing here)...and yet the urge to write threads thought impulses to the fingers along a line of melody (and it is the VERY *PULL* in mind of both tendencies which I'm somehow now wanting—wanting, perhaps, to get deeper into my concept of music as sound equivalent of the mind's moving, which is becoming so real to me that I'm coming to believe the study of the history of music would reveal more of the changing thought processes of a given culture than perhaps any other means—not of thought shaped and/or Thoughts but of the *Taking shape,* psysiology of thot or sumphin'...I mean, is there anything that will illustrate the feel of chains of thought gripping and ungripping, rattling slowly around, a block-concept, an Ideal, as Gregorian Chant, for instance?...and doesn't The Break occur in Western Musical thought in terms of melody, story, carrying blocks, making them events, along a line? (Or, as Kelly put it to me recently: "& event is the greatness of story, i.e., where story & history & myth & mind & physiology *all* at once interact"—and is not THAT the greatness of Bach, the interaction of blocks becoming events as they inter eachother in the act, in the course, of the line of melody? (I'm reminded here that Gregorian notes WERE blocks in manuscript, stems attached later to make flowers of 'em, and then, still later, strung along lined paper, etcetera. And sometime later, when the notes are well rounded, flowering right-and-upside-down, sporting flags, holes, etc., and all planted in the neat gardens of the page, all in rows, it was possible for Mozart to play Supreme Gardener: but there lurked Wagner who would, did, make of each line of melody a block, specifically referential, so that the French could image melody as a landscape, all thought of reference. But then Webern made of it a cube, all lines of melody converging on some center to form a cluster or what composer James Tenney, writing about Varese, does call "a Klang." And it does seem to me that with John Cage we are, thru chance operations, to some approximation of Gregorian Chant again— not held to links, as of a chain-of-thought, but rather to the even more rigid mathematical bell-shaped curve.

Ah, well, Bach is long since stopped: and even the needle in my mind is revolving around a too narrow center now; but it was an exciting spin thru a thousand years of possibilities. (And Olson is right: there is no end-parenthesis...

TO MANIS PINKWATER

Day before Thanksgiving, '64

An artist MUST act on dream instruction (day AND night dream structures conditioning all his being) for continuance of his art. Some have called this "inspiration," some "the word of God," some (more modernly) "sub-conscious feed-back" or what-have-you (without quest shun mark)... it doesn't much matter what-you-call-it—there IS a process which governs the arts, necessities of each medium which discipline the artist's living making it impossible for him to exist in an avoidance of the right, the rite: and it is very encouraging, AND ABSOLUTELY NECESSARY for the movement of works of art into the world at large (not to mention proper celebration of birthdays), that there be others who permit instruction, always dream structured, and act of their given sense of right, thus participate in the rite, in whatever way their form of living enables them. "Art for art's sake" is a term imposed on the, otherwise, opening field of the arts BY a negligent or INdifferent society, a seige, as it were, which does force an, otherwise ever opening, field into becoming a fortress of "ivory towers," etc., and/or (more modernly) a game preserve, wherein the forces of nature may play withIN strictly defined boundaries imposed by most unnatural game wardens, a place where natural forces are appreciated (as if one could applaud the universe) rather than experienced.

TO JAMES BROUGHTON

Mid Dec., 1964

Of His Story, then—when I married Jane, when Jane-and-I/I-and-Jane married?, when (to put it accurately) Jane called her parents, after my three-hour drunken harangue (like: "You're just waiting around for me to cut off my ear and send it to you"—"I'm just your affair with an artist"—etc.) and told *them* she was eloping with *me*, when we got married then (because it was easier than trying to lie to them about how we'd accomplished it, blood-tests, etc., quick enough to be there two days later for dinner where they first met me, etc.) when we were then married (these seven years ago this coming Dec. 28th—our 'contract to marriage' probably, finally, legal this coming anniversary) I didn't really expect to live the year out, couldn't really imagine sustaining myself thru all that illness and those financial impossibilities, let alone the two of us. Then when Myrrena was born, almost a year later, WHEN I was still capable of holding a full time commercial film job, and when I was healthily aware I WAS likely to go on living, I couldn't POSSIBLY imagine how I was going to support the three of us and go on with not only my living but what was/IS synonymous, my being the artist I, after ALL, *AM.* Then when I could no longer hold full time job and WHEN, a little more than a year later, Crystal was born, it was REALLY impossible for me to imagine *HOW/WHAT* I was *AT ALL* going *TO DO!* And, as I can't make expletives greater on this typewriter, and to make a long story short, as you know, we now have FIVE children, and it is IMPOSSIBLE for me to hold any kind of job for practically any length of time, and (naturally) many more films than ever seem to be pouring thru me (in these natural, to-an-artist, circumstances of our being). Sometimes we go hungry for days at a time (a couple times without *any* food): but we share that, after all, with ALL humans—every human hungers almost all the time for SOME-thing or other. I have never had anything NEAR to the technical means my imagination would term adequate for my film work (just this year, as you know, have been reduced to 8mm): but the imagination in any growing human is beyond existing technical means (and I have refused to be "reduced" in any relation with my work other than in technical terms, such as "millimeter"). I cannot tell you how we've managed to go on (except that we have), nor how we come to be where we are (except that we *are*), nor can I imagine (at all) how we're going to continue: but don't I share this with any man who knows the limits of history, and who knows (as you said I gave you some sense of, viz:) "that It is Now & Here it Is whatever is born of this moment, as if there will never nor need ever be any other: immediacy, I mean, and life Now . . . ," and with any man who has given up (as I am only recently come to) all the black magic which prophecy, in sense of 'control of future and/or anything not at hand' IS.

Let me recite what history teaches, History teaches.
—G. Stein

From EX-perience, then, and without re-acting, let me take plants of previous thoughts thru to whatever fulfillment of the moments of writing this: and I hope for growth along these lines thru to seeds for further planting by ALL of us involved in these concerns—the twist of which, if INvoluted, usually comes out as the distort term: money problem. Robert Kelly once answered my use of that phrase with something like: there IS *NO* "money problem," per se . . . there are problems such as "how much do you need," "where can you get it," etc. To take it CLEARLY from there I've found I MUST, at each instant, avoid all temptation of prophecy, must THUS clear myself of ALL considerations of *debt* and/or ANY past considerations which seek to extend themselves thru the present and into the future, thus must clear myself of any such historical structure: and I find I must rid myself of any such sense as *"further* considerations," thus take The Present as a present, gift, with no attempt to prophesy therefrom either. If debt exists in the present, the gift of it cannot be accepted except in terms of *"due* consideration," thus exchanges prohibit change, thus even cash change becomes checked in a counter balance, thus residence in the living body of the moment becomes resi-due: BUT, thus, at least "how much do you need" becomes physiologically CLEAR; and, thus also, "where can you get it" often becomes immediately "how can you pay the debt," the resources of which are often, if not always, to be found in myself's immediate taking action— most often immediately effective if *with respect* to the past . . . and especially (as the word "immediately" can ONLY imply) *withOUT guard* for the future (as the term "regard of" is impossible in this form).

Only a poet can deal with the word "money" as a living term. Only a poet can make a present of it to the world; but I cannot imagine even that possible in those terms "of it" and "to the world" except as he would make it present—no, not that . . . more like: receive the presence of it to the world of himself—NO, still not it . . . too many "of's," I sense . . . something more immediate yet, like: give the word his world present —and/or, to drop "pre": give the word sense . . . dropping "his" possession (all possessiveness tide to future, "securities" etc., prophetic in nature) out of it also. Often poets do this with respect to the past: but a poet's clearest etymological search does seem to me to be with that respect withOUT guard and motivated by—no, rather: being a taking action to pay the debt of the word

> The true test of a work of art
> Is out of how deep a life does it spring?
> —James Joyce

I feel the following, also, to be true: "The true test of an artist's life is out of how deep a work does it spring."

BEFORE *SCENES FROM UNDER CHILDHOOD*

I am involved in a 16mm color film I believe to be called: *Scenes From Under Childhood*, or *Scenes From Under Child Hood*. The latter distinction in title depends, I think, upon the extent to which I accomplish a making of material, of the work, for the prompting of the aesthetic experience withIN the mind of the viewer upON the recall of the individual childhood experiences OF the viewer. As I do not, cannot as an artist, work with any idea of audience in mind, "viewer" means specifically "the viewer *I* am, when *not* making, of my work." I believe that when I am *most* individualistic as viewer I participate to the greatest extent in the communion which unites all viewers similarly concerned, each with his and her individuality, that I share with each other, then, the universal considerations upon which ritual, and thus art, depends, and that my response thus, as primary to these considerations, is as like unto any other's as is possible: and experience with other individual viewers and with audiences of large numbers of people have confirmed this belief. Most of my film work the last several years has created experiences *less* to be watched (as something "out there," which presumes to instruct by example, as the educational or propaganda film) and *less*, even, to be seen into (as something "elsewhere" which pretends to transport the viewer, succeeds in the illusion by creating imbalances which play upon his or her sensibilities for balance, as do most entertainment films. Hollywood or otherwise) but *more* to be invisioned (as something "to be taken in" thru an activated awareness on the viewer's part of a "Want of vision, or the power of seeing," as Webster's Dictionary defines the term "Invision"). The simple distinction is this: I am primarily concerned with making films which can be taken in*to* the viewer, in *thru* his experience of himself in the act of seeing, without his being taken in *by* the film and/or *via* his lack of experience. The crucial word in all this, with regard to my future working processes, is "activated" in relationship to "awareness on the viewer's part of a 'Want of vision, or the power of seeing' "! To what extent can the work of art activate my sense of seeing without educating same or imposing propagandistically upon me? How much can said work exist with*in its* necessary sets of circumstances with*out* pulling on *my* sensibilities thru any lack of vision on my part? In some recent films of mine, particularly *Dog Star Man* and *The Art of Vision*, some highly structured and integrally necessary levels of vision are created in such a way that they can *only* exist *in* the eye of the viewer. For instance, a single frame may be painted red, superimposed with a

From a letter to the Avon Foundation, March 18, 1965

gray toned image and preceded and followed by frames of overexposed imagery in such a way that that frame will be seen as green, if seen at all (that is, if the viewer is "normal" in his creation of after-image color retention, if his optic nerves retain green after a red-flash in such circumstances—the fact that the viewer may be color-blind or may have blinked his eyes in that instant can, obviously, be no more a concern of mine than the possibility he may be blind altogether or may have chosen to go out for a bag of popcorn, etc.). Now I find, with regard to *Scenes From Under Child Hood*, that many of my thoughts these days tend to the possibilities of creating, and depending upon, a level of that film which can occur as exclusively in the mind of the viewer as certain levels of *Dog Star Man*, etc., can only occur in the eye. I have already taken over a thousand feet of images of my children playing, etc.: and this unedited material has inspired the above concept. This concept must *not* impose itself upon my working processes but must *rather* be, if anything, a source of inspiration during the editing and ordering of visions. I am thinking of that particular thousand feet of images of my children's activities as containing the possibility, among many possibilities, of being structured in direct relationship to thought processes so that, as material, they might evoke aesthetically necessary images in me, as viewer, from the memories of my childhood, and that this could happen as primarily and universally as to constitute a source of communion and ritual of response with other viewers. Should these considerations prove impossible, unwise at this time, or simply otherwise in the working process, I shall probably find myself working on a much longer film called *Scenes From Under Childhood* involving photography of "snapshot" material, variously animated moving pictures of "stills" from my childhood, or perhaps an even longer film to be called *Autobiograph*.

TO ANDREW MEYERS

Rollinsville, Colo.
April somewhat, 1965

Dear Andrew,

Knowing the matters of this letter are going to concern Jonas and P. Adams, and Bob Branaman, and having little time for writing letters these days, I'm making a couple of carbons as I go along here.

At Jonas' instigation I've also supervised the making of a double 8mm master (on 16mm stock) and, thus, two prints of some of Bob Branaman's films along with your ANNUNCIATION and SHADES & DRUMBEATS. I have compared ALL these prints, now finished, with the masters and the masters with the originals (along with prints of MOTHLIGHT which I've just made) and it is my opinion that they are ALL remarkably good prints: BUT, let me qualify that statement with respect for your disturbance over the print of ANNUNCIATION.

I remember very well the day I first received a one-lite print, as it's called, of my 16mm B. & W. film, INTERIM, as it was—I was horrified at the loss of subtle detail in grays, the harshness of line, the over-exposure, the under-exposure, etcetera: and I rushed in

anger to the lab, the SAME lab, as it happens: Western Cine . . . only in those days, the lab was essentially John Newell and Herman Urshal and a B. & W. processing machine & a printer in a basement. They patiently explained to me the facts of printing which, in B. & W., are comparatively simple: in order to get a print anywhere near the balance of light of the original, light changes have to be made in the printing to compensate for increased contrasts naturally occurring in any removal, any print made, from the original; and these light changes must be made with respect to the specific print stock being used and even the particular batch of stock IN stock and with respect to the processing (development) of that stock (which is why tests of an incredible number are made daily in every lab right down to and including the relative humidity). The first print made with these light changes imposed IN the printing is called an answer print: and I have yet to find a lab anywhere that will guarantee the answer print to be more than an answer as to how to make the second print, with its second series of light changes, more approximate to the original —tho', for me, Western Cine's answer prints have always been very close to the best that can be expected, resulting in much fewer light changes for the second print than is usual in laboratory work . . . of late, particularly Mike Phillips, an employee there (and the one who timed your prints), has shown remarkable judgment in timing, as it's called, for a well-balanced answer print. When I made my first color print, of IN BETWEEN, thru San Francisco's Palmer Films, I went thru print torments all over again, even WITH an answer print; for the slightest variation in light values of course changes ALL color values and balances: and I went thru fresh tortures with each color print (learning, thereby, the irregularities color tone in the varying print stocks) and an especial *sturm and drang* (thereby) when I transferred some color work from various other labs to Western Cine (the "thereby" referring to the differing methods of processing, etcetera, which would be involved in changing ANY film from one lab to another). For instance, even tho' I am obviously more pleased by Western Cine's work, particularly with reference to latitude of color quality, I HAVE left DOG STAR MAN: PART 1 at Palmer Labs because their particular processing, etc., produces a print which is (HOW shall I describe something so subtle?—), well, "colder," "slicker," of a "polished density" which seems appropriate to THAT particular part of DSM, with all its reference to even the Hollywood drama, and the print quality serves to set it, thusly, apart from the overall tone of ALL other parts of that film. Of course, special measures have been taken all along the working process of each part to set its overall tone apart from each other: but, in the case of Part 1, its major tone is achieved by the special printing qualities of the lab which prints it, qualities which are altogether too (how shall I say?)— "bluishly" narrow for the majority of my work. So you see, Andrew, that I have concerned myself to an unusual extent, since my first betrayed sensitivity in print making, with the particularities of the subject; and, at the same time, I have HAD to come to accept the particularities of prints and the resultant generalities of the medium—(I must confess that, at the present, I am having a rage against "greenish" proclivity of the new Eastman print stock, a MOST picayune rage for one of my experience in the medium and yet, it is that very experience which has increased my sensitivity to the slightest variance and has, momentarily I hope, narrowed the tolerance my experience has also provided for me— "momentarily I hope" because there is a tremendous danger for the artist, and for anyone, in such a critic-type use of sensitivity . . . we need only, here, take warning from Charles Ives' trembling fits over the dropped fork at the table or from Edgard Varese's necessity, for a number of years, to remove himself to the relative silence of Death Valley . . . and for the film-maker, in such a newly bastard medium of constantly shifting values, it would be madness at the second step . . . NO—I must, rather, put up with the green moth wings and, MORE, come to see how perfectly MOTH-LIGHT sustains its original form in these new color balances, and, more YET, how beautifully it grows anew in this new Eastman spring of itself.)

Now, in 8mm printing, we have an additional problem to all those mentioned above (and to all those unmentioned and, even, unmentionable) and that is that there is no lab (known to me) which can make light changes in 8mm; and, therefore, there is ONLY and ALWAYS a one-light print being made (unless 8mm is blown up to 16mm, corrected, and reduced to 8mm again—a rather expensive process). The only control the lab can exercise, thus, is in the choice of the one-light with reference to the particular stock being used. I think Mike Phillips hit it on the button, so to speak, with every single master and print we have just had made. You see, had your complaint been that the

whole of ANNUNCIATION was too light OR too dark, a compensating light change could be made in the second print; but the very fact that it is both too light in some areas and too dark in others confirms the correct medium choice taken for the best print of most of the film. The second title, for instance, is very light on the original, is over-exposed and barely visible on the master, and is (of the course of increasing contrast with each removal from original) completely washed out on the print. Now, you might prefer to order the whole second set of prints a stop darker, which would probably get you the barely legible imprint of your name on that second credit shot; but then, the dark shots you are complaining about might go to absolutely black leader. There is nothing, with existing 8mm equipment at this time, which can be done about this problem—the problem, thus, becomes one of the technical terms of the medium itself . . . I have come to take it for granted in the very shooting of the film; and I'm sure that you will, similarly, benefit from experience which, in this instance, and in some sense always, can only seem an unnecessary frustration.

(Ah . . . "in some sense always" —Jane and I have just been talking about this in relation to our whole life. Yesterday I stood on the porch and raged at the piles of snow around our house, at the mess it has made of the road in its melting, at the length of this winter which the old-timers around here call "one of the worst" in memory—some 8 months out of this year we've had snow here —: and I found myself in the absurd but animistically real position of sputtering: "Poor form!": at the pissy sky, extending my fingers in exasperation at the, to me now, dull blacks and whites of the scene in all directions and yelling: "It's a fucking Andy Warhol movie, that's what it is!": feeling the full force of Napoleon's "Fifth element: mud!" with every glance at the almost impassable road— part of my boredom is due to the extent to which I HAVE immersed myself in this scene, photographing some of the minutest details of winter here, and part is due to my LACK of sensitivity to it, its sameness, its changes, etcetera . . . ah, well, it is beginning to snow, AGAIN, right now today as I sit here writing this to you— those flocks of sheepish flakes!: how do they DARE to show their symmetrical faces to me thru this window; and, yet, if they all started coming down Eastman green, what kind of a rage of fear and anguish would THAT precipitate in me? And then, downstairs, the phonograph is playing; and my increased sensitivity in music listening of late has made me aware of the slightest varia-

tion in mechanical pitch which, when first I heard it, I took to be inadequacy of turntable, have now come to know as variation in electrical current so that, when my neighbor's refrigerator goes on, my ears are critically tortured in midst of new-found listening joy—ah, the curse of John Cage extends in his total gesture— which Andy Warhol extends— which the muddy roads and the pissy skies extend—which anything taken totally, thru to end/beginning, extends—((yes, even Eastman)) . . . which even I, at first ((as they tell me)) torturing people's eyes, can hope to extend in beginning/end/beginning, etcetera. Ah, but it was really the "etcetera" which touched off converse between Jane and I in this: that we can tend to distract ourselves from the "going-onness" of everything AND from the realization of the ultimate "un-ness" of anything with our rages of unacceptance which can ONLY be premised on SOME sense of purpose, touching off all of plot aesthetically and plan realistically control prophetically/blasphemously/etceterally, the very etcetera of which thwarts purpose naturally from scratch—and it IS strange, and somehow encouraging to me in this moment, that man tends to be about equally distressed about birth AND death, seeking to sense the former as change ((transformation)) and the latter as, at least, X-change ((transfiguration)), both proclivities cancelling each other into the feelings of the moment, the "going-onness" of that, the "going-on-unness" of the past, the "going-un-onness" of the future, "going" becoming "being" in all that, and—oh, my, these words becoming more and more black-flake answers of mine across a page to the sift of the sky outside my window . . . and you'll have to forgive me for that, Andrew—it is my way of satisfying the monkey-chatter instincts in my origins . . . what would human beings be like if they were descended from cats, I wonder?)

And that's the best I can do for you, Andrew, at this time; and I hope it's the most I have to do at the moment for 8mm AT LARGE, because I have a most specific little "song" calling me into a techne of its own, informed in its coming into being with/ and/of Eastman green and no-wise concerned, now, with other/ later-Eastman in-clin-tone-ations and/or with costs and my, no doubt, future cussing thereabouts —"Song 11" . . . and so the songs ARE, yes, of a "going-onness" beyond my previous imaginings which clutched, but didn't brake, at "10."

Blessings,

TO ABBOTT MEADER

Beginning June, 1965

Dear Abbott,

Apropo yr very fine close-questioning of my statements on "engagement" in the experience of art, in "Metaphors on Vision":

I had found myself already saying, on that last speech trek, in answer to such-like questioning: "I don't think an artist should get engaged unless he intends to get married"; but then, as I mean something much different by "married" than, apparently, most

people ("7 out of 10 marriages end in divorce," a lawyer friend tells me), I'd better be more specific than I have, heretofore, been:

Jane and I live in a perpetual state of divorce-and-marriage; that is: we separate (in all senses save that we live in each other's sight, sense surroundings, under the same roof), make it FINAL (proclaiming the intolerability of some characteristic in one or the other—usually several-such in the divide of both of us); and then we come together when each has shaped new sense of self and the other (the tentative lace of words/fingers, etc., in acknowledgement of the inevitability of attraction, an "engagement' period in all this, "marriage" that inevitability.) Most others, it seems to me, lie about their feelings, hedge the "intolerable" IN (7 out of 10? . . . only?), the self trying to take it upon it's ("take it like a man" . . . like a woman?, etc.), finally, in self's "failure" (strength, actually, to resist self's suicide) they come to believe too much in externals, providence-as-self's-servant (what'all will "drop from heaven": other women/men?, happen/ing/ness?, etc.?) and, that failing, in societal means (go to court as they once a'courting went, cancel preach-err with lawyer, etcet-er-errr) and start superfishing again (the man dangling his cock in the waters/she drifting him to her/his next natural falls.)

Now, as to "making it"—art and/or . . . :

He hear her, she hymn, they come in form, he Ho!, she Hummmm, he Haw!, she He!, He's-he, She-she, each miss tree in which:

He hear her, etceter (ahhhhh over all of it).

Thus, the "engagement" to me is simply sensing (hearing/seeing) the other (and so for-th): "marriage" ultimate of good sense (one that leads to source): permitting all self's senses to experience singular senses' attraction; and "making it" (opposite of "making it up" and other than "last," etc.) the actual feed-back, the exercise (play) of source IN self (AT large).

Only value of this writ-(you-all) is as it stands against The Right(ch'us) on grounds that don't exist around a missed tree. Only those who care to give an *UN*RE-(hersed)-*DANCE* in the sheer aire-(ear)-y of it can live in this (IN-Stan't this lettering IS). I no longer care for over-see-errs and under-stand-err-errs.

TO JONAS MEKAS

A snowed mid-Sept., 1965

Dear Jonas,

The world utterly white outside now—flares of aspens, even, snowed. This freeze thaws me inside, somehow . . . some *very* NEW work willing up. I find myself feeling that it is the total physiological impulse of a man must be given form in the making of a work of, thus, called, art. I think all subject matter is a peg to hang this impulse on, that outside source of a work is simply that which excites the entire physiology of the man, and that he cannot commission that from himself anymore than he can decide to be impulsive and have that decision affect more of his physiology than the "derangement" Rimbaud writes of/out of. A prime drive of all contemporary arts seems premised on many individual needs to get inside one's own skin—via dreams (Surrealism), via some duct or other: the finding muse/source in physiological sense: as has painting (Abstract) in closed-eye vision, as has music (Electronic) in ear's hearing, as has poetry (Black Mtn.) in breath's measure, etc.; and in this sense, the art of moving pictures is the oldest art of living times in that it was the medium wherein you'll find first works dependent totally on the eye . . . that, THUS, the art of moving pictures is LEAST subject TO—MOST object of—ALL OTHER ARTS . . . that, THEREFORE, it defines itself most completely in all THE MUSE *MEANS* / THE BRAIN'S *IN*-FORMATION, as painting does as it ceases to BE information AS illustration, as music does as it ceases to BE information as mathematics, as prose does as it ceases to "make up stories," as poetry does as it ceases to "tell" and is as words as it ceases to mathematically measure as it ceases description, "making pictures" . . . that, ANDSO-FORTH, the art of moving pictures is further along the backbone than all other arts: BUT, most men abort this drive by taking information OF physiology as source of sensibility, take mind's impulse as total, thus utter thought only, bog down in brain matter, etc., AND/OR commission excitement in arrangements of color, pattern, shape, into what turns out to be for brain's sake only (Bach, for instance, got much further "for God's sake": thought extending, thus, thru faith into the unknown for source of impulse innards—subject matter? . . . the variously inner impulses taking shape in sound, the term "fantasy," as with the works, thus called, of Swelinck particularly, Vivaldi also, etc., but especially Bach, helping to defeat dominance of brain wave's math in music, giving excuse perhaps for ear-regularities and/or impulses of an un-brain-known origin.) I believe in THE NEW PHYSIO-LOGICAL MAN Michael Mc-Clure writes of, and that an artist can only hope to become something of that man He TOTALLY *IS* and then, in order, to create out of *more* than he's a mind to. I believe each person's absolute necessity to inhabit the present will make it finally impossible for an artist to accept even the commission his own memories' urgency prompts—that, thus, all subject matter (as impeg hanging

pulse up) all content ("AS A WIFE HAS A COW ((*IS*))* A LOVE STORY"—G. Stein) all *referential* source (as excitement is a past tension available only thru *brain's* immediacy) will cease to in - form the work . . . ex - ternal means could thus (perhaps for the first time in a million years) be IN - direct/dance-touch with a man's IM - pressed/pulse - EXpression.

Well—wow . . . how I've made a bend for your eye-ear this morning, dear Jonas. I only intended, at start, to write thru a flurry of snow here and tell you how we all are. We're happily fine.

Joy to you,

*my addition

TO JEROME HILL

Late March, 1966
Winds everywhichway—
Jane and I just hung a
kite in a pine tree. . . .

Dear Jerome,

Your film strips are BEAUTI-
FUL! The color quality of them
is so very much "yours," as I remember from your painting, that
I am moved to considerations of
style as soul and of man's particular sphere/environment of color
possibilities *as soul's tone*—you
are, perhaps, familiar with some
of the 19th century drives in this
direction . . . Rudolph Steiner,
etcetera . . . all of which, alas,
washed out in world consideration
because of the fake mysticism of
a few . . . Madam Blavatsky?, etcetera?! (I use question marks
here because of Robert Duncan's
recent defense of Blavatsky, in
issue of Aion Magazine, defense
of the beauty of the world of her
imagination and the perfected
synthesis of earlier image-birth
definitions she'd made—which
naturally, as Duncan finds it, she
was forced to "fake" in the face
of the so-called "real" world's
demands . . . the question mark
ought, really, to occur after the
phrase, "fake mysticism," a possibly unlikely combination of
words). Anyway, it is interesting

that the deepest considerations of
the word "style" (historically, for
instance, as it comes out of the
Latin "stylus," referring to the instrument of writing—which is,
after all and finally, the human
being himself—and keeping close
to its phallic origin clear thru the
Elizabethan Era, taking on the
Teutonic "stellen"—to set or
place . . . "self-styled" being possible out of this . . .) lead one in-
evitable to the sense of it as a *most*
personally definitive piece of our
language—that, for example, a
man's penmanship is unlike any
other's enough so that money can
pass on it, that "style" is precisely
what cannot be translated from
one language to another *unless* the
author himself makes that translation (then it is *exactly* STYLE
which IS translatable), that a
painter's color tone (like ghosts,
visions, etc.) is unphotographable,
unreproduceable, etcetera . . . (I
will use your film strips in reference to the photographs of your
paintings to remind me of the
true-to-your-soul / sense of the
color of the originals, however,
because color style is—as these
prove—translatable if the painter
involves himself creatively in the
photography/reproduction, etc.—
as you have here done . . .) And
I, all the same, marvel that you
made this magic—the startlingly/

Film Culture 40, **Spring 1966**

uniquely beautiful color in those pieces! —by painting on color negative . . . perhaps the perfect "once-removal" mechanism, or "angel-interstice" I call it, needed to permit the passage of your soul's tone onto film . . . the "mysterium" for "soul's passage," the ancients would have called it, working thru "Blind Faith," a middle - ages craftsman would have called it (the kind of "blind" Homer was said to have had)— (and you surely were, in a sense, painting in a kind of "color blind," when you had the courage/faith to work on the negative, taking all your technical knowledge of color translation, thus, as only the religious knowledge in your possession . . . useless for soul-stuff with-

out some celebration of the mysteries premised on faith.)

Jane put the films up on the mirror in the dining room, where the light reflects thru them, their bouquet of frames, most marvelously.

Joys,

Stan

Postscript: Did you know that the FIRST censored movie (in this pre-Civil-War Country) was the early 19th-century whirligig hand toy, the crucial one of whose movies flickered the dozen-pictures-or-so of The Devil throwing a small boy into the flames of Hell?

TO NED O'GORMAN

April Fool's Day, 1966

Dear Ned,

A Child of the Times, which I take myself to be, lives this (every instant anyday) poised in immediacy and posed upon The Present as gift from an unknown benefactor—lives *op*-posed (out of "seeing is believing") to The Past as more than memory can make immediate, and posited against any more than a *pre-*

tendency of control over The Future . . . avoids, thus, both Debt and Prophecy (Faust's problems) . . . lives, therefore, very much in his/her skin (kinship centered primarily on sex) . . . and, heretofore, heralds what I take (without predicting) to be The Physiological Man—as defined most clearly/immediately in the writings of Michael McClure ("Meat Science Essays," "The Surge," "Poisoned Wheat," etc.) out of Charles Olson ("Proprioception," etc.) and taking whatever of the 19th century is presently useful via the dedication to same of Robert Duncan (the "H. D." book, etc.).

The arts of this Man take Sense as Muse so that poetry arises in direct relationship to the word as a cultural-memory particle (Duncan), the breath of the man writing (Olson), his changes of throat, tongue, lip, etc., in rendering it into sound (Zukofsky) and the tantric reverberations of same in the various areas of his whole body giving utterance (McClure) —so that music orients itself to the emotive ear (all tape music utilizing dramatically evocative sounds) and/or intensities and rhythms of thought (all "purely" electronic music, most "twelve"— and more—"tonic" music) rather than mathematical formulation— so that painting arises out of the physical act out of emotion (Action painting) and/or takes shape according to those mental processes creating "closed-eye vision" (Op Art), etcetera.

The Film-Maker of this Time inherits these, and many other, physiologically premised directions as possibilities of influence on an essentially "open" medium and is inspired by one or another of the arts according to personal necessity. Film is, thus, either *not an art at all* or it is *the oldest art of our times*. In either case, it was the first medium of this century to shape itself primarily thru the sense necessities of the individual makers dedicated to it and to begin to define itself, thus, by way of its shared physical relationship to all other arts and, thus, to seek its outgrowth thru inspired intake without more regard, or guarding against, historical aesthetics than came in the wake, or death, of those forms it necessarily fed upon and sustained in itself. As a public medium, it has been the last/first source of ritual in our time: but some few children have played privately enough with it to engender what I like to call unipersonal visions wherein The Persona ceases to be Mask once it is known as flesh and The Ivory Tower of inwardness takes shape again on Public Domain at the outermost limits of physiological awareness.

Blessings,

Stan

TO DOLORES DANIELS

Dolores E. Daniels
Principal
Rollinsville Elementary School
Rollinsville, Colorado

Dear Dolores Daniels,

I can understand something of your position—I can, yes, understand enough of this incident from your standpoint to sincerely address you as "Dear," as above: and if you had simply written us and stated, as some school rule you'd felt the need to make, a requirement that we, say, bathe Myrrena once a week, we would certainly have found it easier, I suppose, to comply than to take issue . . . to be specific about our "individual philosophy," as you call it, I think that if you'd required a "once-a-day" bath, I'd have felt inclined to fuss this matter right into the law courts, if necessary (you might as well find out *right* now that I'm a dedicated man when it comes to my beliefs, that I'm one of those humans concerned enough with every individual right I am often in conflict with most of the current trends of this society, that I am thus one of those individuals it is popularly convenient to dismiss as "trouble-maker" and/or, as of the last several years, "beatnik"—the latter term expressing more of the hope, I think, of the satisfied "middle-class" that its dissenting children are "beaten" at their individuality rather than, as is more true, that they are "beating out" some paths of more sanity than were left to us by the previous generation . . .)

But your letter is more than a request, states more than a simple requirement you might have felt your position forced you to impose— indeed, you do not finally state any requirement at all, will not take that responsibility (as is so often the way with those who act, in the name of the social order and in terms of its "unwritten" laws, to infringe on the rights of individuals) . . . and, instead, you express indignation ("because of the odor, which is offensive to the point of nausea"—really, Miss Daniels!) and seek to shame us ("It seems grossly unfair to penalize a child in this way") — etcetera. As you seem to me to be primarily a good person, I suppose you have taken the tactic of this letter because of your own doubts in this situation—that that made you delay in writing "because we want to respect your individual philosophy" . . . and yet, and then, when you felt compelled to write us finally (because of your position, the complaints of those in your—or rather Myrrena's environment) you passed not only the burden of this responsibility onto us (and that we can justly assume) but also the vestiges of your frustration (which we cannot assume).

Let me be clear, therefore, about our lack of shame: my wife and I both cherish the human senses, have developed them in ourselves (and hopefully, in our children) to a high degree. My life's work, as a film artist, particularly qualifies me to search out and create thru the finest qualities of human vision: but we do also cultivate, naturally in our love of living, all other senses. The sense of smell has been particularly delightful to us—an area of sensibility rich in surprises to the searching human precisely because it has suffered such common human neglect, has been so suppressed in most people's upbringing. As a result of our opening our nostrils, so to speak, we have come to be aware of the *fact* (now scientifically established by Ray L. Birdwhistell and others in the field of kinesiology) that the human being, and indeed every living thing, participates in the communication with others very largely thru the emitting of smells specific to individual emotion. My wife and I, for instance, have learned to consciously differentiate the smell of fear (a sour-milk-&-burnt-fat effluvium) from, say, hate (somewhat like moistened-charcoal-of-burnt-meat, sometimes coupled with sea-weedly-salt). These emotional-emits *are* repulsive to us, but *naturally* thus—that is, because they are *biologically intended* to repulse . . . they are those indications of necessary-(if fight is to be avoided)-creature separation. We respect every human smell *particularly,* as we take it to be our responsibility (ability to respond) to participate *meaningfully* with others: BUT, we do NOT respect the evasions deodorants are—we do not know any more how to meaningfully accommodate these than you, I think, would know how to accommodate a person who intentionally distorted the exchange of language for the purposes of evasion . . . I hope to think you would dismiss such a person as a liar and would be distressed at all such proclivity in current human activity (and I like to imagine, at this moment, that you *are* distressed at the hypocrisy in, say, the average television deodorant ad . . . as well as, say, the more subtle, but no less lying, journalistic usages of our language, the destruction of specific meaning thru sloppy usage, on the one hand, and intentional propaganda, on the other—in fact, I would have the right to expect you to be concerned with these matters, as you are a teacher and, more, a principal: one who, I believe, should be primary guardian of the *whole* heritage of education AND as *against,* or at least resisting cautiously, the too-easy proclivity of the present—you see, if you understand me, that I am actually very *conservative* in my attitudes . . .).

But then you are of necessity, also, a principal in the popular liberal sense: a representative of the popular trends within the institutional environment, a mediator in democratic procedure—and, as such, somewhat of a benevolent dictator too (as has always been necessary to the liberal concept of democratic procedure): and, thus, you find yourself representative for, from my viewpoint, a soap-and-deordorant-crazy society and as against, in this instance, this individual drive to retrieve human *animal* sensibility. You may find me selfish in this matter, wishing *my* way rather than simply condescending to the will of the many, making my child suffer (as you suggest) because of personal peculiarities: but I would ask you to consider, please, what is the *traditional* responsibility of the artist. It would be easy, selfish, of me to conform: but if all did, there would be no arts, nor sciences either, nor *any* of the traditional historical forms—there would, then, be no formal education either . . . there would be nothing for you to teach or be principal of. My way is shaped, as is traditionally so for artists—a condition of their work, you might say— by an ever-increasing knowledge of historical aesthetics AND, as is of primary importance, a being true to my senses in all my experiencing of the present. From that standpoint, and with whatever authority I deserve for my position, I find the society deranged with regard to "hygiene" (as you put it) and in danger of psychologically destroying, for its individual members, one of its most precious senses, the sense of smell. In search of the possible cause for this, that I take to be a cultural insanity, I've come across the following passage by a very great artist of our immediate past (a man much despised in his lifetime—but one coming now to be respected enough I expect you'll be teaching him in your school within a decade) . . . D. H. Lawrence— and I quote:

"Once the heart is broken, people become repulsive to one another secretly, and they develop social benevolence. They smell in each other's nostrils. It has been said often enough of more primitive or old-world peoples, who live together in a state of blind mistrust but also of close physical connection with one another, that they have no noses. They are so close, the flow from body to body is so powerful, that they hardly smell one another, and hardly are aware at all of offensive human odors that madden the new civilizations. As it says in this novel (he's referring to the novel, "Bottom Dogs" by Edward Dahlberg): The American senses other people by their sweat and their kitchens. By which he means, their repulsive effluvia. And this is basically true. Once the blood-sympathy breaks, and only the nerve-sympathy is left, human beings become secretly intensely repulsive to one another, physically, and sympathetic only mentally and spiritually. The secret physical repulsion between people is responsible for the perfection of American 'plumbing,' American sanitation, the American kitchen, utterly white-enamelled and antiseptic. It is revealed in the awful advertisements such as those about 'halitosis,' or bad breath. It is responsible for the American nausea at coughing, spitting, or any of those things. The American townships don't mind hideous litter of tin cans and paper and broken rubbish. But they go crazy at the sight of human excrement."

Yes, I believe much of the American "heart is broken": but I also believe it means to mend itself and, more, to grow utterly new—but very *real*—tissue . . . I mean, I believe we are entering an era of physicality, that we are taking from our whole animal beingness, and that I am personally responsible to/and/for the sense aesthetics of this: the experiencing of the senses fully in whatever present living, and the tradition of this. How, believing that, can I possibly encourage my daughter in the ways you indignantly suggest I *ought* to . . . and still be true to her? No—if you had succeeded in shaming me, you would have introduced hypocrisy into this household. I *don't* expect hypocrisy from you—I emphatically do NOT "expect that Myrrena be given individual attention by the teachers"—I do NOT expect you to "strongly suggest that the other children work or play with her" . . . both of those ideas, and all the false social benevolence & hypocritical human behavior implied, horrify me.

As we did never *prevent* Myrrena from washing or bathing (as, in fact, she has the example of myself bathing about 3 times a week with joy— I enjoy the water and relaxation—) I can only inform her of the exact situation, *as I see it,* and encourage her with the joys I find in bathing. If that does not satisfy you, then please feel free to be *direct* with me in this, and all future, matters.

Sincerely,

TO MICHAEL MCCLURE

March '66, quoting
from his poem, "Power"

A few more words about *Scenes From Under Childhood* — Viz, say, the sense of some particular power remembered, I'm after the rhythm of blinking of:

> "A black rainbow in 3D
> curved and solid blinking
> black neon
> in a chrome box":

and after the particular colors this black pulse takes upon itself—for the colors are INdrawn, one color always more than another at each pulse, while all of such a mix as to engender the sense of black OR white (why you call the box "chrome," natch): and in this working, I have had black & white positive and negative prints made of much of the color film so that there can mix in exact superimpositions, pulsing according to need, in the editing.

It is that the work itself, the finished film, should be source only for what occurs in the mind of the viewer . . . as is always the case, natch, but never before (or hardly ever) premised so clearly in the making, taken as such exact assumption in the creative process. But, to be clearer yet, this process is actually opposite of the PREsumptions of Op Art (where I find the intention is to affect the viewer, his affectation necessary to pull off, so to speak, the effect the work is—that he must be optically bugged, as it were, for the work to exist) because I am simply here involved with a process so naturally always existent its workings have been over-looked: that the light takes shape in the nerve endings and IS shaped, in some accordance we call communication, thru physiological relationship.

March '66

I slept 14 hours last night! awoke this morning full of thoughts of *The Feast,* have just re-read the play . . . God, what a masterWHOLE it is, the space it makes in THE critical religious tension of our TimePIECE. The whole thing flares in my imagination as in the space of 35mm Cinemascope, PRECISELY BECAUSE THE WHOLE SPACE WOULD NEED NEVER BE USED, would be a being there as SPACE for the filling-(with)-IN the imagination of the viewer; so that I envision the entire work occurring in the mind of the viewer, only your words and visual illustrations, in the purest sense of the word, coming in from the OUTside of him/her/whom/ever. Actually I sense the vision of the work occurring, ESSENTIALLY, in two spaces: (1) above the heads of the viewers, in the movements of the strings of light from projection booth (and this would be the space I would directly bring into being) and (2) within the forefront of the brain (taking eyes as brain at surface) to such an extent that the thumbs of the viewers (as thumb area of brain overlaps eye motor area) would surely join the dance of the work. Your words do already give specific DIRECTION, sound the ear with air that knows of its taking shape, thus touches all knowing DIRECTLY. Thus:

"The light of Blessing is meaningless there's no light
in the closed rose but a tiny black cherub
sleeps there and sings to the creatures
that walk in the cliffs of the Lillys pollen
moving from shadow to light in the drips
of rain.
The seen is as black as the eye seeing it.
What is carved in air is blank as the finger
touching it.
All is the point touched and
THE RELEASE.
Caress."

It is the impossibility of making *Nolight* that permits black rose (as there IS a rose tinted black-leader) as it is the impossibility of the eye to retain any but complimentary color that permits black-blue to make an other-color of rose (as retained blue light will make a rose which can only bloom in the EYE of the viewer), etc. (*Dog Star Man* ends on the dying shapes in fields of changing tones of variously tinted, so called: "black": leaders.)

A move "from shadow to night" *in negative* means the swallowing up of shape so that a bringing into shape can ONLY occur in the mind of the imagination extending itself upon the given possibility. If the change occurs at the instant of taking shape, and the change be visually from positive to negative, only the sense of shape will ever occur (and that only in the transformation); and thus shape will only occur in the extending of the imagination of the viewer feeding upon what was sensed (in transformation).

"What is carved in air is blank as the finger touching it." Give me a finger moving in air; and it will be picture of finger for *one frame only* (1/40th of a second), will become a carve of solid shape in air, thus: each frame is exposed full-time length needed for the movement (say: 20 seconds), and first frame finger is still at starting point, second frame finger has retained its position and then moved a fraction of an inch during the exposure, third frame finger returns to starting position and moves two fractions of an inch during exposure, and so on for 480 frames—finger carves solid shape OF itself in space of picture area . . . is finger-picture ONLY at time-source of itself, thus only in the referential mind of the viewer.

THUS: Illustration, MOVING illustration, which, taking language as source *only,* cannot possibly interfere with the images language engenders in the mind of the viewer but only encourage that activity further by being TOUCH-(upon the optic nerves)-TONE upon the eyes of the viewer.

But, I must temper the above with THE FACT that *The Feast,* thus: as a film: would AT BEST cost $100,000.00.

GOD DAMN THE MONEY PROBLEM, the hard solid million years old UTTERLY MISTAKEN at source PICTURES, dirty pictures, of it interfering with every turn of my imagination these days.

But, then, pictures too, in filming this work, would be of essential source for imagination. Thus, a Cinemascope space which was never filled but only implied the given set of *The Feast* would reply upon Leonardo's Last Supper in the minds of the viewer. Perhaps I, in some such living awareness, even at this difficult time, can draw a blessing from these considerations. The other way would be, of course, to do away with Leonardo & MONEY altogether, forget Last Supper & Cinemascope completely, and dig this vision out of trash baskets behind Western Cine Labs. But I fear, in all my life these days, being *driven* to a coming to terms with JUNK, being driven from the clearly beautiful visions my present surroundings engender to a coming to terms with the constructed ugliness and rotting junk debris of it which is my sight of the city; for I sense, in that exchange, in my seeing the works of all artists who thus "make it," that it is only the struggle to find beauty in ugliness which is, in itself, beautiful; and I fear some devil-pact is being slipped over & eventually *upon* us all, in this exchange, wherein the artist sensibility will, finally, be tricked and/or *driven,* as most other human sensibilities in our TIME-piece, to DISTORTION in which ugliness *is* beauty and, ULTIMATELY (wherein even the beauty of the struggle would be lost) VICE VERSA.

S.A. # I

*IT IS MIND MOVEMENT which finally, vitally, concerns me IN another man's art

NOT that I am THAT interested in Gloucester BUT that Olson's breath breaks *tempo*ral constructs in THIS brain

   it: ART: (not BRAIN) but THAT interested/constructs THAT

   that it is man's art (not that this brain)

   IS mind move me in ANOTHER MAN

   that I AM that construc*tion* IN this BRAIN

   IT: that is man

   THAT: brain

            - - - - - - -

TEMPO ION?—the eyes have it . . . *viz*:
ability to trace Greek-columnar (I)'s from the first space-place,*
string second, third (I)'s as verticals along-the-(first)-line, etc.
find second (I) roofed (T), fourth two (II) supporting "v" for
(M) etcetera.

   tempoR All?—ear-responsibility . . .
   that "*v*" *is* (not pronouncable)
   that "IT IS" are like (Germanized)
   that my : mine : : I : eye (in Eng.)

   i on?—
   (IN mind) . . .

vis-ability

OF relationship between columns & lop-sided pedastals with
balls a'top (°) of 'om (i)

"which fin . . . vit" allies ears to eyes
AND bodies
               2 back-throat Ichy CAPS, a double
               unpro-*noun*-cable uncap-v"-CAP aye-aye,
               and a first person singular "I"

F Acts

I make IF of it . . .

As I make It of it . . .

As IF I make It . . .

As if "as" were "A-Z" . . .

As "it" "is" . . .

"Is" "As" . . .

            and so for THE: Axe:
                       AXE: :the

S A won, mind moving now axiomatically, viz:

    (won):   of script of brain, say: *"gray matter."*

    (too):   (d) scrip (of Chaucer) mine(d: bray IN as)
                  print(or: IMitater) a(ver((b)) as handwriting),
                  say: *"Coll or* as sociate mat."

    (the re):   (see) script (see Shakespeare) my(((e))nd:
                  "T,/But now 'tis made an "H") refer (((h))ence:
                  Anthony and Cleopatra, IV, vii,8) other(((X))YZ:
                  Zukofsky's *Bottom on Shakespeare,* page 33, top),
                  say: *"Dis cull* or dis A-Z ocean ma(h)."

    (F, or):   (be) scribe (be((e)) Milt-) Im eye (be I((n))
                  Whit-) "cookie-" (be eye in((g)) -on -man)
                  "pusher (be in((g)) Pound), say: *"Disc all*
                  or 'dis a sew see on 'em.' "

    (F I've):   (a) scri(m) and (a((m))) a (ma((n))) and
                  (((S))((A))): *"Fire of waters."*

AS Kelly

      "The truth of the matter/is this:
                           that man's body

           lives in a fire of waters
           & will live forever in
           the first taste."

AS Collage   "The taste"

F AS   "The truth"

forth   1 backthroat itch, 2 tongued-to-lips-
out "i" 's (as here a-pos-trophied distinct
from double & half quoted), and double-double
lop-sided columns after, etcetera.

SEE quence: not to MORE than mention "v" to
"V", "M" "M", "MOVEMENT . . . concerns"
such as M : M : : 1 : 1 displace-space)-
ment, in telling, which intellect will
seek to balance, in spelling, with "i" to ","
"eye" to "comma" and an eary Ooooo-Ehhhh to
ooh-eeh for a "meIN", etc.

resiDUE? INconsideration! (*VIZ*-a-"V") :

"Olson's breath breaks"

"in Gloucester"

(and a few other particulars)

F A-Z   "of the matter"

IF   "is this:
                       that"

I   "man's body"

F Acts   "lives in a fire of waters
& will live forever in
the first taste."

      F aXe, thus, makes bode of man's
                    makes waters subject to his
                    (and particularizes Z)

8MM SEEING VISION

Before I actually began working in 8mm, I had talked about it for several years. Then at one point, when I had come to New York with my whole family, things were very bad: we [independent film-makers] were pressured on questions of censorship and couldn't get a place to show films anywhere. Some were speaking of going to jail and being martyrs. I said, why fight for the right to show our films in the auditoriums? They never have been of much use to the film artist anyway, for most works of film art are designed to be seen many times, and your auditorium experience is never anything more than an introduction.

I have said for years that showing a film that is a work of art once in an auditorium is like a single flashing of an Ezra Pound poem around the old *New York Times* building's electric news sign. They've got to stop this business of never considering a film something which needs to be seen several times in order to understand it. Television has made the one-shot a primary way of encountering visual experience. If you miss a TV show, it'll probably never be on again, so there's no possibility of study. Therefore, there's no room for a work that exists on multiple levels.

If this sort of presentation were true of poetry, poetry couldn't exist. In the language that poetry requires, study and involvement and an ability to manipulate language back and forth are necessary. If film got into the homes it would suddenly open up all those possibilities. A man could not only have the film and look at it as many times as he wanted to, which is important, but also—perhaps more important—exactly *when* he wanted to. Maybe at home he could even stop the film and look at an individual frame, or run it at any conceivable speed and move it backwards and forwards to study it.

This is something the foundations could help make possible, and they absolutely refuse to do it. The foundations have the perfect opportunity to buy a *finished* work of film art from an artist (instead of *commissioning* nonexistent work, as they seem to prefer, and which, not surprisingly, often turns out badly, or not at all) and put it into 8mm cartridges. Then they could give it to libraries and institutions where people can simply pick it up and stick it in a machine, there or at home, and look at it as often as they want to. And the foundations would, in the process, have paid for that work to support the artist so that he could go on and do whatever he's doing, and give the work to the people in a meaningful way.

Soon after that mess about censorship, we went to live in an 1890's cabin in a ghost town at about 9,000 ft. on the continental divide. Just before we left New York, some of my 16mm equipment had been stolen, so when we got settled, I went into town and found that I could buy—with money that wouldn't even begin to buy a 16mm editor—all the used 8mm equipment I needed. For about $25, I could get a camera, editors, rewinds, lights, and even a roll of film.

My work had passed through the influence of other media: the theatre, Hollywood movies and educational movies. All those are rooted in drama. The distinction makes very little difference. The fact that the camera moves around doesn't make a film profoundly different from looking at, say, a Tennessee Williams stage play through a pair of zoom-lens binoculars controlled by Elia Kazan [its director]. He would zoom in on the actress's face at one point and swish over to the actor's and so on back and forth. He would control the exact area, in size and shape, of what you were seeing, but otherwise you would be watching a stage play—and that's basically what's still going on in the film medium.

As the influence of drama passed out of my work, then came painting, poetry, and music. The poetic idea that meant something to me was the word "song." It really rang to me and made association. But it bothered me that the art of film was always leaning to some extent on these previous arts; so I needed a base, a source of inspiration, a form that had run clear through film from its very beginning, that was more clean of these other older arts. That's where the home movie is an inspiring thing, because a man—for all his embarrassment—when he's working with his 8mm home movie camera is usually trying to make a record of what he cares about. He has to get over his embarrassment and stop trying to imitate Hollywood or TV, and simply use the camera with the sense of what is in his hands. It's good if he wants to put something in it of how he feels about the things he photographs—how much he's enjoying the trip he's taking, how much it's bugging him, too; and how much he loves his wife and his children, or how much or to what degree he hates one or the other of them at that moment. If he could let all that come into it, then what he made could be expressive.

So these things, home movies and song, involve me very much with 8mm, and I knew that through them I could restore the film form to what it was at source. So I began to try it, and *Song I* is "Portrait of Jane," my wife, just as she sits around the house and reads. As *I see* her sitting and reading. I knew I had to get something of the sense of what her world was like to her, so I kept track of the footage numbers as I ran the film through the camera for the first time; then I went back and laid in two levels of superimposition. I tried to do it very subtly, to give some sense of the passage of the world through her mind's eye, as it was imagined in *my* mind's eye, of what she was thinking and doing. It was always a mystery to me what this woman that I loved was doing when she was so much in her own world—reading, sitting by herself. Not to presume more in what she was actually thinking about, but only to put myself in it enough to say, well, here are the rocks that pass through her mind and that I know she loves so much, and here is her parents' shadow moving, and so on.

Even the limitations of 8mm are interesting: that you can't do A and B roll printing, that there wasn't much that could be done in the labs. You work with "8" as does a still photographer, who never depends on the labs in that sense. When I came to the editing—and I edited quite a lot—I could splice: I could change and shift around.

I get very excited, too, about the colors and textures of 8mm: 8mm is very grainy and "grainy" means that you can blow up the small image so large that you are, in fact, seeing the grain field of it, the crystals of its silver haloids. This is important to me because I feel that graininess is part of vision—especially closed-eye vision, in which you see the dot field and grains and shapes moving around. So there is a correspondence in 8mm to closed-eye vision; this grain field in 8mm is like *seeing* yourself *seeing*.

I have always thought of 8mm as something that had particular forms unto itself which, if they were fully gone into, would make it an expressive medium utterly distinct from "16" or "35." We can always take those 16's or 35's and reduce them so that they could be distributed in "8," but that never has interested me as much as the film that was made for 8mm from the beginning.

FILM AND MUSIC

Dear Ronna Page,

Jonas Mekas will have whatever material has been salvaged on and/or by me—old clips, "stills," etcetera—as I make a practice of sending them all to him for Film-Makers' Cooperative files.

As to quotes out of my past, I imagine you have ample material in FILM CULTURE issues and my book METAPHORS ON VISION. I am presently working on a long film (16mm) to be called: SCENES FROM UNDER CHILDHOOD. It would probably be of particular interest to your Parisian readers to know that this work-in-progress is to some extent inspired by the music of Olivier Messiaen and, to some lesser extent, Jean Barraque, Pierre Boulez, Henri Pousseur, and Karlheinz Stockhausen (all, I believe, former pupils of Messiaen).

Fifteen years ago I began working with the film medium as primarily shaped by the influence of stage drama. Since that time, both poetry and painting have alternately proved more growth-engendering sources of inspiration than either the trappings of the stage or the specific continuity limitation of any "making up a story," novelistic tendencies, etcetera: and the first departures in my working-orders from "fiction" sources gave rise to an integral involvement with musical notation as a key to film editing aesthetics. Some ten years ago I studied informally with both John Cage and Edgard Varese, at first with the idea of searching out a new relationship between image and sound and, thus, creating a new dimension for the sound track, as Jean Isidore Isou's VENOM AND ETERNITY had created in me a complete dissatisfaction with the conventional usages of music for "mood" and so-called "realistic sounds" as mere referendum to image in movies, and Jean Cocteau's poetic film plays, for all their dramatic limitations, had demonstrated beautifully to me that only non-descriptive language could co-exist with moving image (in any but a poor operatic sense), that words, whether spoken or printed could only finally relate to visuals in motion thru a necessity of means and/or an integrity as severely visual as that demonstrated by the masterpieces of collage.

The more informed I became with aesthetics of sound, the less I began to feel any need for an audio accompaniment of the visuals I was making. I think it was seven/eight years ago I began making *intentionally* silent films. Although I have always kept myself open to the possibilities of sound while creating any film, and in fact made a number of sound films these last several years, I now see/feel no more absolute necessity for a sound track than a painter feels the need to exhibit a painting with a recorded musical background. Ironically, the more silently-oriented my creative philosophies have become, the more inspired-by-music have my photographic aesthetics and my actual editing orders become, both engendering a coming-into-being of the physiological relationship between seeing and hearing in the making of a work of art in film.

I find, with Cassius Keyser, that "the structure of mathematics is similar to that of the human nervous system" and have for years been studying the relationship between physiology and mathematics via such books as Sir D'Arcy Thompson's ON GROWTH AND

Written in April 1966; published in *Guerrila*, June 1967, and in *The Avant-Garde Film: A Reader of Theory and Criticism* edited by P. Adams Sitney, 1978

FORM: and following those "leads" along a line of music, I've come to the following thoughts (which I'll quote from an article of mine which appeared in the magazine WILD DOG) :

"I'm somehow now wanting to get deeper into my concept of music as sound equivalent of the mind's moving, which is becoming so real to me that I'm coming to believe the study of the history of music would reveal more of the changing thought processes of a given culture than perhaps any other means—not of thought shaped and/or Thoughts but of the *Taking shape,* physiology of thought or some such . . . I mean, is there anything that will illustrate the feel of chains of thought gripping and ungripping, rattling slowly around, a block-concept, an Ideal, as Gregorian Chant, for instance? . . . and doesn't The Break occur in Western musical thought in terms of melody, story, carrying blocks, making them events, along a line? (Or, as poet Robert Kelly put it to me recently: "& event is the greatness of story, i.e., where story and history & myth & mind & physiology *all* at once interact"—and events as they enter each other in the act, in the course, of the line of melody? (I'm reminded here that Gregorian notes WERE blocks in manuscript, stems attached later to make flowers of 'em, and then, still later, strung along lined paper, etcetera. And sometime later, when the notes were well rounded, flowering right-and-upside-down, sporting flags, holes, etc., and all planted in the neat gardens of the page, all in rows, it was possible for Mozart to play Supreme Gardener; but there lurked Wagner who would, did, make of each line of melody a block, specifically referential, so that the French could image melody as a landscape, all thought referential to picture, i.e. to something OUTside the musical frame of reference. But then Webern made of it a cube, all lines of melody converging on some center to form a cluster or what composer James Tenney, writing about Varese, does call "a Klang." And it does seem to me that with John Cage we are, thru chance operations, to some approximation of Gregorian Chant again— not held to links, as of a chain-of-thought, but rather to the even more rigid mathematical bell-shaped curve."

J. S. Bach has been called "the greatest composer of the 20th century": his current popularity is probably due to the facts that (1) he was the greatest composer of his own time and (2) most of the western world has, in the meantime, come to think *easily* in a baroque fashion—come to think *naturally* baroquely, one might say were it not that this process of thought is the result of these several centuries of cultural training. The most modern baroqueists in music were, of course, the twelve-tonists: and my ANTICIPATION OF THE NIGHT was specifically inspired by the relationships I heard between the music of J. S. Bach and Anton Webern. The crisis of Western Man's historical thought processes struggling with the needs of contemporary living (technological as against mechanistic) has never been more clearly expressed than in Webern's adaptation of Bach's MUSICAL OFFERING (which piece has inspired several films of mine, most dramatically the sound film BLUE MOSES): but the most essentially optimistic (if I may use so psychological a word) force of musical thought has come from Debussy, Faure, Ravel, Roussel, Satie, and even Lili Boulanger, etcetera—all moving along a line of hearing into the inner ear (the sphere of "music of the spheres" being now *consciously* the human head) . . . just as all visual masters of this century who've promised more than a past-tension of The Illustrative have centered the occasions of their inspiration in the mind's eye (so-called "Abstract Painting" having a very *concrete* physiological basis in "closed eye vision").

I seek to hear color just as Messiaen seeks to see sounds. As he writes (in notes for the record of CHRONO-CHROMIE).

> Colour: the sounds *colour* the durations because they are, for me, bound to colour by unseen ties.

I find these "ties" to be sense impulses of the nervous system and find them to have exact physiological limiations but unlimited psychological growth potential thru the act of seeing and hearing, and/or otherwise sensing, them. Messiaen goes on:

> When I listen to music, and even when I read it, I have an inward vision of marvellous colours—colours which blend like combinations of notes, and which shift and revolve with the sounds.

I recall first hearing shifting chords of sound that corresponded in meaningful interplay with what I was seeing when I was a child in a Kansas cornfield at mid-night. That was the first time I was in an environment *silent* enough to permit me to hear "the music of the spheres," as it's called, and visually specific enough for me to be aware of the eye's pulse of receiving image. John Cage once, in a soundproof chamber, picked out a dominant fifth and was told later that he was hearing his nervous system and blood circulation: but the matter is a great deal more complicated than that— at least as much more complicated as the whole range of musical chord possibilities is to the, any, dominant fifth . . . for instance, any tone of the inner-ear seems to be hearable as a pulse, or wave of that tone, or *irregular* rhythm and tempo, "waveringness" one might say: and yet these hearable pulse-patterns *repeat,* at intervals, and reverse, and etcetera, in a way analogous to the "themes and variation" patterns of some western musical forms. External sounds heard seem to affect these inner-ear pulses *more* by way of the emotions engendered than by specific tonal and/or rhythmic correspondences: whereas the external pulse perceived by the eye does seem to more directly affect the ear's in-pulse. But then that's a much more complicated matter, too, because the eye has its own in-pulse—the color red, for instance, will be held, with the eye closed, as a retention-color with a much different vibrancy, or pulse, than red seems with eyes open, and so on—and the rhythm-pattern-flashes of the eye's-nerve-ends, making up the grainy shapes of closed-eye vision, are quite distinct from inner-ear's "theme and variations" . . . so much so that no familiar counterpoint is recognizable. Well, just SO— for these fields of the mind feeling out its own physiology via eyes and ears turned inward, so to speak, are prime centers of inspiration for both musical and visual composers of this century who take Sense as Muse (as do all who recognize the move from Technological to Electrical Era of 20th century living) . . . and there is very little historical precedence in the working orders, or the achievements, of these artists.

Well, all of the above essaying (which grew way beyond any intended length) should at least serve to distinguish my intentions and processes, and whatever films of mine arise there-thru, from most of the rest of the so-called Underground Film Movement: and (as you asked specifically about this in your letter) I'll take the opportunity to emphasize that I feel at polar odds and ends therefrom whatever usually arises from that "movement" into public print, especially when journalists and critics are presuming to write about myself and my work. I'm certainly nothing BUT uneasy about the any/ everybody's too facile sense of mixed-media, which seems by report to be dominating the New York Scene, at the present. Whether the "mix" is per chance (operations) or per romance (opera) or per some scientific stance (Op) or just plain folksy, Grand Ol' Opry, dance (Pop), I've very little actual interest in it, nor in The Old Doc-(umentary) school, with its "spoon full of sugar help the medicine go down" either—all these socio-oriented effect-films being related to "The Cause" rather than Aesthetics . . . and some of them, naturally, working beautifully in that context; but most of them, these days causing sensibility-crippling confusions in the long run, because all are sailing into import under the flag of "Art," leaving that term bereft of meaning and those films which are simply "beautiful works" (which will "do no work" but will "live forever," as Ezra Pound says of his songs) lacking the distinction that there IS that possibility for cinema, as established in all other arts, or works that *can* and *must* be seen many times, *will* last, *have* qualities of integrality to be shored against the dis-continuities of fashionable time. I do not ever like to see a "Cause" *made* of, or around, a work of art; and I strive to make films integrally cohesive enough to be impregnable to the rape of facile usage (shudder at the thought of Hitler shoveling eight million Jews into the furnace off the pages of "Thus Spake Zarathustra," etcetera, for instance).

To be clear about it (and to answer another of your questions about my attitude toward increasing censorship): I've many times risked jail sentences for showing films of mine which were, at the time, subject to sexual censorship laws, and will do so again if the occasion arises: but I *have never,* and *will never,* force said works upon an unprepared or antagonistic audience, have never made them party-to/subject-of (and/or)/illustration-for "The Cause of Sexual Freedom" or some-such. I made those films, as all my films, out of *personal* necessity taking shape thru means available to me of historical aesthetics. I risked imprisonment showing them in order to meet the, as requested, needs of others. To have *forced* these works upon others, because of my presumption of the good-for-them in such occasion, would have been to blaspheme against the process out of which the works arise and to have eventually destroyed myself as instrument of that process . . . freedom, of expression-or-other, can only exist meaningfully out of full respect to the means of its becoming: and a work of art does never impress, in the usual sense of the word, but rather is free-express always —and it does, therefore, require some free space, some fragile atmosphere of attenuated sensibility, in which to be received . . . the social strength of the arts is rooted in human need to freely attend, which demonstrates itself over and over again in that people finally DO create such an UNlikely (free of all likenesses) space wherein aesthetic (shaped with respect to his/somebody-else's and history's means) can be received. Let society's sex-pendulum swing "anti" again, if it will (tho' I hope it won't), the works of art of sex impulse will continue to be made as surely as babies and to have an eventual public life as surely as babies grow up.

A MOVING PICTURE
GIVING AND TAKING BOOK

This book is dedicated to

Michael McClure
who spoke to me of the need for a short book
on film technique which could be read by poets
and

Bobbie Creeley
who gave me a beautiful sense of Home in
her home-movie making
and

Joan Kelly
who made me aware of the word-root of
amateur
and so,

with love

PART ONE:

This is a moving picture giving and taking book. It will begin
with those areas of moving pictures where the gift of the maker is
most easily accomplished, and move toward those areas where taking
is predominant—but always with the view in my mind of encouraging
giving . . . my sense of accomplishment being determined by the extent to which the moving picture maker can continue to *give* when
increased technical knowledge permits him to *take* more and more
from and of moving pictures, bless him.

I begin with very few assumptions about you, reader, but I must
presume some interest on your part in becoming a moving picture
maker; and I'll refer to you as maker, for short, and for the long view
of your historical origin (as instrument of giving of yourself) in *the
poet*. I'll thank you not to presume on this title—I invoke it to help
inspire the writing of this book . . . I leave it to the powers of your
being to determine whether or not you have and/or will have earned
it. Thank you.

I assume that you have no tools for moving picture making, and I
must begin, now, to ask of you. Provide yourself with a strip of moving picture film. It may be called 8 *millimeter* (*mm,* for short), 16
mm, 35mm, or any other mm#, so long as it has the kind of holes in
it which make it possible to move it and thus make moving pictures
of it. The film may be:

(1) *Black Leader*—
(Unexposed and developed film
—opacity: the result of retained
emulsion.)

note whatever other color the
black is tinged with: brown, usually, or if color-film-black-leader:
blue, green, etc.
(Sometimes referred to as Opaque
Leader) note it is not opaque, how
much light passes thru it, how it
can be seen thru.

(2) *Clear Leader*—
(Exposed and developed film—
clarity: the result of the removal
of emulsion.)

note whatever color its clarity is
tinged with: blue, purple, yellow,
etc.
(Sometimes referred to as Blank
Leader) note it is not blank, how

many dust motes, scratches, imper-
fections dot its surface and interfere with the transmission of light.

(3) *White Leader*—
(Unexposed and undeveloped
film—it has been fixed:
hypoed.)

note whatever other color the
white is tinged with: yellow, usually, etc.
(Sometimes referred to simply as
Leader) this is the material most
often used at the beginning of a
film to be projected.

(4) *Gray Leader*—
(Unexposed and undeveloped
and unhypoed film.)

note whatever other color its gray-
ness is tinged with: usually deep
purple, etc.
note also its possible color changes
as it sits exposed to the light day
after day.

(5) *Moving pics*—

which, I assume, you didn't take
but an interest in, perhaps only to
the extent that they were given you
free of even the small cost of the
above-mentioned leaders.

Your strip of film will, in all cases, have a dull side and a shiny side
(tho' you will find it difficult to tell the difference if using clear
leader). The shiny side will be referred to as *the base side,* and the
dull side will be referred to as *the emulsion side* (which accounts for
your difficulty with clear leader from which almost all emulsion has
been removed—tho' the emulsion side still remains stickier when
moistened than the base side). I will now ask you to make some
marks upon the emulsion side of the strip: (if you have either black
leader or gray leader, I suggest you scratch the emulsion side of the
film with some sharp instrument of your own choice)—(if you have
clear leader I suggest you use india ink applied with some point suit-
able for making both small dots and fairly even lines)—(if you have
any of the other types of strips of film listed above, I encourage either
scratching or inking and/or both if you choose) . . . please do not be
inhibited by my suggestions as they are are only offered with specific
reference to forthcoming text—that is, if you are excited enough, at

this time, lay aside this book and go to work. And good luck to you if this is our parting point.

Your strip of film will have a series of evenly spaced rectangular holes punched along either one or both sides of it: these will be referred to as *sprocket holes.* Film with sprocket holes on both sides will be referred to as *double-sprocketed*—film sprocketed on only one side: *single-sprocketed.* Hold the strip so that it dangles, vertically, down. With double-sprocketed film, the space between each set of double sprockets (or, in single-sprocketed film, that space you can define if you imagine an identical set of sprocket holes on the side opposite of those you have) is the *picture area*—that is, each set of sprocket holes defines the area of an individual, unmoving, transparent picture . . . and when you hold the strip vertically, with its emulsion side facing you, it is in position for the correct projection of a series of individual, unmoving, images of exactly what you see on the film when looking thru each window defined by sprocket holes (except that, in order to project the image you see, to enlarge it brightly and sharply on some distant plane, you would have to concentrate bright light thru it and focus it sharply thru some lens which would, given an average lens, reverse left to right and vice versa, but *not,* ordinarily, top to bottom). If you focus your own eyes sharply upon it, you will notice irregularities in whatever kind of film strip you hold, in even the most so-called opaque or blank; and these nicks or scratches in black, dust motes and hairs in clear, etc., are, given controlled light and a lens, eminently projectionable (tho' usually considered objectionable) pictures. Similarly, any mark you make, whether scratched, inked, or both, can be projected (*and* objective—dependent on your thoughtfulness, the precision of your mark, and your precise knowledge of the picture area which will be projected—so to be both more precise and, of necessity, general about it: the top and bottom lines of your *frame,* as picture area is also called, can be imagined as equally dividing the sprocket holes on either side, the right and left framing as continuing the inside vertical line established by the sprocket holes . . . tho' generally, this picture area is dependent upon the projector, etc., so that all edges of your frame are somewhat indeterminate). Now you, the maker, are qualified to make still images for projection; and all those interested in making black and white, hand-drawn, slide films can discontinue reading this book.

And now it is time for a story. I do not know whether it is a true story, in the sense of fact; but it is certainly true in a mythic sense . . . and it is wonderful that so young a medium as motion picture making already has its myths. It is said that Pathé, great 19th century inventor and photographer, invited his friend Méliès, a famous stage magician, over to his house to show him a new gadget he'd created. He projected onto the wall a picture of a beach scene with incoming waves. Méliès must have fidgeted, as image-projection, or transparencies, were nothing new to him (did, in fact, date back centuries to the undetermined origin of shadow-plays); but suddenly the waves in that image began to move, were actually seen coming in to splash dramatically on the beach (and these moving projections were not mere shadow silhouettes in movement but composed of photographic detail). Méliès must immediately have taken the phenomenon as Magic, and then as "magic" in his business sense of the word; for, so the story goes, he at once tried to buy whatever gadget produced this effect, and then he asked how it worked, etc. But Pathé would neither sell his marvelous gadget nor would he reveal the secret of its workings; for he said that, to his way of thinking, moving pictures were not for entertainment but for serious scientific purposes and to be used only as a recording device, etc. So, Méliès went home and, simply out of his knowledge of transparencies, and his realization that they were capable of moving picture transformations, created a motion picture projector of his own. As I find the origin, or at least the mythological origin, of all moving picture making, other than as defined by Pathé's way of thinking, in this stage magician Méliès, I will refer to him often—of which this is an introduction . . . to be engendering a: how did he do?

As I am assuming that you have no moving picture camera, I suggest you draw, by ink or by scratch, some representation of Pathé's beach scene as you imagine it; and as you are probably finding the finger-nail size picture area somewhat restrictive, I further suggest that you draw, however sketchily, a single in-coming wave. Move down the strip of film one frame and re-draw your wave as exactly like the one in the frame above as you are able, only make it a little, very little, more in-coming—very slightly closer to whichever edge of the frame its crest is pointing. Move down to the third frame and repeat this process, drawing-in your wave a little further. Etcetera. If you choose to become elaborate, you might attempt to draw, in each succeeding frame, some simulation of the increasing collapse of your wave upon some beach or other of your imagination; but this would probably require a more careful study of ocean waves, if you have an ocean available, than you have ever before imagined. In any case, you have now begun the creation of a potentially movable picture universe of your giving. It is a simpler matter for you to set your universe in motion than it was for either God or Méliès, for there are a number of machines ready-made to engage with your basic material, the strip of film, and to automatically project the gift of your incoming wave to a distant enlargement, *and* to project the whole series of waves in such a way as to give them the appearance of being a single wave in movement. These machines can be divided into two types: *moving picture projectors* and *moving picture viewers*. But before I introduce you to these two types, and the various kinds of machine within each category, I would like to make you familiar with the essential process which is common to all so that no matter which kind or type of machine you encounter you will always be able to engage it with whatever film strip you have for the most successful marriage of the two in operation and the simplest possible birth of moving pictures.

If you were drawing on paper, as indeed Méliès must first have done, rather than a strip of moving picture film, as instructed, I would have asked you to make each drawing of your wave on a different sheet of paper and then to have flipped rapidly through the whole sequence to produce a moving picture. This is indeed, an adequate method with which to practice sequential drawing and serves to illustrate three aspects of the moving picture process:

(1) What you can most readily notice from thumbing thru flip-pics is that the success of the illusion of movement depends most critically upon the flips: those split-second interruptions between pictures, when one picture has vanished in the blur of the page turning and the next picture has not yet become fully visible—were it not for those interruptions between pictures the pics themselves would blur into an unintelligible mass of lines.

(2) You can also note that the timing of the flipping, or flip-rhythm, is crucial—when flipped too slowly, the series reveals itself to be exactly what it is: a series of still pictures . . . when flipped too rapidly, the potential movement blur one into another. . . .

(3) You can further note that the tempo, rate of flip, is dependent upon the number of pictures involved in the production of each movement—too few pictures (with too great a jump between each extension of the lines of movement pic. to pic.), require a slow flip page to page . . . and too many pictures (with too little extension of lines of movement) require fast flipping for a move to be mentionable at all.

If you prefer this thumb-in-hand method of motion picture making, take your pick, your paper-pics, and be off; but as the movable picturing obtained by this method is not easily projectionable, I'm returning my considerations to the strip of celluloid and moving picture machinery.

(1)

The flippist part, of the above mentioned process (in the moving picture projector, and in some viewers) is called: *the shutter*. It is (in most projectors) a thin piece of metal cut approximately to a half-circle (cut so it looks like a metal pie almost half-eaten). It is located in the machine somewhere between the light source (the place where the light from the bulb is most concentrated by a condenser lens) and the place where the film strip passes, called *the gate*. The shutter whirls around a number of times a second, allowing light to pass thru a single frame of the strip of film in place at a rectangular window in the gate called *the shutter opening* (when the cut-out, or eaten part of the pie, is passing) and then blocking all light (when the metal, uneaten piece, is having its revolution past the shutter opening). The actual picture-mover is of course not a thumb but a relatedly named instrument called: *the claw*. This is a movable metal part which, when the machine is in operation, jerks out beside the top of the shutter opening, and disappears at the bottom only to appear again at the top to repeat the process a number of times a second. When a film strip is loaded in the gate (that is, between the two plates of smooth metal designed for film passage) the claw will engage with each sprocket hole on the outside edge of the film, pull the strip down a frame at a time, and repeat this process with regularity for the length of the film. It essentially controls the stop-and-start movements of the strip of film, but its actions are dependent upon two wheels, one on each side of the gate, whose outer edges are spoked by a number of little claws which, during revolution of the wheels, convert the continuous unrolling and rolling-up movement of the film into a stop-start movement for precise control by the claw in the gate. These wheels, so crucial to moving pictures, have remained essentially unnamed, but I call them: *sprocket-wheels,* bless them. Where you have a continuous movement converted into a dis-continuous, stop-and-start, movement and back again, you need two areas of slack in a strip of film. When threading a strip of film into a projector, leave a loop on either side of the gate, between the gate and the sprocket-wheels, for this purpose.

(2)

The timing of the flipping, flip-rhythm, is dependent upon inter-action between the shutter, the claw, and the sprocket-wheels. The shutter and the claw are synchronized so that the shutter is only open when the claw is disengaged from the sprocket hole and the frame is held perfectly still in the gate, so that the light passing thru the shutter opening and the film frame projects only one picture, held absolutely still, at a time, and not the movement of the strip of film. When the shutter closes, cutting off all light, the claw engages the next sprocket-hole and moves the film strip down one frame and disengages again before the next revolution of the shutter allows light to pass. The sprocket wheels, on either side of this process, keep unraveling and rolling up the film in time to the shuffle of the claw and the whirl of the shutter, insuring space enough of top and bottom loop for the stop-start dance of the film thru the gate.

(3)

Flip-tempo, the speed with which a film strip passes thru the gate, is determined by the speed of the motor controlling all synchronous movements; and (in most projectors but only a very few kinds of viewers) this speed can be set at either 16 frames per second, called: *silent speed:* or 24 frames per second, called: *sound speed.* (Some silent projectors run only at 16 frames per second; and a few silent projectors run at a variety of speeds which are essentially undeter-minable—the latter being also true of most viewers, which have no motor and are dependent upon the speed with which the film is pulled thru by hand; but a few, very expensive, viewers are motor driven and are both variable as to speed and also able to run at silent and sound speeds.) The determination of proper speed is dependent upon the film strip. For instance, if there is a great leap between each move-ment of your in-coming wave, you will find the illusion of continuous movement, and speed of movement, more believable if the film strip is projected at 16 (or even less) frames per second. If you have taken a long time, and many frames, to draw your wave in, then 24 (or even more) frames per second may be required to speed your movement up to believability. Naturally, this is also a question of taste, a deter-mination of style, and ultimately an altogether individual matter which I leave up to you.

[(Viewers are also called *editors;* and, as that name implies, they are principally used while editing film strips into a larger continuity. As they do not project the image across much space (and are essentially for identification purposes rather than show) they approximate the motion picture effect much more simply, and less effectively, than the projector. The film is threaded between two metal plates, *the viewer gate,* but usually engages only with one sprocketed wheel, on either side of the gate, which completely replaces the claw of the projector. No loop is needed because *the claw wheel,* as I call this viewer wheel, turns a cylinder (under a window in the viewer gate) which contains a prism that scans the frame of the film strip (as it continuously moves) in a way which gives each frame the appearance of remaining still (while light is passing thru) and reflects these seem-ing-still pictures thru a series of internal mirrors and onto a frosted glass called: *the viewing plate.* Thus the film strip passes, from left to right or vice versa, emulsion side down or up, depending on the kind of viewer, in as straight a line as possible thru a gate and over, or under, a clawed wheel. Motor controlled viewers, usually called: *Movieolas:* thread much the same as a projector.)]

If you are more inclined to *take* machines for granted, and have thus *given* very little attention to the foregoing, admittedly difficult, description—I offer the following simple, push-button, instructions to permit you to thread your film by rote, by hook or by crook, or whatever:

(1) Place the emulsion side down, usually.
(2) Engage outer sprocket holes with the spokes of the upper sprocket wheel.
(3) Make a small loop above the polished metal plates.
(4) Slip the film, emulsion side out, usually, between the two polished metal plates, or into what is called the gate.
(5) Make sure your film is in position where the little claw be-side the window on the inner gate plate will be able to engage with your sprocket holes.
(6) Find the lever which presses the outer gate firmly against the inner gate.
(7) Make a small loop under the gate.
(8) Thread your film around the sprocket wheel under the gate.
(9) Find the shortest route around whatever wheels are left to get the head end of your film onto the reel for winding it up.

PART TWO: ON SPLICING

Dear Gregory:

Your letter affords me the opportunity to go into some details of film technique which might be of use to many film-makers; so I'm making a carbon of this letter to send to The Co-Op—heaven knows I dislike writing about technique (I mean, it is so much more exciting to allow the lettering mind to explore imagi-nation, aesthetically adventure, etcetera); but as many a mountain climber has perished for lack of skill with a pick-axe, tangled himself in his own rope, and so un-forth, many creations are still-born out of technical inadequacy. I am *not,* heaven also knows, referring to any of your work; for you have always mastered whatever techniques were needed to fulfill your creative needs—it is because you will make good use of whatever information I send you that I am thus herein moved to detailing techniques which *might* be of more general use also. I have long felt there ought to be at least a section of Film Culture devoted to exchange of technical information between film-makers. While this might prove dull reading for the purely audience readers of that magazine, it oughtn't: for I have discovered it impossible to communicate certain aesthetic information to technically ignorant audiences, have found it like trying to explain a pun to a child who doesn't even know the same sound can have several meanings, have felt audience frustration similar to the frustration I had when forced to attend a foot-ball game at Dartmouth and expected to cheer or groan at certain intricacies of the game which remain obscure to me to this day because I never learned the rules: for there is a vast area of any art where the grammar of that art and its technique are inter-related and even synonymous (in the sense of: to be taken for granted); and one of the definitions of any medium could, and perhaps best *ought,* to be in terms of the technical limitations of that medium—a great deal of wishing-washiness would be drained from aesthetic criticism were such an *actual* taking-measure of the medium prerequisit to any pie-eye-in-the-sky-isms.... I mean, at least a critic *ought* to carry the standards he refers to for every put-down of a creator as heavily as if he were bearing a very real flag in a windstorm.

I encounter very few problems inter-cutting color and black & white. I always shoot, and (as I too edit original film) use in editing, reversal film—unless I want a negative image as the final screen image ... and/or unless I might happen to be shooting color negative to be making positive prints therefrom. I assume what's worrying you is whether or not color & black & white film bases will splice together; and I would like to pass along certain splicing tips I learned the hard-way (and hope you'll reciprocate). To begin with I always use double-perf film, if possible, in photographing. This always permits a four-fold use of any strip in relation to any other strip in editing for greater flexible handling of any (particularly abstract) image in movement, albeit the two uses of that strip of film (that is: when turned over or base-up, as its called) will soften the image slightly in printing (as the focusing devise in the printer is set on assumption that the emulsion side of the film is consistent throughout). Many times, in editing, then I'm forced to make a base-to-base splice—this is actually, if well made, a stronger splice than the regular emulsion-to-base splice. Now, as you know, in the usual splice the emulsion is scraped off one of the over-lapping bits of film to be spliced because the cement will not weld any but base material; so, theoretically, one wouldn't have to scrape in a base-to-base splice at all; but I find it advisable *always* to "rough-up" the base side to be spliced, even in regular splicing. In emulsion-to-base splicing I put a small dab of cement on the base piece and immediately wipe it off, then lay down cement on the scraped emulsion side and weld the two. In a base-to-base splice I scrape one of the bases just the same, with perhaps less scraping, as if it were emulsion—then proceed as usual with the other base side. I arrived at this procedure out of the necessity of splicing many different kinds of film—for instance, certain different kinds of black & white film go together very difficultly and there is a bluish base B&W film which won't splice well *at all* unless its base is "rough-ened-up" with either cement or scraping. For these reasons I am also drawn to use scrapers which roughen film unevenly while scraping—find a fine grain strip of emery-paper (not board or cloth) best in this respect. Base-to-base splices also leave an often noticeable bar of dark across one of the images (of double emulsion, so I often turn the film over after splicing and meticulously scrape off the emulsion of the intruding picture. This brings up the problem of the noticeability of the splice in 16 (&8) mm. The commercially professional way to make the splice invisible is the one I'd guess you usually use, that is: "A&Bing" as it's called where two synchronous rolls of film are created with black leader always on one roll & picture on the other, splice always tucked under black leader, pictures over-lapping only where a dissolve from one to another is wanted or where the two are to be superimposed . . . but I have found this method altogether too distracting while creatively editing original and, of late, I usually have multiple superimpositions going on AB, ABC, and even (in Part 4: *Dog Star Man*) ABCD rolls with no room left on the synchronizer for splice-hiding rolls even if I wanted it. During Part I of *Dog Star Man* I became particularly concerned that the splice SHOULD show (as a kind of aesthetic counterpoint to the plastic splicing and the fade-out-fade-in, etc. . . . . The Splice, that black bar breaking two kinds of white, operating aesthetically as a kind of kick-back, or kick spectator out of escapist wrap-up, or reminder ((as are flares, scratches, etc. in my films)) of the artifice, the art, et set-TO) and I became very invloved in the splice-bars as operative visual cramps upon, for instance, the baby's face in Part 2 of *Dog Star Man* . . . and you can imagine (apropo my comments on page one of this letter) my difficulty in explaining how splice-bars compress that face and then break-up into the hand-drawn lines struggling for verticals to an audience which, for the most part, doesn't SEE splices, even in a white field, or have the vaguest notion how individual moving pictures are put together. Of course, aesthetic involvement WITH the splice does increase the need to be able to hide the splice when it isn't wanted (as it mostly isn't in Part 4); and the best technique, aside from A&B rolling, for *that* is the use of splicing tape, so that the cut can be hid exactly between frames; BUT, to the sensitive eye, the splicing tape lays down a wavery pattern particularly noticeable on white fields where there is usually the *most* concern for hiding the splice. Kenneth Anger told me he used this transparent tape exclusively on *Scorpio Rising* and that, by pre-arrangement with the laboratory, he only had to use it on the emulsion side, thus decreasing tape-glue image by half. Next best for hidding splices is The Negative Splicer (so named because it's used almost exclusively when splicing negative film because all splices thereon will turn out very noticeable white bars when positive print is made) and this makes a very much narrower splice but one which also requires much more care & ability for it to hold in printing. Every time I go to make a splice regularly I decide which of the two joining frames will carry the splice bar. If I want to semi-hide it, I'll usually choose the darkest and/or most complex image; but very often a lighter but more rapidly moving image will hide the bar better and/or an image mainly composed of horizontals, etc., etc., etc. Sometimes, for instance, I choose to leave the double-emulsion bar in a base-to-base splice because it cuts off part of the preceeding image and makes a plastic flow into the following image, etc., etc., etc. Sometimes in cutting B&W to color the partial superimposition of over-lapping emulsions creates a one-frame transition of aesthetic smoothness, etcetera . . . and, in other words, all these etceteras stand for one whale of an aesthetic involvement in The Splice. Even splicing cement doesn't just mean to me "that which holds two pieces of film together"—I know it's a dissolvent which welds film and this knowledge has led to its use in chemical treatment of film—that is, I've dissolved images, "painted" with it, mixed it with paints and clorox and salt and lacquers, etceteras. I found, for instance, that the glue of splicing tape crystalizes into certain recurring patterns when heated (with an iron) to certain temperatures (which I can only specify to the extent of "low" "medium" and "hot" on the average iron as corresponding respectively to "large, overlapping 16mm frame in most cases, unwieldy aggragates with large center & fine snow-crystal points," "clusters attached to eachother," and "even textured small crystals in a field." *Mothlight* was made without recourse to heating; but *Dog Star Man* Part 2 involves the packing of material (even mica, which raised temperatures and scattered crystals like explosive material from it) & punched-out pieces of film packed between a *very* thin clear leader & splicing tape, all packed also with chemicals, Elmer's Glue, Nu-Skin, etc., depending on the piece, and (in most cases) heated with an iron welding all into a pre-determined crystalline pattern. (It should be mentioned, for the record here, that I had no less trouble getting Part 2 printed than I did with *Mothlight*. *Mothlight* original, packed between splicing tape, was too flexible for the printer. Part 2, using thinnest leader available & tape, was too INflexible . . . part of this problem being mica shavings & the stiffness created by crystallized glues. There is also one hell of a problem getting splicing tape to lay down evenly onto clear leader, a less-flexible material, for any length—I'm next going to try exclusively filmy glues (like Nu-Skin) and cut up the splicing tape every foot or so, *that* the sprocket holes can be realigned at center of every second-and-a-half of film. Well, I see I've diverged a bit from The Splice; but I sense it's a divergence which may save you some time and repeated effort—as P. Adams told me you might be using film collage techniques in your *Illiac Passion* . . . and PLEASE send me any information you gain from working with these techniques—names of glues, for instance, would probably be worth thousands of words of aesthetics to me.

Now I sense the desire to close off *this* letter and hedge on the major question of *yours* because I cannot offer much encouragement regarding your current felt-needs of two-size screen simultaneity in projecting *The Illiac Passion;* AND YET I DON'T WANT TO DIS-

COURAGE YOU FROM ATTEMPTING ANYTHING, no matter how impossible-seeming, WHICH MIGHT PERMIT YOUR MUSES TO SHOW US ALL *SOMETHING NEW*, even if utterly other than what *you* think *you* want to be showing. So then, the following is simply to give you an idea what you're up against. For the rest: FOLLOW YOUR A MUSE MEANTS ... okay? As you already know, unless you can get your entire vision onto one strip of film (no matter how many separate and separately framed images thereon) you run into almost impossible problems of distribution, etc. I think you're right to feel that THIS shouldn't stop you if your feeling of necessity urges you into a technically difficult area, particularly if the technical difficulties are only reflections of fulfillable lacks in distribution (after all, you and I made films for years when there wasn't really anyone to distribute or much of any audience to distribute TO)—BUT there are limits to this consideration ... If I make a collage film which can't be printed or projected at all, then it is, after all, more of a necklace or wall decoration than a film. Kenneth Anger's *Inauguration Of The Pleasure Dome* was finally edited into a Tryptich version (one large center screen, two small screens winging either side) requiring 3 synchronized projectors (and 3 screens) for screening. I worked constantly with Kenneth for a couple days in Brussels in 1958 attempting to bring this Tryptich screening off. All projectors came out of sync during all rehearsals & the public screening. Finally 3, out of the 7 judges, agreed to give up their lunch hour one day for a final try—which succeeded. There were about 15 people who saw this performance. These are the only fifteen, to my knowledge, who have ever seen the completed version of *Inauguration of the Pleasure Dome*. The experience was so incredibly beautiful that I would never for a moment consider the single track as more than a teaser of the total experience—NO MATTER *WHAT* THE PROJECTION PROBLEMS OF THE LATTER, all of which I'm *very*, painfully, aware of from the experience. ... Okay? At Brussels, 1958, there was also a 7-synchronized-projection (involving 7 differently shaped screens) as a semi-constant attraction in The Polish (I believe?) Pavilion. The film they showed was a so-so travelogue; but the technique was fascinating—for instance, a dancer would leap from one screen, cross another, and land on a third, while four others were flashing scenes of audience, other dancers, orchestra, etc ... there being a real attempt to keep sense of integrality. Kenneth and I were particularly intrigued to find out how it all worked; and we were not too surprised to find an electronic computer

was operating all 7 projectors on a stop-start basis, a vast room of
equipment constantly supervised by several german-types rushing
from one computer component to another and cursing constantly,
apologizing for everything being "out-of-sync." My point is that
synchronism (which is here synonymous with aesthetic perfection)
is dependent upon getting the experience onto one track, one strip of
film, WHICH COULD ACTUALLY HAVE BEEN DONE, by
either Kenneth or The Polish Govt., BY PHOTOGRAPHING
ALL IMAGES THRU MASKS IN THE APERATURE and/
or, if money enough, BY HAVING FILM MASKED IN THE
PRINTING STAGES, using the usual superimposition techniques,
but so masked that no image ever superimposes on another. But, dear
Gregory, it doesn't sound to me as if you could afford to so treat the
material you've already shot and/or re-shoot material using said
masks. I don't know just where, from your letter, you want to put
your larger picture in relation to your smaller; but when we saw
Harry Smith's *MARVELOUS* film at the Co-Op, Allen Ginsberg
told us that he, when showing the film, would project slide images
around his frame—and I remember thinking how expensive it would
be just to get this simple device transferred onto single strip of film:
it would involve shooting the slide image (masked accurate in center)
into 35 mm film, then A&Bing the two together & making a final
composit print, the expenses being in accurate masking of the external
to internal image, even tho', in his case, it wouldn't have to be too
accurate as all his images occur in a black field, so that the shape
of the image makes its own variable screen . . . something I've been
working on in Part 4: *Dog Star Man* by laboriously painting out, a
frame at a time, all but the image desired—and the painting can never
be perfect enough to avoid a wavering edge which, thus, I extend
into expression, viz: my masking becomes black sky breaking into
stars, multicolored patterns (closed-eye visions) and scratched out
shapes and objects (re-call visions). There is a masking tape you
could block out some areas of your frames with; but you could never
lay it down carefully enough to avoid a wavering line which would
also be constantly fluttering with the irregularities of spilled under
glue—a dynamic visual which would constantly pull the eye away
from the photographic images to its vibrant edge. No, effective masking really has to be done in the shooting stage unless you're after effects
similar to hand-painting or unless you can afford the expenses of laboratory optical effects which can only be achieved by step-printing
(frame-at-a-time printing) . . . which would be the staggering ex-

pense of Harry Smith's film—because, you see, he would have to have his central images (the only ones I saw) reduced in size to leave room for the surrounding images on the frame, or else get some laboratory to re-tool for one-to-one printing of 16mm image in center of 35mm frame, then superimpose this onto 35mm shots of his slide images . . . then, as you know, reduce the whole thing to 16mm for distribution.

Well, I hope all of this has been of some help to you; and I very selfishly hope you'll reciprocate with technical information of your own, particularly if you get involved in masking during the shooting stages . . . I am very definitely being drawn into the area of multiple imagery and image shapes within the field of the frame (have, for instance, punched and/or cut holes in black leader and dropped images into isolated black spaces in Part 2—a MORE laborious activity than hand painting) and am much inspired by Harry Smith's work, which I hope you'll get a chance to look at.

PART THREE: MAKING LIGHT OF NATURE OF LIGHT

"Any fool can see for himself—," like they say. . . .

It is the light we share.

I had meant, since beginning "The Moving Picture Giving and Taking Book," to write about the taking of light, the use *of* it: taking a light reading, so to speak—*with* a light meter, as it's called . . . *for* the figuring out, like they say, the where-abouts, on the movable ring of the lens marked with "f," the numbers of it should be placed so that a picture may be taken. As I came to worry the subject in my mind's eye, came to see where I'd left off writing this book altogether and to foresee how impossible it was becoming to write what was left of it, I finally arrived at the thought that the book had perhaps better be called: "The Moving Picture Giving Book:" and that I had better let it go at that. In that light then, if you'll pardon the pun/fun of it, I've come to the beginning of wanting *to make light of* all of taking—of *light,* of *pictures,* of *others,* of *myself* in this "take", as an "exposure before development" is called, this taken then of my mind's eye moving thru thought to language in this writing.

My first instruction, then: if you happen to have a light meter— give it away . . . otherwise: give over reading this further and get on with the game of numbers you're playing and its absolute sets of what is *scene:* for I am going on, from here, with *seeing*—any/everyone's ultimate gift to the motion picture medium.

Beg, borrow, or buy (I do not believe in stealing) a moving picture camera with at least one lens on it (a "used" 8mm camera is perhaps most in need of your blessings and will, thus, very likely come to you easily in the family attic or for ten to fifteen dollars *at most* from a store—but please don't accept a magazine camera, even as more than temporary gift, as it will cost you more money for film in the long run . . . and please NO "automatic exposure" photo-machine, either —that "seeing eye" dog of a camera). Get a roll of film, *any* film that is the same millimeter as your camera. Somewhere on the box of it, or on a paper on the inside of it, or from the store proprietor, you will find a number coming after the letters A.S.A.: and if your film is a "color" one you will find the information as to whether it's a "Daylight" or a "Tungsten." Keep all this information in mind.

Let us suppose to start with a "black & white" film, as that is usually less expensive. Let us even suppose, to start to begin, that you have not yet given yourself a camera. Collect yourself a handful of tiny objects, such as would sit neatly on a fingernail, and also an empty spool and film can the size and millimeter of the full one you have in hand, and a small or "pencil" flashlight. Find the darkest room available to you; and sit in it for awhile, some ten to fifteen minutes say, looking all around for the light. You will find yourself, thus, fulfilling the initiation rites of many religious cults: but you need not let that worry you. Look for any light coming in under doors, thru curtains, or wheresomever; and cut it off with old rag stuffing, thick coats over windows, etc . . . and you need not worry about that, either, for, as you cut off the light you're *used to,* you will come to *be given* to see many kinds of light you may not have known existed before.

If you begin to feel foolish in this darkened room doing these things, please continue; but if you've only come to find the me-in-your-mind as foolish for the above writing, then please stop reading and try, rather, something on your own until you've managed to make a fool of yourself—for the writing, from here on out, is specifically for the "fool" who can "see for himself" . . . no other than that in mind.

When the room is dark of all light you're used to, and before you begin to look for more light than may come to you, open the box and/or can of film and place it on the one side of you, with the empty reel and its can on the other side of you. Unwind some film (a good five feet or so). Attach the end of it to, and wind it up on, the empty reel (a piece of tape will help). Then place both reels in their cans, bending the film carefully over the edge of each can, so that the lids may be put on without more than gently folding the film, without more than a soft diagonal crease in the film, without tearing, etc. There should be, then, several feet of film between closed cans. Place this firmly on a flat surface (tape, again, will help) so that the sticky side (when moistened to test it between fingers) is up. Place your tiny objects along the length of the film. You may, of course, do this as carefully or as haphazardly as you choose. If you choose to give your care you will remember that each space between sprocket holes (which you can feel with your fingernails in the dark) is an individual picture which will when projected flash in some other darkness at a fraction of a second—the area between and to the direct side of any two sprocket holes in 8mm and "single-sprocket" 16mm, the area within the rectangle of any four sprocket holes in "double-sprocket" 16mm, the area to the side of any four sprocket holes of "single-sprocket" 35mm or between the four on one side and four on the other of "double-sprocket" 35mm, etc. The more you think of these things while placing your objects on the film, even in the dark of your first endeavor, the more you give of form, of yourself thus to form, of the medium in the eventual projection of images, as always, about to be made.

Think of your flashlight, then, as a wand, for it is something more magic than a flash that we want of it, something more than any simple light, as we're used to, use of it. We want to make a ray—a Man Ray we'll call it, in honor of the man, so named, who first made it—directed by all of the thoughts, as above, and conditioned by two pieces of information kept in mind: the "A.S.A." number and, if color, the indication of "Daylight" or "Tungsten" . . . but, assuming again "black & white" film, let us assume a number after A.S.A. A small one, say between one and ten, will tell us that the film will take a lot of the light we give it to make an "exposure." A large number after A.S.A., say any number above fifty, will tell us that the film is very sensitive, so to speak, to light and will over-expose, as they call it, with the slightest bit of our illumination. Let us assume, to start then, an A. S. A. 5—the American Standard Association's average exposure rating for most motion picture "sound stock" film . . . this low rating will permit us a great deal more play of/and/with light in our giving exposure to the film. We can possibly even use the pencil flashlight to write directly upon the strip of film, if we write quickly and if the point of light of it is sharp enough, focused enough. As we move our wand away from the film, its beam spreads till, finally, evenly over the whole length of the strip, its exposure interfered with only by the objects we've placed on it and their shadows. As we think of its beam as a ray, we may come to direct it elsewhere and only indirectly light the film; and as we come to think of the ray as a Man Ray each one can then, honoring tradition, become aware of what's undone and, being that self each is, direct the particular ray in hand, wave that wand wheresomever, as is most wanted, around whatever particular room in relation to the strip of film, writing directly upon it in one place and never permitting the light to shine other than indirectly upon it in another, creating a dance of the shadows of the objects placed upon it, throwing shadows of objects in the room across it, etcetera. . . . BUT, whatever each chooses to do with this instant, *we* ALL *share* in this: *the light* can only illuminate that room for a very few seconds for the film's exposure, film's take, as it were. Even with an A.S.A. of 5, I would guess that more than two or three seconds of direct light, from however small and dim a flash wand, would expose the film to the extent that, when developed, it would be clear leader (if reversal film) or black leader (if negative film) as defined at the beginning of this book: and we would thus—for we all *do* share the

light, share thus the conditions of time of light in relation to film—
be back where we started from, with no trace upon the film, no sign
or record even, of the magic each was making in the room of his or
her most individual dark. The higher the A.S.A. number of the film,
the further must the wand be kept from the strip and/or the quicker
the speed of illumination. But if all has gone well, each will have
(when the film is developed) what is called "A Rayogram" for moving picture projection. But before developing, I would suggest that
the process, as described above, be repeated for the entire length of
the roll of film, each exposed strip being taken up into the can on the
one side as the unexposed strips are unraveled from the other. As
should be obvious, the whole length of film need not, indeed *should*
not, be done all at once. Other than tiny objects may be placed upon
the film, as say cloth for texture shadows, glass for refraction patterns, etc. And, assuming your film is color, various colored glasses or
filters may be placed upon the strip, the point of the wand, or around
the room, even, for a play of hues. If the film is a "Daylight" one, all
whatever-colors will transform on film to completely other-colors,
because the film was exposed to flash wand rather than the sun wand
intended—generally speaking, there will be more yellow in everything (unless it overexposes) because the flashlight will not be passing
thru the blue of the sky as the sun's light does before exposing film
. . . and you can, thus, put a "sky" in front of your wand in the form
of a bluish filter taped onto your flashlight to render more approximate colors with "Daylight" film. If your film is marked "Tungsten,"
you'll know that word refers to the filiments of your flashbulb or
electric-light-other and that the "sky" or blue of it has been put already into the film itself by the manufacturer, so that without your
adding a filter the colors will be rendered more approximately—tho',
in truth, they will still be transformed utterly into colors other than
those of the objects placed upon the film, or between the light and the
film, etc.: and I would hope you have the good sense to be aware of
these differences when the film is developed, bless you.

Now if all the above does seem an end in itself, have patience for
I, too, am tired of these mechanical limitations, would have us share
more mysteriously in the light, am about to fool *with* the camera
(rather than professionally fool it) and, for the sake of illumination,
become the fool *of* the camera and all its means (being amateur—
lover . . . at heart). But if the above be beginning for you, quit reading and get on with it . . . joy to you!

Now, a camera can be thought of as a small closet (box) into which the film may be put (with pegs to hang the full and empty spools upon and a gate, much like the projector's described earlier, to thread the film thru) which has a wand-like light focuser (lens) screwed into it so that whatever external illumination which is "gathered," as it's called, by the wand *can* be focused into an image on the surface of the film, can *be,* thus, recorded by the light-sensitive grains of the emulsion of the film so as to be developed, later, into a picture which is projectionable. The motor of the camera simply conditions the movement of the film in relation to the shutter (the same as in the projector except that, in camera case, the film is always stilled for the ingathering of light, at shutter's opening, rather than for the projection thereof thru the film). When we hold the camera, therefore, we have the whole closet as well as wand in hand, stand IN the light and condition whatever of it and of images of objects reflecting that light we wish to affect the surface of the film. The motors of most cameras will permit us to flash light onto the strip of film at a variety of speeds by pre-setting a dial on the outside of the box which conditions and indicates how fast the film is moving thru the gate (usually marked: "8-12-16-24-32-48-64," etc.—meaning: "8 frames per second-12 frames per second," etc. because the speed with which the shutter opens and closes is conditioned by the number of times the film is stopped-and-started-etc. each second. We can also control the dimness and brightness of these flashes of light by setting the ring marked "f stops" around the lens itself (typically marked: "f 1.5-2-2.8-4-5.6-8-11-16-22"—meaning, for all intents and purposes, that when the lens is set at its lowest number, say "f 1.5," its iris, as it's called is *wide open,* like an eye in the dark, that at "f 2" it is a little bit closed, permitting less light, that at "f 11" it's about half closed and that at "f 22" it's almost closed, like the iris of an eye looking straight into the sun or at sun's direct reflection on a beach or bright snow scene) because, for *our* intents and purposes the "f stops" are like distances we keep between the flash light and the film according to the A.S.A. of it. If the A.S.A. is a low number, such as A.S.A. 5, then we can set our lens at a low "f," say "f 1.5," on a bright day even and still get an image upon it. If it is a high number A.S.A., such as "A.S.A. 120), closing our lens to "f 22" may not suffice under the same circumstances to make other than white or black leader: but then these "circumstances" also depend, for picture, upon the speed of the film and, thus, shutter, and of course upon whether one is under the sun of this bright day or in the shade of it, in a house, etc. These many circumstances cause most photographers to use a light meter to determine their exposure, the setting of the "f stop" ring, etc.: but I suggest you play the fool, along with me, fool around in the light *with* your camera, be the fool *of* both (fool neither) and come along on an adventure, the nature of which is the nature of light itself.

First we must deal with the light *of* Nature, then with Nature of Light. And set your science aside, please, as we've no more use for it than what is *of* it as embodied in the camera in hand—an ordinarily closed system (as any machine) for taking pictures . . . which I am about to cause to flower (as my usual) wide openly in a gift of in-and-out-sight to the means of it. The camera will try to give back simply taken pictures (as that's what it's made for) but in the exchanges between us (myself and machine) there'll be, if I'm lucky as usual (and for you too if you're able as anyone) *a made thing* (an un-pic'ed image) which gives as much as it takes, *an illumination* (made as much *of* as *with* light) which should be a joy to see. I might, as I often have before, make a discovery (called "creation" most usually): and you, too, might, if you can but give your eyes to the medium (as any maker finally must) as a gift *beyond* any desire, to see or other, any re-quest, etc. "We shall see" refers to conditions, such as technical limitations, which we share, as we share the light. "I see" is an unconditional surrender to the light for a fool's vision. When giving sight to the medium, *"with, not through,* the eye" (William Blake*), *with,* rather than thru, machine, *with* any means at your bestowal (rather than disposal), *with* the light, and naturally then OF all these things also as in any gift, the term "moving picture giving" takes on a blessed (and necessary to me) dimension, viz.:

If you will, but listen (give your attention) to the camera motor (as you press its button—*never,* please, at speeds higher than 32 frames per second when there's no film in it, as that will often snap its spring) and you will *hear* some semblance of the speeds of film's run thru it . . . if you will, then, think of yourself as collector of light, thru wand of lens, for gift to film, you can then come to know your-

---

*For when William Blake writes:

> "We are led to believe a lie
> When we see *with* not *through* the eye,"

he proclaims his possibilities as a great "still" photographer and, as such, of extreme opposite inclination from a moving picture maker.

self as conditioner of the light entering the magic box you hold in your hand—that you can slow or speed up the flashes of it, on the film's surface, by changing motor speed—that you can collect the most of the light you stand in by turning the "f" ring to its lowest number, opening the iris of the lens widest, and/or can limit the power of the sun itself with each "stop down," as it's called, to the highest number. And if you can, then, but give yourself to the light around you (keeping *sense* of the above conditions on circumstances) till you are attracted to one area or another of the direct or reflected light (taking a *stance* in relation to your surroundings), you will be able, by a pointing of lens and a turning of its rings, to give some of your inner illumination to the surface of that film (give the song of your *sensing,* what you've seen AND thought of it, to the film's heard movement in the camera), viz-a-viz:

If you want the light you're sensing to take shape upon the surface of the film, to etch itself there in sharp lines of the edges of its reflecting forms, you will guess at the distance *from the film's surface* to the most of the objects within the rectangular space of your looking (thru the "viewfinder") and will set the numbers of the "foot" ring of your lens (usually numbered from "1 ft." to "∞," a symbol standing presumptuously for "infinity") accordingly; whereas, if you want the light to affect the film's face more impressionistically, you can "soften the focus," like they say; and, therefore, if you want light's tones unenclosed in shapes, you can set close object's image in "infinity" or obliterate landshapes and distant forms with a "1 ft." setting. Wherever you would interfere with the light, take account of shadows as exactly as if they were objects placed upon the film emulsion in a darkened room, as if a setting of the lens to the exact distance of the shadow were a placing of the object flat upon film surface, etc. A breath upon the lens will often add the Western eyes'ed sense of halo, or the mystic's aura, or a whole fog even. A drop of water, or some similar refractor placed before the lens, will split the beams of any direct light into the very lines tunneling out of it which must, once, have given Western man the idea that the sun was in harness, or reigned, and then caused him to later create a way of seeing called "Rennaissance perspective" we take too much for granted; and a soft focussing of these lines will spread these lines to rays, as clouds or dust storms often scatter sun. And many things may be put before the lens to simulate something of mind's eye, thought's light, on film—if you use a "Tungsten" film in the daylight, for instance, an orangish filter will render the colors what we call "truer," just as a blue filter is used with "Daylight" film to put some sky into electrical illumination, etc. . . . but all of these conditionings I've written above are a hatch of hindsight, a taking of light for some use or other—not much more of a gift to the medium than the taking of a picture. Not being a poet, I cannot write much other than "about," write out of some past en- deavor, whereas a gift is always a present, so to speak . . . it will take some very creative you in the gift of reading this to make this writing more than a take. Permit me to illustrate, become the reader myself of the below, now, blank of page in seeing search of nature of light, viz-ability:

"blank" (as all words) interfering with my read of the texture of the paper, the shadow blackened creases and spots impressed on the white field of it— "white" coming to mind to block any seeing of the yellow of the lamplight upon it, reflecting from off it, and as if lying heavily across the whole surface of it—"yellow" blanketing the mind's eye as if to cover up the sense of the blue, as it's collected in each shadow, like pools with deep purple centers, or flaring palely blue over the whole surface and almost flickering at page top nearest my window in instreaming daylight—"blue" (as "purple" and "black" and all earlier color words) finally giving way to eye's sight of an other-than electric yellow whirling within blue on page and sky out my window in some as-if struggle with blue, an eddying all thru the air of these environs, which I follow up the margin of the page I'm reading till blue takes shapes surrounded by yellows of skylight, but shapes that are almost invisible under apparently shifting folds of "Tungsten" yellow, each blue whirl taking general shape of ball with curved comet-like tail, all shapes blackened in focus of concentration on the page, tho' easily seen bluishly out my window, all tailed-spheres spiraling as if in the heat of liquid gold (these being Reich's "Or- gones" in, say, C. S. Lewis's "yellow space?")—"Orgones" taking away all sight-sense of the vision, "Reich's" taking the experiencing away from me, and "C. S. Lewis" as literary reference intellectual- izing my seeing beyond any sense of it . . . thus, all within that last parent-thesis disperses the vision, making sense *of* what was a sensing (do not, please, permit me to do that to you, dear reader)—my sense of "reader," "dear" or otherwise, interfering utterly with my reading of this page, blocking me in a lock of attention to the inks of its letters . . . but then . . . but then, the type marks—they wink at me—not as letters but, rather, as surfaces rainbowed over: and as my eyes open to them, relax into softened focus, the prisming lines bubble open into streams of colors infinitely varied—"infinitely" (that presumptuous word again) tips me off and into a searching concentration wherein the black-born colors *tend* to arrange themselves as follows: oranges, blues, greens: and, thus: oranges in curved lines or circles, with yellow at inner or center and red at outer or perimeter; and blues in lines graded to purple one side or the other; and greens as a weave throughout—"throughout" checking my concentration, causing a spread of vision across the whole page until I see similar-to black-born prisming colors moving, according to the first *tendencies* observed, among the comet-blue shapes and molten folds-over-folds of electric-yellow and in shadow pools, concentrations of prism-blues tending to impress upon me large (several inch once) *always elongated* shapes, ingatherings of prism-oranges *always forming circularly,* and green weaves shaping fields of their predominance *always* as *irregularly curled* as vines—three underlined "always"es demonstrate to me that I'm about to make a science and/or a religion of this endeavor, damnit, about to really try to *convince* someone else (some "dear reader" of the imagination) of my own eye's sightings, make sights of them in sets of laws and dogmas to *convict* all other (in a "damn your eyes," as the saying goes)—forgive me . . . I tire, viz:

. . . goodbye again, dear reader—I'm off to work: to try to gather light this particularly, even if (as in the past) I can finally only paint some approximation of these miniscule occurances upon the film's developed surface . . . for film is never hypoed by the lab, "fixed" as it's called, beyond a maker's giving—his adding to it, thru paints and chemicals and superimpositions in editing, his senses of the light as seen—until that maker himself becomes too long exposed to the light of any particular piece of film and, thus, ceases to see *it* any longer . . . then, and then only, might a work be called "finished." As I've ceased to read myself herein, then, and have other livelier things to do, permit me to make (not "the" but)

an end.

EIGHT LETTERS TO GUY DAVENPORT

Early April, 1966

To Guy Davenport,

The winds feint with bitty puffs of snow against my window, as if the sky were half-heartedly throwing confetti. "Cheep Donkey" is singing wildly in the kitchen—he's as inspired as I am these days by a whole new (to us) order to great musical experience come our way*—the music of Messiaen and his disciples (or former students): Boulez, Barraque, Pousseur, Stockhausen . . . actually, Boulez and Stockhausen were quite well known to me; but somehow even their music has come into new earshape since I've discovered the grand old master and source of this impulse: Messiaen, surely one of the VERY greatest living composers. The music of Debussy, Ravel, Satie, etc., was reaching toward *image,* the evocation of visuals thru sound—I should say SOME of their music was, for this was only a small area of concern albeit one which could be written about and, thus, receive much critical attention . . . anyway, Satie came the closest in this direction because he always kept his eye on the picture and his ear planted firmly in the orders of music: thus the hearable impulse engendered by image shaped the music (I'm thinking particularly of "Sports and Diversions") rather than that there was any attempt to evoke image thru sound. His impulse inspired music cross-pollenates perfectly with the master twelve-tonists—Berg / Schoenberg / Webern—along with elements of recall/collage techniques (which must surely come out of Ives) in the sensibilities of this great man Messiaen and flowers, thru him, into a whole new (yet firmly traditionally rooted) order of music: and this music, directly inspired by vision—and most specifically by the movements in and of vision (imagistic movement AND images moving the mind)—does naturally come closest to my working orders these days . . . for years I've been increasingly inspired by music in my, particularly, editing processes: now I've worked thru to proximity of music and vision at brain-wave source (know "sphere" and "music of the spheres" to to be skull) and am now close to knowing the exact difference of the music of each. It

---

*That bird teaches me more about music than any person (including, as you know, Varese/ Cage / Subotnick / Tenney / etc.) I've ever known—you should HEAR him accommodate, for instance, an electronic piece by Stockhausen or one of Ives', etc., in his musical orders.

is a very exciting time—for instance: the other night I was working away at *Scenes From Under Childhood* in the late & early hours and forced to listen to the dogs barking continually, and with particularly regular insistence, as they chased what we're pretty sure was a mountain lion (as he had been seen earlier in the evening not more than 50 feet from our house) all over the neighborhood: and the rhythm of that bark came to seem directly appropriate to my working orders of that moment and definitely evocative of something in art which I desperately needed sense of to arrive at some exact clear comprehension: and then, suddenly, I had my key—it was a particular section of Kurt Schwitters' sound poem which goes something like this: "Fums Be-ve . . . Fums Be-ve-te . . . Fums . . . Fums Be-ve-te-ta-oo . . . Fums Be-ve-te-ta-oo Pa-giff!", etc.: which source unlocked a whole recall area in me so that I could relate the rhythm to the crying patterns of a week-to-six-week old baby: and, as such, it poured as an impulse into *Scenes From Under Childhood* in some *perfectly* beautiful way.

Late May, 1966

Dear Guy,

You DO connect here—the "pain, distractions" you write of take some shape here too: and

intimations of same from friends all over the country these days are tending to confirm my belief that people of like nature in a given culture are on SOME kind of telepathic line . . . it is the war that finally gets us down, each via his and her personal daily demons: but it is the war, all the same, all the same as it's always been in a culture fighting a war when/wheresoever—all of sentient living gets crimped in the backwash, all of sensibility tortured . . . it is as if some spirit force we do not consciously recognize, but *do* very much depend upon, began to flicker, rather than burn steadily, in the wind of war's thought, to smoke-over the mind of even the most innocent—and are any of us really innocent?—in a war breathing culture . . . I remember this sense of it well from Korean War days when, like now, creativity came in desperate bursts of such consciousness needed for making rather than in waves of some total-continuity-feeling as all-of-a-piece as breathing, as the name "inspiration" implies, and as is usual to me and my friends in all our creating when there is no war storm to disconnect our sense of the sea-surge, our source of being, in living.

I try, these days, to maintain *stabile*—look at rocks . . . and take FULL advantage of each burst of force that can father-in vision. I am husbandman of all I love in some more careful sense, these days, than ever before: and I steer *into* the wind—having completed the first section of *Scenes From Under Childhood,* having come to some clear place of discontinuance there, I set it aside for the time being and turn to *23rd Psalm Branch,* all the footage in 8mm shot in Europe: and I just bought a set of 8mm newsreels from 1938 to 1945 to go into this work out of all my senses of war as a child, all memories which were prompted by that trip to Europe: and I've just finished reading *War & Peace,* Toland's *The Last 100 Days* (of the Third Reich) and *The Rise and Fall of The 3rd Reich* . . . and thus I begin to weave the eye's sword among all the discontinuities that threaten my soul.

And the goat grows fat and pearl white on horse-chow and powdered milk: and Rosco the donkey trims his form to some colt likeness in the spring frisk: and Durin the dog smiles and smiles these days as he grows sure of summering: and the children inherit the outsides fully and the bright sun right up to bedtime; and they fill the air even to the horizons with their shouts: and Jane, being with me, is all in a brave struggle these days to keep us from getting hung up on anything less than the stars: and the stars grow brighter every day we polish them with our looking.

Come see us then, when you can—come soon as possible.

Blessings,

Mid-Sept. '66

Dear Guy,

I've just survived the two most depressing / dulled / deadly pessimistic / "wound bore" (as Michael McClure calls 'em) days in years—I feel, today, a very centered quietude . . . I look back on these 2 days with fearsome awe, as if looking down the receding mouth of a tiger shark I'd somehow managed to crawl out of.

* * *

I feel in that hot-wire state rather regularly—it is when the wires begin to melt, when you can *no longer* be "a solid moving thru an inferno" (as McClure once described it) that better describes being back-of-the-tiger's-teeth, to put it another way, or the most "frightening" and, thank gods! "rare": BUT, I do go very much in the sensory feed-back at nerve these days. I'm so much involved in the sensory feed-back at nerve ends that I do hear, in my inner ear, the little bastards twanging (or more like "tinkling") away; and I do attend their "harmonizing" (shifts in "tone" which must be at the rate of hundreds a second, if one could hear one's own physiological song that completely); and sometimes I am hard put to turn this off (this, which those who only heard it rarely on some few attentive occasions—such as Jung, of late—called "the music of the spheres," I'm sure): But I take care to control myself, my "input" in this area *because* the inability to shut this inner sound off is what finally broke down Ives and sent Varèse to "Death Valley" for 10 years to recover from breakdown—Ives never did recover, poor man—and is probably what broke down Schumann as well, etc. . . . and I'm trying, primarily, to deal with the eye's sight of it—the rapidly shifting rhythms of optic nerve-end output, the colors thereof it, their shape-making, and so forth: and all this is integral to the form *23rd Psalm Branch* is taking. Last night, at bottom of funk, I tried to convince myself (via declamation to Jane) that I was "abandoning the damn 'war film' "; but this morning I know I'm more than ever dedicated to it, whatever the mental cost, and *because* it is somehow absolutely necessary for soul's sake!

* * *

I'm listening much to Debussy these days, re-reading all the Freud I know—Jane reading Henry James . . . and Neowyn (2 years ahead of herself's place) reading Crystal's and Myrrena's school books.

Joy to you,

Oct. 1st, 1966

Dear Guy,

It is a bright, absolute blue, hard sun, shiny day: and the last fragment of the children's snow man is all that's visibly left of yesterday's winter at this height—tho' the high mountains have taken on more white than will melt easily—: but we're probably in for a month or two of Indian-ing summer.

Illness plagues me still these days—a 'cold' turns into asthma and then asthma into 'cold' again . . . each diseaseful thought infecting the lungs and, thus, puffing itself beyond mentality's measure and assuming a physiological proportion as absurd as a nightmare would be if it knocked upon our daylight door . . . I think the devil you write of in your last letter is trying the trick of rolling a veritable avalanche of translucent-*seeming* grains of sand thru each day's hours to conceal from me the one Blake writes of which Satan cannot find: for all does *seem* of such a beauty here, and of such joy, that I cannot imagine why I wheeze with such neurosis in the midst of this—except that it be all attributable to the *23rd Psalm Branch* in its making as surely as were the similar sicknesses I suffered while making *The Dead* ("sim . . . sic . . . esses . . . suf" as sure as alliteration of my asthmatic estate as I could express in language—for it has taken the form of a cough more often than not, these days, as distinct from the long hiss and whistle of my steamed up insides while making that previous meditation on death: and I cannot help but chuckle at the appropriateness of my affliction's express-noise, that I do 'explode' and spit, now, in accompaniment of war's thought, rattle-in-the-throat this daily "song" exteriorizing mind's rat-tat-tat-*tat-tat* of martialing armies' shapes' cluster / thus / rhythmically and criss-cross of each other's continuities on the strip of film I am now editing, as I give meaningful form to the newsreel pictures of 1938–'39, treating the 'movements' and 'massings' of those times as exactly as a scientist would edit the microscopic images of germs to show-forth their germination and, thus, the history of a particular disease; but, then, too, I am editing *in* the rhythms of remberence thereof, the most personal (which I believe, as always, to be the most *uni*-versal) meaning which thought-in-time can give to these, otherwise, 'Opake'/ 'dirty' pictures (believing that the very rhythm with which they burn in the mind's eye, being 'fuel' of the optic nerves' 'firing' in the act of remembering, will reveal their true substance clearly if attended carefully).

And, thus, . . . we go on, here,

with what grace we are afforded amidst war's turbulence. Jane's strength and wisdom, is, as always, the major sustainence of the household: and the children grow in their various ways, looking at us often with wide marvelling eyes and then again, at times, thru slant askance.

Blessings,

Early Nov. '66

I mean: Why *must* The Devil and his Watch Fiends have all that optic luck on *their* side? (Why are there "sides" in the 1st place?)—Why isn't it just the other way around? . . . I mean, I'm pretty good at finding that one moment (as I think you'll agree) and even filming there-thru it; but I'm getting tired of the whole stupid game and am coming to think The West has made some Golum of itself just thru treasuring its found and/or made moments . . . its "PRE-CIOUS" . . . "precious"—moments!

Mid-Nov. '66

Dear Guy,

Well—the more I work along a line of film called *23rd Psalm Branch*—the more studying I do of the 2nd World War . . . dozens of books now—the more convinced I become that we/(U.S.) live now in a closed dictatorship in all respects— in/and/to-depth similar to Hitler's Germany and all previous and subsequent focuses of power to some centrality . . . even tho' we do obviously inhabit a culture that is superficially/ (surface-wise) completely different from any such. It is visually apparent in that the crowds shape up to that similarity (whether in opposition-to or agreement-with the government): and it is audially apparent in that the tone of speeches does suck-in the eyes and ears of the world by phonetic implication–for instance, both Hitler's and Mussolini's rhetorical success was largely due to the fact that their speech patterns revolved in the back of the throat (Mussolini had a language edge, in that Italian lends itself to this proclivity via the peculiar nature of its roll of *r*'s . . . a phon/ phenomena that takes its similar course thru *o*'s in German, tho' to a lesser extent: but Hitler more than made up for this by a gutteralness which was so pronounced one would have called it a speech defect in any but rhetorical circumstances—Johnson's accomplishment of this in Americanese is no small feat: and his sacrifice is visibly apparent in the whole decayed aspect of the lower half of his face . . . and perhaps in his recent throat sickness as

well)—and the trick in terms of choice-of-words is simply to lace all speech language heavily with those syllables which depend primarily upon the roof of the mouth for pronunciation, excluding all the outgoing sounds possible: and the trick phraseologically is to rely on the cliché as much as possible because it sounds natural when mumbled inwardly (as if to be taken-for-granted—which is, of course, also its psychological advantage) and also, simply, need not be pronounced outwardly as it is so well known that its meaning will be heard even when very *in*articulately pronounced . . . anyway, these are some of the means whereby politicians create speeches that primarily suck up sensibility ("Romans-countrymen, lend me your ears" is an excellent example—"Romans" is a very outgoing word, and very deceptive, thus, in the context, because it is obliterated by its immediately following synonym "countrymen," all syllables of which are thrown against the roof of the mouth . . . "Romans" is thus the tossing out of the net and "countrymen," with its syllabic edge, is the drawing in of that net of national identification . . . and the, of course, "lend me your ears" is a masterpiece of a lapping back and forth of syllables in the mouth—"me" being the only word which isn't pronounced with the tongue as an absolute guard against the escape of anything from roof and tongue tops).

Hitler's (and Mussolini's) gestures were, as Bertold Brecht demonstrated beautifully for me in the East German (his direction) production of "The Resistable Rise of Arturo Ui," straight out of 19th century melodramatic stage-style —the Nazi salute a direct extension of standard "discovery" gesture (all salutes, interestingly enough, partake of this idea—the flat-hand-to-forehead being only a tilt from the shade-of-eye gesture for looking into distances, such as Keaton played upon naturally with his dead-pan additive to the gesture in, say, *The General*): and Mussolini was, of course, shadow-boxing with his closed-fist gestures with a perfection of acting that would have immediately marked him as the hero of even an American silent-era serial . . . tho' he lacked the "humility" of the American archetype hero—a quality Hitler accomplished beautifully during his "peace" speeches and that Johnson is an absolute thespic master at, so consistently so that his eyelids have become as if permanently weighted and his eyeballs sunken thereto some *now* physiological downcast attitude . . . and it *is* a real terror when the mask of a man has closed over his eyes —the only pictures of Hitler I've ever seen to have "eye-holes" are some recently discovered 1925

snaps of him published in the August '66 (#33) issue of *Der Spiegel*.

Ah well—I could go on and on (write a book even) in this vein (or in this "vanity," I might say— vanity of disclosure of the top secret of the age . . . "secret" only in the sense that no one writes or speaks of the American dictatorship, not even in the "whispers" we can credit most Germans with . . . not "secret" in the sense that people don't *know* what's going on—why one need only point out that the acknowledged restriction on our "freedom of press" does absolutely mark our government "despotic" ((and I quote)) in the exact terminology our "Bill of Rights" uses to recognize such suppression and presumably forbid it ((or am I quoting the honorable Gov. of Virginia, or was it Mason's wording—I must re-read "The Bill of Rights" now that it has become a purely aesthetic document and see how it stands— in *that* light, that is: see whether it might ever be of inspiration and/or whether it was "loaded for bear" from the first))).

Well, I am bitter-sounding, am I not? . . . but then, I was never raised to live thru a reign of Caesars; and I must learn how to survive in this time *from scratch* —and I am *not* able (like most of my fellow Americans) to scratch my eyes' sense out of my considerations to accomplish my survival in some play of innocence or some-such: I must, apparently, look upon the horror and then devise some dance with it, like "the side-step"—must, in all probability, learn to keep my mouth shut (Mark Lane convinces me it's come to that as he tabulates the number of Dallas murders surrounding the Kennedy assassination *and then,* when people call into the T.V. program asking what they can *do,* advises "write your congressman," convincing me that he's either a Judas sheep of this whole investigation or the biggest fool of all and/or both: and Hitler *did,* you know, employ many men to stir up trouble against him whose express purpose was, of course, to collect names for the concentration camps to come).

Well, I had meant to write you a letter more directly answering the last two beautiful correspondences of yours: but all of the above did seem to just pour out of me this morning (I can only hope some similar doesn't pour out of me from some public lecture-platform or other in the future: and, in that sense, the *23rd Psalm Branch does* inform me that any public gesture in this time will inevitably contribute one's energies to the despotism of The Times (whether one carries a "Peace" sign or marches in a militant parade)—only acts of most personal privacy and works

of deepest aesthetics will stand against the wreckage inflicted by the West's death-throes . . . and *that* only by withholding energies therefrom that lemming-rush to the cliff's edge.

Blessings,

20 Nov. '66

Dear Guy,

I am so alone at these heights of my findings that I am afraid of distorted vision in this area—that, perhaps, the very fact of my working on *23rd Psalm Branch* does cause me to see *as if* I were living in the Nazi Germany of the 30s, whose news-reel images right now figure so largely in my editing procedures: and yet, if it were *not* for some exact correspondences, I don't believe I'd have ever been inspired (that is—found it necessary) to do this film in the first place. As to exactitude of correspondence—per example: Johnson speaks of each subject monotonously (as bespeaks of and to an "all but created equal" sensibility) and he speaks softly (out of a tradition of "speak softly and carry a big stick") and he approximates facially the "strong and silent 'American archetype'" (in the poker-player attitude and/or the tradition of "the Fireside Chat"): these *are* the basic forms of the new rhetoric and create the subtleties of tone most effective for the radio and T.V. medium—T.V., really! . . . (Hitler had, after all, to make the voice stand for gesture to make the fullest use of radio: Johnson only has to slightly raise his eyebrows to powerfully alter the entire visual field.)

Yes, "the tone," as you suggest, is "the message" (as McLuhan would call it): but the visual equivalents of "tone" (barring color) are texture—meaning: any grain-shift over the whole image-scan . . . a shift of a thousand dots along the brow of the speaker in close-up is more meaningful than the shape-shift of his whole head! The new oratory is primarily a matter of shifts of whites into dot-pits and dot-creases along a facial scape which does thereby powerfully invite the only real participation by audiences in this (as McLuhan rightly calls it) primarily "cool" medium —(except he, as his usual, calls it that and *that only . . . not so!,* I say: rather, T.V. is a medium that pulls on the spectator primarily thru its emphasis on closed-eye-vision's grain field and does create its imbalances ((for spectator to shove in his psyche to fill)) thru slight darkenings, or grain-holes in the basically grayed-over pattern *AND* thru, thus, rifts in the basic horizontal make-up of this pattern . . . try, for instance, looking at a T.V. image *side*ways—that is, by tilting your head sideways) . . . it is a "cool" medium for looking at old movies because they—and most T.V. dramas which so far only imitate them—rely basically on gesture, and the imbalances of composition-as-gesture, to draw the audience IN for "escape," etc.: but the politicians—especially Johnson—have intuitively realized the real nature of the beast that carries their impulse; and they may also—by this time —be using sub-liminal flashes of messages, etc. (that *proven* psychological hypnotizer which became a controversial issue with the F.C.C., etc., shortly after its discovery and has, since then, been suppressed as even a topic of public conversation).

Okay! . . . well—I have to, and do easily, have *some* faith in the subconscious' ability to cope with subliminal advertising: it is the more conventionally deceptive taking on the forms of the new media, which troubles me more: because, for instance, Johnson's or any other leader's stance as "great daddy" does undermine each human subconscience at its root under childhood: and the only possible remedy for the manifest ills of this proclivity *does* seem to be in the shake-up of the whole human social condition.

We're all struggling along here —tho' this is by no means a happy time . . .

Late Dec. '66

Dear Guy,

The question doesn't seem to me to be whether or not we're living in Germany's 30s (as we *certainly* are not) but whether or not there's enough *basic* difference between this and that time to trouble noticing . . . I tend to think/feel that *politically* there is not—that there never *has* been *that* much (worthy of notice) difference in politicing in the whole recorded history (nor *that* much difference in recording history—excluding Spengler, for the nonce . . . therein him: *first* truly ego centered 'historian' I've come across) . . . that *politics* is a static form (both senses of the pun good: that is: it is an inorganic medium composed primarily of chaotics/noise—Pound was being idealistic when he proposed so natural an outlet as an ass-hole for a politician's language . . . would that the form were capable of so human a proclivity as anal-oral transference!) —and that *history* is, similarly, cookie-shaped in its development as a 'form' . . . neither takes root in the human physiology—but, rather, each IS the product of cerebral impress and does behave in the 'world at large' *as* such . . . neither, nor religion either, grows out of creative need—but both, rather, express prime human rock consciousness *as wall* (between consciousness and UN—both 'coming on' in terms of alternatives . . . religion, of the three, only occasionally penetrating into itself complexly enough to touch its crystal-nature and thus root itself in a growth process—tho', still, one of secondary necessity to human being, as we do not, cannot, recognize our chemical existence nearly so much as our organic make-up) . . . thus, all these 'forms' (which should really be called 'shape-makers') damn themselves: and, I'm afraid, aesthetics (at least as it is preserved—chemically fixed—) is part-and-parcel of this damnation . . . I'd certainly rather talk thru my ass, my Bottom nature, than thru the political, historical 'forms' of aesthetics: and yet I find tears forming in my eyes as I write this; for I *have* been one of the foremost of my generation to defend and refine(d) the concept of art . . . I can no longer do so—*23rd Psalm Branch* has shaken all my metaphors thru to their non-roots. It is a terrible time for me, as I now go on with "Part 2"—"to source": and I come to such simple crystal clarities as that the *only* way to end a war is UNconditional surrender —some passing completely thru even 'UN' as is, after all, only the 'other,' the 'unholy,' the 'unwhole,' the UN — UN — UN — ETC., alternative . . . and I am very much afraid, these days, save that my body begins to delight in the trembling such fear engenders: and I am asking Jane to teach me to dance.

Mid-Jan. '67

Dear Guy,

It's alright—you're closer to seeing the film than you think, viz: "I found myself watching *23rd Psalm Branch* with an utterly different feeling" . . . I mean, that's it!—that those shots, "used as troop training films," as you say, and on T.V., etc. *are,* in this *Song 23* transformed. The military *wants* to sicken you, vacuum-ate you, with those images—the government, too, to get you impli-cated in the guilt, etc. . . . where-as the *23rd Psalm Branch* is cre-ated out of my need to restore those images, through an act of memory as intensive as prayer, to individual sight. You write: "I suppose I'm just not FEELING enough": but, that's a natural enough reaction—for of *all* my films, this one can *least* afford the risk of superficial feeling, or sur-face emotions . . . your feeling for it will, I'm sure, come thru seeing it in-depth, after many viewings, after living with it awhile—and "I'm sure" of this because you do seem very much on the right track of it except that you quest-shun your own response.

Where you seem amiss—and

where, thus, I might 'save you time,' is that you don't seem to take the newsreel images at 'face value,' so to speak—I mean, *I* take war, herein, *as* natural disas-ter (hence my shots of floods, etc.) and the images of Hitler as very *close* to those of Benes, the kings and queens, the crowds (the people masses actually prepare the way for the appearances and gestures of their heroes, as well as being prepared by them) . . . all these images being retroactive upon each other, etc. I *don't* see "Then war as a superstructure *above* the people"; and I don't think you can find visual source for that idea in the film . . . it is a superimposition you bring to the work and must work-thru in order to see *23rd Psalm Branch* (and I *don't* think "a work of art ought to be effective in spite of one's opacities"—a work of art requires a very fragile landscape in which to exist . . . its strength is that people feel the need of it strongly enough to provide that landscape —it does then illuminate what was only dimly known: but it can no more penetrate opacities than light can).

But you know all this better than I and did, I'm sure, but write these doubts because the film engendered them in you as it did in me and has in most people first time viewing, 2nd, still, for some and 3rd and 4th for me, for instance—the fragility of the landscape of the imagination *it* requires is primarily composed of *time*. Oh, and another thing it *is* a *most* "particular statement"— in *no* sense to be taken as anymore "general" than *15 Song Traits* . . . again the lifetime's viewing of newsreels, etc. pulls on you too much: but give *23rd Psalm Branch* only a *little* time (3 or 4 hours as against years and years of your exposure to those same shots in their guilt-engendering form) and I think *Song 23* will whistle more ghosts to their proper grave than all the rest of my films together. At least, that's how it's now inspiring me: and I was, a year or even 2 months ago, about to be done-in by Hamlet's father, etcetera.

P.S.

I don't know what you mean by "little T.V. fellow" unless it's these two ⚊⚊⚊ 3500 B.C. Upper Egypt figures representing a war in two movements . . . earliest example of double image I could find—thus first "movie" was a war 'film,' a racial struggle in which the white guy wins. Also —when I write "I can't go on," I then do . . . still *am*—now 30 min. into "Part 2—to source."

March 31, 1967

Dear Guy,

Ah, what shall / *how* shall I write you of all that's been happening here these last several weeks? I would call and talk with you but that I must, for money's sake, refrain from my telephone as surely as an alcoholic from 'the bottle'—yet how shall I justify that "for money's sake" when Blake says that any consideration of money whatsoever destroys Art and engenders War . . . I ought surely to make the telephone ring from one end of this country to the other: for I have such hopeful news these days as all the Nat'l Networks horse-operas and all the Nation's newsmen cannot put together now or ever: I, Stan Brakhage, declare that the war is over!: and with the last splices of *23rd Psalm Branch: Part 2* the year-and-a-half long quarrel between Jane and I abated, fluttered out in some final spits (one of which sent me to a motel in Boulder for a few days) and ended altogether during the making of the "Coda" of that work . . . let this house nevermore be temple of Mars on *any* pretext whatsoever—at least nevermore than enough to salt the occasional blandness we may fall into: but let the sweet peace reign like cat and dog cookies and elaborate French pastries upon us . . . at least as just deserts to any mealiness we may in our sadnesses engender.

I have held up sending you the sections of "Part 2" until it shall be complete and with "Coda"—

now all at the labs being printed
. . . and now that the work is done
(and I've even gone on to *Song 24*
and *Song 25*), what do I think of
all this Quixote windmill I've
been whirled around on and
reeled up into? . . . I don't know
more than that I can no longer attend what used to be my favorite
kind of Hollywood movie— (the
war / paranoia / spy / para-cum-
laude-hero plotter)—without becoming physically ill (asthma
and/or stomach cramps) and, usually, being thus forced to leave:
and this inclination holds true for
noose-reels, T.V. or otheruswise,
also: and it therefore seems to me
that *23rd Psalm Branch* has freed
me from all the propagoosing-
and-gandering this society has
stuck me with since I was a child
and thus taken to be voodoo doll
of its Nat'l stance and war-shaping
messages. Otherwise, I don't know
of what use the work is but that
it, in its final form, will free others
viewing it as it has me in the mak-

ing of it. Kelly writes: "History
(at least the range of subjects,
theses & opinions that word means
at a university) is the enemy of
cosmology, & only strife-loving
warriors (Archilochos, or that
nameless angel who shook his
spear & ranted thru the lips of
fiery Plantagenets & David's un-
forgiving god) make song-sense of
war. *All art is image-fixing, & cel-
ebrates what it 'portrays'* whether
its maker wd have it so or no."
And Kenneth Anger tells me that
we should have had a shrine dedicated to Peace in our house all
this year to balance the temple of
war we had made it, for he says
that artists take entirely unto
themselves what they are creating
out of, etcetera. For myself, I am
confused about all such issues except as I note the very real changes
in our life now that we are out of
it, as well as those which its making and viewing have engendered.

Joy to you,

ON MARIE MENKEN

Marie Menken opened for me (1) a sculptured and very heavy filmic door (in VISUAL VARIATIONS ON NOGUCHI) by "swinging" it, (2) a garden gate (in GLIMPSE OF A GARDEN) by "swinging" *on* it, and (3) my microcosmic or "inner" eye (in HURRY! HURRY!) with a kind of lid-swinging technique. The heavy door, which was at the time (about 1956) weighing very heavily on this young film-maker, was the influence of Hollywood in dealing with its ponderous technical equipment which almost automatically (a well-chosen word) forced the *most* individual film-makers to try to make "smooth" pans, dollies, etc. even tho' they were economically forced to accomplish this with hand-held equipment. We were trained, so to speak, from childhood film viewing that the "heavy door" with the eye in it MUST move slowly and smoothly. Marie Menken's "Open Sesame" to me was that VISUAL VARIATIONS ON NOGUCHI was the first film I had ever seen which completely not only admitted but capitalized on the fact that the camera was hand-held. She was, at that time, the purest disciple of Jean Cocteau's advice to young film-makers to take advantage of the freedom of the hand-held camera (*Cocteau:*

On Film or some such title). This was, in one sense, a very simple contribution by Marie; but in another sense it led me to begin questioning the entire "reality" of the motion picture image as related to a way, or ways, of seeing, so that by the time I saw her GLIMPSE OF A GARDEN I was prepared to accept the far greater reality, to the film artist, of the strip of film as opposed to the images it makes (under certain conditions of extreme mechanization) on the screen. So you see, in a great way Marie's influence on my work has been more social (or even moral) than aesthetic—that being one reason why I classify her influence with that of Gertrude Stein (who continually draws me toward the material of my daily living rather than "literature") and my wife. I say "moral" because her path to the garden led *me*, as distinct from the experience provided by an aesthetic viewing of her work, away from being screen-centered (surrounded, in considerations, by auditorium audience, public-event, publicity, fame, etc.) to being film-strip-centered (or centered in the "reality" of the working process, in isolation, even to the extent of being just as concerned that the strips of film cohere as strips, and as variably moving images thru an editor, and

From a letter to Gerard Malanga; *Filmwise 5-6,* 1967

as even individual frames, and as material for possibly projecting backwards or reversed, as I was with the projector-cast image at 24 frames per second. As to HURRY! HURRY!, you cannot imagine how difficult it was, for instance, for a film-maker of that time to even consider images which he couldn't somehow justify as related to ordinary visual perception—being, as we all, even unconsciously, were influenced by the first aid kit of Old Documentarianism. It was, of course, not just that Marie used microscopic footage, or even that she superimposed it with flames, but that she employed these images in such a strictly personalized manner, charging them with her own most individual psychodrama, that HURRY! HURRY! occurs on the screen with the authenticity of documentation of her inner spirit in a way far more successfully than the psycho-dramas which I attempted to similarly document by using actual people reenacting their experiences expressively. I had previously used many photographic devices in my work to heighten the expression of the "reality" around me (tho' they were usually couched in dream sequences—the influence of Surrealism—or crises such as blindness, an old favorite of my dramatical films). In fact, you can see my dilemma most clearly by realizing that I felt a necessity to "blind" my dramatic protagonists in order to allow my camera eye to range expressively into new areas of vision . . . and even these were so Surrealist-ballasted as to be limited in scope. I remember, for a fact, that it was the influence of Jean Isadore Isou (VENOM AND ETERNITY) and Marie Menken's NOGUCHI which gave me the courage to actually scratch the eyes off the film-base in REFLECTIONS ON BLACK, an act performed the same month I first met Willard and Marie and saw their work. McLaren, for instance, could never have so encouraged me because the line, with him, whether scratched or drawn on film or otherwise, is a means to an end, an ego-centered finality which his work calls forth from the audience. Marie's line, whether painted, scratched, animated or not, is as unpresumptuous as that of a stalk growing, and fascinates for the same reason, because of its unpredictable formality. (It is no wonder McLaren admires her work because a McLaren feeds off growing processes being incapable of them himself). In other words, Marie is a "natural," her world the world of openings. (While I, too, admire her work, am grateful for the opportunity to stroll thru her stone foundries, gardens, and microcosmos, I do not [like a McLaren] shut the door, gate, or eye-lid after me, am not aesthetically influenced). It is the ideology, if you can call it that, of Marie's working processes which have influenced my work. She made me aware that I was freer than I knew, that those chains were daisy-chains, those locks free flowing hair, etc.

MASTER WILLARD

once gave me the following recipe (I paraphrase):

> "An old beat-up magazine-load camera
> With one lens
> Plus scotch tape and
> Magnifying glasses (bought in a dime-store),
> War-surplus film (50' spools),
> Marie,
> Her body,
> My body,
> The various parts of bodies of assorted friends,
> George Barker's body,
> His poetry
> And voice reading it,
> Plus some Balinese music,
> One hell of a lot of patience . . .
> And love . . .

The result was, of course, GEOGRAPHY OF THE BODY. By now most film cooks in the country have tried to stir up such a brew. They've substituted finer technical equipment (pressure-cooker sex-pots, etcetera), but mostly to indulge their own impatience. Most of them lacking either a real woman, or even lively-looking friends, as well as lacking The Poet in any sense whatsoever, have tried to substitute one hell of a lot of selfness, mostly indulgence (the smut-pot in the closet-drama, etcetera). Most, of course, lack love or they'd be making their own films rather than quest shunning Will, mimicking the Maaster piece. Even those few (and I count myself among them) who've been more inspired than simply influenced by GEOGRAPHY OF THE BODY have lacked proper balance between the last two listed, and essential, ingredients. It is love of the

work itself which Willard implies in his "patience," making of GEOGRA-
PHY OF THE BODY the finest cinematic approximation to living flesh
in a work of love. That sense of time, when on the make, which extends
the flesh adventure into the area of love, without which (and only at
best), comes rape of a kind, of a kindlessness, lacking even satisfactory
release. It is the brilliance of this work that it releases the spectator into
the areas of his own sensation, permitting him even to reject the film
itself altogether (something neither the Hollywood film nor the Don Juan
in any form can afford to permit), the film remaining prophetically,
crystal-clearly, within itself—a ball to dance with rather than make
something of. The sound track treks across forbidden territory, yet giving
continually that balance of assurance of the circus barker advertising
freaks—that the ears hearing, and (as implied) the eyes seeing, are
distinct from the experience of the traveloguing. The audience is taken
in, alright, but never allowed to identify. They're also never allowed to
identify with object matter, the source material—"eye of newt, toe of
frog," etcetera. Or, as Ben Moore once loudly put it, in the darkened
Cinema 16 Needles Trade Auditorium, during a public screening of the
film: "Don't worry, Willlllll. Nobody will recognize your balllllls." All
material is subject, as photographed, and has been transformed by an
act of love. Cognizance is within the viewer by way of the film images
before his, or her, eyes. Even "his" and "her" towels are thrown out,
along with the babies and the bathwater. The film is certainly not sexless,
but hermaphroditic in the deepest aesthetic sense of the word.

Once, early in the month of December, Willard Maas remembered a
thing past, a German Christmas cookie not tasted since childhood; and
in a most un-Proustian way he set out to re-discover this experience by
actually baking the cookie of his mind from scratch. Batch after batch
of mixtures were tested by fire and found wanting. Odor of cookie
drifted out of the penthouse apartment and down the elevator shaft; and
anyone arriving was immediately sent to the delicatessen for additional
ingredients, while the master himself rushed from mixing bowl to oven
with each subtle variant on a cookie theme. Between bakings, Willard
was either tasting, testing each result with a mysterious enclosed sense
to all his being, an inward budding, or else talking frantically on the
phone to grocers near and far demanding exotic and, sometimes apparently, non-existent spices, etcetera. Soon there was no place left to sit
down in the pent-up cookie house; and warlock Willard's atmosphere
was all of the next-to-the-last scene of Hansel & Gretel. This drama

continued into the night, and day and night (with little sleep) for three days. Finally Willard, exhausted beyond endurance, surrendered to the Proust-process, rolling all ideal cookie back into his mind, boxed all the "edible" produce of his labor, labeling "with love," and sent them as Christmas presents to his friends. This is how Willard Maas subverted all of what Ezra Pound calls "the cookie pusher" in art, which Willard found within himself, to rid himself of it in his work. He exhausted it in every conceivable debauchery of daily living so that only "wine, virtue . . . (AND) . . . poetry" were left to make drunk the world of his expression . . . or at least, this was his driving *intent*, as I saw it. Naturally, he met, and continues to meet, with failure; and I now fear that he has reeled up the ideal film into similar reveries and canned the "visible" works of his labors, as always "with love" and as always "for friends" wherever they are, and let it go at that. It has been a long time since he has completed a film. It is a particularly German neurosis, this sense of "perfectionism," the I-within image which can deal death-blows to all external realization. Does he understand that it is really the struggle, his struggle, which inspires, spiraling often to heights of vision previously unknown, in his work? Could he comprehend Gertrude Stein's: "Every masterpiece came into the world with a measure of ugliness in it. That ugliness is the sign of the creator's struggle to say a new thing in a new way . . ." . . . ? Did he even believe me when I told him, that long ago December, that those cookies, which he was rejecting to the right and the left of his German self-centeredness, were the best that I had ever tasted?

> Willard used, often, to say (and I paraphrase):
> "If they would round up all the Germans in the world
> and herd them into a gas chamber,
> I'd be glad to be the last one in—
> just to be rid of the whole race once and for all . . ."

But in my mind's eye, I always saw Willard standing outside that slammed door with a mischievous child's smile on his face.

Every year or so, Willard would give an award, verbally only, called "The Maas Award For Neurosis Above and Beyond The Call of Duty," or something of that sort. I remember 4 of them, which particularly seemed to satisfy his qualifications, as he delighted in giving these awards over and over again:

> To a Mother and her son (the boy had actually

once been in one of Willard's classes) who had de-
vised an extraordinary way to avoid the draft. The
mother kept her son hidden away in a covered grease
pit in her garage, in so small a space that he was not
permitted to either stand or even stretch at length.
She lowered food to him and removed his excrement
daily for a period of several years which extended
beyond the time of all danger of draft.

To a negro who had been undergoing psychoanalysis
for 3 years and who, one day, shot and killed his
psychoanalyst. When questioned by the police as to
why he had committed such a crime, he replied: "It
would take me 3 years to explain it to you."

To a young man who put a bomb in his mother's
suitcase, took out insurance on her in the airport,
and not only succeeded in killing her but also everyone else on the same flight.

To the Mad Bomber of New York, who began his
notorious activities in revenge against the Con
Edison Co., and subsequently extended his anger, and
his bombs, to the city at large.

Willard always had a way of growling:
    "Gawwwwwwwwwwww wwwwwwwwwwwwd ! "

which extended his rancor from the person being addressed in the given
moment of frustration to, as the tone both deepened and became more
resonant, The Creator Himself—that is, also, Willard himself, as he
found the "awe" there being created, having spat "ga" out at the source
of his annoyance . . . but then, also, always addressing the "god" in
anyone else and addressing his self-ends with an abrupt "d" turned to
a "t" almost "tut." I have heard sounds like it in the bass parts of
Bach fugues.

"Gawwwwwwwwwwww wwwwwd" and "love" came into direct contradiction in Willard's life when men became the objects of his desire.
His "patience" was taxed to the extreme of IMAGE IN THE SNOW,
perhaps the only really traditional morality drama of the experimental

film movement to date. In this work, sound track contradicts pictured image, and vice versa; the accumulation of images contradicts the image seen, continual see-saw of visualization; and stage drama intrudes its forms in contradiction to the image-making eye of the film artist, the "I" of Willard struggling with his self-idealization. This *is* its beauty—ugliness of that struggle . . . unresolved. Only guilt over homosexual desire leads the protagonist to "love" of "God"—and only in the sense that he can die *of* it . . . "The End" of the film. But Willard, himself, went on living, carrying the strands of that romantically severed Gordian knot like a net about him. I have never known him to sit thru a complete screening of the film. He always excused himself and could be found pacing frantically back and forth beyond the exit door waiting for the last sounds of Ben Weber's musical score to free him. The film itself certainly could not. Long before he had finished filming, he knew that it would not. Yet for five years he had spread the nets of his criss-cross desires and followed every thread thru to inconclusion. I quote (as nearly as memory serves me) some of his statements on the cast his characters had taken:

THE PROTAGONIST:

> "Ah, he went off and got married (the poor bastard)
> in the middle of the production. A couple years
> later, I had to drive him back from some New Jersey
> housing development to finish the film. He was bald
> in front. His face was puffy. He had a paunch.
> I couldn't really take anything but a long shot.
> Gawwwwwwwwwwww wwd—he *had been* so beautiful . . ."

THE MOTHER:

> "Can you imagine—Marie playing The Mother? I
> couldn't help it . . . she was so *perfect* in the part.
> I *love* the way she peers out of the window, after he's
> run away, with tears streaming down her cheeks. We
> rubbed onion in her eyes; and then, imagine, she
> couldn't stop crying."

THE FAIRY GODMOTHER:

> "Ahhhh—Hawwwwww . . . We kept covering her with

veils of white. Nothing would help. If only I'd
had the sense to cover her face. She seemed so
beautiful until it all ended up on film."

THE BLACK DANCER:

"That dinge!"

THE DOVE:

"It flew away too quick. Couldn't get a good shot at
it to save our lives."

THE SNAKE:

"Couldn't get anyone to touch the thing. I wanted to
get a close-up of it in his hand."

THE VOICE OF THE POET:

"I *love* the way Ben read it. But I'll never forgive
him for one thing. You know it was his idea to say
the little prayer which he wrote for the scene at the
crypt. Something bothered me about it. Then one day
while I was teaching in my classroom, I took up Joyce's
Portrait of the Artist As a Young Man and suddenly
realized where he'd stolen the whole idea and half
the words (you know: 'Ding dong! The castle bell!/
Farewell, my mother,' etcetera). Gawwwwwwwwwwd,
was *I* mad, and did *I* let him have it!"

Thus, Ben Moore entered the scene; and Willard was almost always
mad with it and letting him have it, whatever he had of love and hate
to be giving him. And Willard worked continually at making A Portrait
of Ben as the Artist as a Young Man. And this all went on, and off and
on, longer than IMAGE IN THE SNOW. And somewhere in the midst
of all this, I met first Ben and then Willard; and each in turn, and continually, on and off, attempted to make me the object of desire which
would free each from the other. Had either one really meant such a
separation, each would have chosen someone of homosexual inclination, and certainly someone unknown to the other. Instead, I became just

another one of their mutual frustrations. And this became, for awhile, the center of Gryphon Film Productions, Headquarters in an old lower east side loft above a dressmaking shop. The loft itself was dominated by the most enormous bed I've ever seen, surrounded on three sides by film-making equipment, the most expensive being locked in a chicken-wire enclosure to prevent its theft by questionable pickups who might gain entrance to the rest of the room. Most of THE MECHANICS OF LOVE was shot within the confines of this makeshift studio. It was Ben Moore's and Willard Maas' first complete "collaboration." I quote "collaboration," because to me the film has always seemed more Ben's utilization of Willard's idealistic conception than anything else. Maas, the perfectionist, was certainly more intent upon making Moore, and perfecting love, rather than upon making film at this time. When a perfectionist gives up, he tends to give up altogether. This suspicion was later confirmed for me when Willard related his original idea for the film. I quote from memory:

> "It was supposed to be a color film. A boy and
> girl are seen making love in a forest beside a
> pond. Raindrops fall in the water. Trees are seen
> falling to earth . . . lightning . . . planes crashing
> even (I wanted to use lots of newsreel footage).
> Balls, on wrecking cranes, demolish whole buildings.
> Birds and animals are seen fucking—elephants even.
> A train enters a tunnel. There is an explosion. A
> cloud uncovers a kite flying. Plants are opening
> (single-frame animation). A bee is entering a flower.
> All the world is fucking!"

Ben always wanted everything, that he wanted, to have been; so he was always in a hurry. (In this sense, his and Willard's relationship was a remarkably perfect example of the attraction of opposites.) He wanted it to be a studio production, photographed in a remarkably short period of time, with the black and white film which was immediately available. All symbols of mechanization utilized were those within easy access in the confines of the city, most of them small household objects shot in close-up. Ben Moore wrote the narrative sound-track. Later, when THE MECHANICS OF LOVE was entered in a contest for educational film, Willard added a footnote on the entry-blank:

> "Especially recommended for children under six."

Finally Willard gave up all thought of Ben as an artist and conceived the idea of making The Portrait of Ben Moore As a Young Man, or: NARCISSUS. Tho' this was still not (to my mind) a collaboration, it did give them a better working relationship, with The Maaster at the helm again and Moore's ego calmed for the act of being reflected upon. All the same, there were continual outbursts, projection equipment once thrown from the 3rd story window of the studio, Willard more than once kicked down the stairs, etceteras, followed by long periods of separation. Almost everyone known to Willard in New York was, at one time or another, called upon to witness and help immortalize this titanic drama. I clearly remember my contribution to the scene in which Narcissus is beaten to death by Echo's boys. Willard had photographed it in medium-shots; and the effect was utterly unconvincing, despite some very real bruises Ben had acquired from the beating. I suggested taking some extreme close-ups, photographed at 8 frames a second to be inter-cut with the already existing footage. I agreed to photograph these. Willard was to supply the close-up fists pummelling various parts of Ben's body. They were both quite drunk at the time; and they insisted upon shooting all this at the open edge of the penthouse roof (an 11 story building) so that, ostensibly, only slate-gray sky would show beyond the action. Not only did Willard strike Ben with a force too swift and strong for the 8-frames-per-second running camera, but Ben lashed back with completely un-scripted blows of his own to liven the occasion. NARCISSUS was over four years in the making; and then Ben Moore and Willard Maas separated for, presumably, the final time. The film had not only completely exhausted their emotions toward each other but had also exhausted all the techniques of the experimental psycho-dramatical film movement. It is, at least in that sense, the masterpiece of the entire genre. But, there is not one asthetically revitalizing element within it. It is Willard Maas', and Ben Moore's, last film to date.

I had intended, as I put it, "to set the record straight" as to Marie Menken's contribution to all the above mentioned films: that is, that (to my mind) Willard's only integral and continuing collaboration was always, and only, with Marie. But a listing of her specific contributions (from carving soap bars into Roman Emperors; thru all her assistance with photography and editing; to her being the body, personification and soul of some of Willard's imaginings) would in no sénse portray the real nature of the collaboration. Willard and Marie's whole relationship is of such personal and enigmatic love that I am immediately cautioned from continued attempt at description by a feeling akin to Robert Creeley

"I would not credit comment upon gracefully." As to setting the record straight, Jane, my wife, reminds me of something Creeley recently said to her: "Only the dead are interested in credits." "Besides," says Jane with a smile, "isn't this FILMWISE issue dedicated to Willard AND Marie?"

As I re-read all I've written, I see that there's so much left out: Willard The Poet of the '30's whose poetry I hardly cared enough about to understand in the least, let alone the man of that time who wrote it; the Will of social-consciousness who automatically defended almost any underdog and just as automatically berated any personage invested with a sense of power—the Will who arrived drunk at the C16-Stanley-Kramer evening and, during the question-and-answer period grabbed the microphone away from a horrified Amos Vogel to berate the pomposity of Kramer's speech. yelling so loudly into the microphone that his statement was drowned in ear-splitting loudspeaker feed-back:

> "KRAMER (EEEEEEEEEOWOWOWOWOW) –ucking
> phoney (EEEEEEEEEEEEE), WHY (OWWWWWWWOH)
> –on't you do SOMETHING DE— (EEEEEEE) —cent (OHE
> EEEEEEEEEEEEEEEEEEEEEEEEEOW) a change, (OWWW
> WWWWWWWWW WWWWWWW) . . . give some monEY
> (EEEEEEE)
> —help young FILM-makers (oooooooooOWOWOWOW
> OWOWOWEEEEEEEEEEEEE EEEEEEEEEEEEEEOH)"

                   .　.　.　.　.　.　.　.　.　.　.　.　— ;

the socialite Willard Maas who gave the most indescribable parties in his penthouse (a kind of ship-like structure atop a Brooklyn apartment bldg. overlooking the river, the ocean, The Bridge, Statue-of-Liberty, and the distant harbor of Manhattan, aerially approached, as always, by Willard—all acquired in The Depression and tenaciously held-to), the Willard who was host, in the most sacred sense of the word, to all guests from richest to poorest, ranging sometimes into the hundreds and over-flowing down the stairs and out onto the rooftops and, God-knows, perhaps some of them over the sides, the Will, who always celebrated the human being and who loved the human being in all celebrities, who could crack jokes with Charles Addams, drink champagne from Marilyn Monroe's slipper, and hold his own with Reinhold Niebuhr, all in the space of the same evening, the secretive "W" who would hock his "Picasso" to buy suckling pig for a Christmas party and then, as easily,

help clean up the vomit of his starving N. Y. artist friends overflowing
with this sudden richness, the man who once said:

> "I thank Gawd for one thing—that Marie and I have
> always been surrounded by beautiful people";

the consciousness of the Maas who was always tutoring tarnished-angel-
hoodlums to rise to his original assumptions, his regard for youth
unending—his one most often repeated statement being:

> "Ahhhhhhhhhhhhh . . . — The Young !" —

who could assume, in an instant, the entire guilt of what he considered
his "generation" to the point of weeping as if the burden of the whole
world's woe were upon him individually—as for instance once when
confronted by a young man with "The 2nd World War" and "The
Atomic Bomb" as excuse for youthful immorality (meaning to Willard:
betrayal of a cause, the brotherhood, of friendship, or of love) to which
he replied:

> "Alllllllllllll Right! WE fucked it up. You fix it." —;

the symbolist Willard Maas who insisted upon living his life as if it were
a work of art, surrounding himself and Marie with objects which exactly
reflected both all their accords and dischords till the harmony of all penthouse atmosphere was aesthetically faithful—from the sand-painting of
Adam And Eve (by Marie) over their bed (with rattlesnake-skin
implanted) which dripped continually "with tears," (due to some
chemical reaction between sand and snake-skin) to the black-panther-
like Labrador retrievers snarling and growling continually and slinking
about in the jungle of Victorian filigreed table and chair bottoms, to each
furnishing and decoration included in the space of living, extending to
the entire effect which was as of some Flying Dutchman, seen both sunken
in the ghostly peace of browns and marine-greens on the inside and yet
still aerially approaching N. Y. harbor on the outside but never ever
bobbing about chaotically on any superficial surface; and then (most
impossible to include in any statement) the Dear Will whom I love . . .
For I see that almost all this biographical sketch is in past tense. How
sad that I have seen so little of you, and Marie, these past several years.
How equally sad (to me) that I've seen no films from you. But I know
just what you'd say to that, my friend, as you said so often before:

"Gawwwwwwwwwwwd! BRAKHAGE, you're always yacket-
ty-yacking about FILMS. Why don't you go sit
on a beach for a while, fuck all the girls, or
boys, or both. Lie in the sun. LIVE a little.
Think about things. Read poetry—the classics.
You're making too MANY films. Go have yourself a
Balllllll. LIFE is SHORT. THERE'S OTHER THINGS
TO DO, you know, BESIDES MAKING FILMS   ! "

Ah well, Willard, perhaps you're right—for yourself, that is. And as I
re-read this much worked-over article, I see that what you AND your films
really always meant to me is utterly missing, neither left-out nor at all
right. You were, and always will be, the closest I ever came to A Master
from whom I wanted to learn the craft of my art. You taught me much
of living, instead, and became one of my dearest friends. Your films,
particularly GEOGRAPHY OF THE BODY, and your ideas for the
unrealized MECHANICS OF LOVE were direct inspirations upon my
work clear up thru my FLESH OF MORNING and LOVING. By the
time I saw the completed NARCISSUS, I was already abandoning The
Psycho-drama; but even that film may yet surprise me. I was most
shocked to realize that a film as recently completed as THE DEAD owes
some homage to the graveyard scene of IMAGE IN THE SNOW. But
then, all our relationships to others in this most difficult (so-called: US)
culture are so complicated ("fucked-up," you would say) that it is practically impossible to describe the effect that anyone really has upon
another. I've, herein, approached your memory with paraphrases,
quotes, film and personal criticisms, histories, anecdotal moralities, jokes,
descriptions, scenarios, credits, characteristic studies, and now open lettering . . . So let's leave it an open end—perhaps the next time I get to
New York, I will get that long proposed film portrait of you and Marie
completed at last.

Until then . . .

                    With Love,

HYPNAGOGICALLY SEEING AMERICA

SPELL "Vietnam" backwards and you do get "ManT (ei) V"—and it does seem like that: that "the medium IS" McLuhan's apologetic "message" . . . that the optic war-of-nerves occurs in anybody's very real living room as a feed-back to/fro the fat Spartans that American-'middles' must take themselves to be. The U.S. airplanes trail cocoons of defoliation and hatch white owls offering suck to mouths which "feel so clean." Stamens of flame leap up in the jungle offering a light to "America's favorite cigarette," bombs blossom smoke—belch which dissolves in flavored seltzer, et cetera: but this is all Dada's doing, hangover of Surrealism— bad European nightmares dazedreamed by 'aunty' movements which began in Continental newspapers and ended in American museums . . . the collage of it spilled out of colleges and into Mad. Ave's 'tea-party' (U.S.-style . . . Bostonians playing 'Indian') and created a conned-tent for television . . . okay, so far so bad: but the actual technical means each man woman and child is at the mercy of in T.V.-land IS the crystal —square prophecy inherent in the medium itself—that your life is all before you . . . BOTH senses of 'before' robbing any-every one of presence and/or the pre-sent as a gift. The T.V. viewer becomes center-of-the-universe 1st time thru medium because the image-carrying-light comes directly at him (or, as McLuhan puts it: "The viewer is the screen") and comes en-meshed, or made-up-of, the television-scanning 'dots' which closely approximate his most private vision—his sense of his own optic nerve-end activity, seen as a grainy field of 'light'-particles when his eyes are closed, particles which seem to cluster into shapes in the act of memory and, thus, make-up the picture being re-membered as if it were a slide cast from the brain against closed eye-lids, particles which seem to explode into brilliant coloration and, often, geo-/sym-metrical patterns when the closed-eyes are rubbed and/or the head struck (or—so they tell me—the brains are treated to that internal crisis L.S.D. is . . . mind banged inside-out, etc.). Andrew Lang (19th Century fairy-tale author) called it "hypnagogic"—this seeing of your own sight's apparatus in-the-works: and the 19th century began the process of fixing pics. for newsprint via some approximation of it (as the 'impressionists,' culminating in the 'pointilism's of Seurat, inspired them') and thus extended one of the most internal senses of man.

THE 'movies'—working along a line of reflective experience—resisted the 'graininess' of film with all the laboratory techniques at its disposal . . . as did the great "still" photographers dedicated to the perfection of the 'original print': but ARTISTS of the film medium began, long before T.V. was widespread, to utilize whatever techniques would augment the emulsion-grain and even painted on film, sprayed it with chemicals, etc., to approximate this 'interior' vision—"Closed-eye Vision" I called it, mid-50's, trying to explain my use of paint on film, etc., and television, of course, exteriorized this sense-ability as a moving phenomenon and made it as hypno-(gogically)-teaching a form as possible . . . (is it only a technical fault, as a result of being 1st with T.V., that makes U.S. television show its "scan' far more than European television which, being developed later, uses systems of broadcast which deliver a MUCH more

Los Angeles Free Press, February 3, 1967

'solid' un-dotted picture?) . . . viz: the T.V. screen scans linearly, thus 'coming-on' with all the authority of a book-page, wrapping up every reader's habit in its 'take' on Lit. and taking-up, where 19th century landscape painting left off, on the whole Western eye(z)ed sub-conscienceviewing process . . . the T.V. 'dots,' backed by the light-source and the pale blue-ish tone of it (prime color of closed-eye vision in deep memory process, blue tinting the whole grainy field when the eyes have been closed in a dark room for a long time), do pre-tend the brain of the viewer is IN THE "SET," a tendency that soon makes him feel as if what he's watching had always been stored in his own memory banks, as if he ought to act on instructions from T.V. as surely as he would on his own experiences as remembered. Thus, thru mimicry of memory process and thru prophetic hypnosis, the viewer's life is all before him.

HOW to defeat this phony deja-vu? . . . sharpen the eyes! I've been primarily making silent films for years now—since I discovered that the eye's sight of anything was automatically dulled when any sound was attended to . . . especially since the discovery that the inner-eye (hypnagogic vision and all consciousness of visual-memory's superimposition on any external scene being looked-at) was impossible to attend to, WITH THE EYES OPEN, when and ONLY when a sound was being heard consciously. So, turn the sound down on the T.V. set-to and put your inner-eye back in your own head immediately —see, then, how the television, and movie, directors cover up a poverty of visual imagination by lulling the eye to sleep with sounds continuum . . . see, for instance, how President Johnson ap-proximates with minute facial changes (as befits the medium) Hitler's most exact gestural—(movie) stances (how the rhythm of Johnson's slight head tilts and the shifts of his facial muscles marshal a specific television attention . . . how the scanning-dots cluster and scatter with each shift of light and shadow across his T.V. 'hyp' face with all the force of ordered crowds of people toned to his 'benevolent' expression breaking into rioting mobs—particularly at his each questioning look—and then lining-up militarily on cue of frown, etc. . . . an attention that an un-grainy medium, like 'the movies,' could only command thru violent 'stage' gestures backed by actual crowds of people behaving on cue, as in 30's Germany).

I ALSO suggest tilting your head while watching T.V.—an act which turns 'linear' to some verticality and, for some mysterious reason, makes the dots much less visible. But, these are finally only 'tricks' played on the machine itself and, as such, a too-simple patch-work against ultimate disaster. One must become aware of one's own inner-eye workings and thus, come to know television for what IT is, defeat ITS hyp-goggles at source in self.

ONE of the most useful meditations, in this respect, is the conscious act of remembering a T.V.-image—a careful and deliberate attention to the process of memory itself in calling forth a television scene . . . a seeing of it taking shape on the grainy-field of your own closed eyes, the pulse with which it comes back at you, the coloring it takes onto itself, et cetera . . . this, at least, restores the T.V. 'original' to your own physiological consciousness. I discovered the effectiveness of this process while making "23rd Psalm Branch," a feature-length war film; and I found it to be the only way I could experience the newsreels of my childhood AND that 'staged' slaughter in Vietnam which T.V. brings daily into my home, in a creative way—that is as an existent reality. Otherwise, it's just the old pea-and-the-nut trick: I somehow KNEW the pea was up the politician's sleeve; but I didn't know how it got there: and the politician's hand is faster than the preconditioned eye, but NOT faster than the inner eye's ability, thru memory, to play the whole trick back in extreme slow motion, with personally creative interpretation (in the mind's edit of the parts of the image re-membered, the order of objects called-forth having a meaningful continuity, or personal message, akin to any wordless comic strip or silent movie sequence) and 'colored' to suit, or express, your own deepest emotional response (the closed eyes flashing banks of color rhythmically in the act of memory thus, express the feelings of the person as surely as rhythmically-structured 'tones' of music express a composer's feelings). TELEVISION dumped the implication of monstrous war guilt into my living room; and every conceivable hypnotic means of that medium seemed to imply its filthy (striptease/top-seek) pictures originated in ME and that its, thus, prophetic imperialism was/will-be an absolute necessity of my continued living. I was, thus, 'bugged' in the fullest sense of the word and had to go back, memory-wise to the source of that trick in my life: the somewhat similar noose-reels of my World War II years under child's hood—1938 thru 1945 . . .: and the "23rd Psalm Branch," the film I created OUT of these struggles, does illuminate the whole process of pictured war sufficiently to enable me to say, with Michael McClure (from "Poisoned Wheat") "I AM NOT GUILTY. I AM A MEAT CREATURE": and to watch my T.V. set from where I AM.

LECTURE INTENDED

. . . for Denver Friends of New Cinema showing on April 2, 1967 . . .

I have been asked to say a few words to begin this program—this which is, so far as I know the second public (that is: non-club) showing of any of my films in my hometown of Denver . . . the first Denver public showing of any of my work was at the Vogue Theatre last night—April Fool's Day, appropriately enough.

All right then—Hello! Denver!, after all these years . . . I'm now living in a ghost town a good hour's drive from these streets and have been residing peacefully here several light years away from the bitter memories of my early struggles as dog/artist in this city: and I have given up most of those hopes I'd had of any kind of cultured community in these environs, those hopes I'd wasted many of my young energies upon (their final 'dash' came when a mailing to 4,000 Denverites advertising the U.S. premiere of Erik Satie's "Sports and Diversions," played by Bob Tipps, with slides of the original paintings he'd composed them to and dramatic presentation of the text, at the North Denver "Theatre Innovations," netted an audience of one person—and on a warm spring night, at that: but that was only the last straw in a series of such chaffings . . . I'd started with enough enthusiasm to stage Chekhov, Maetterlinck, Strindberg, Wedekind and othersuch, in an army surplus tent in Central City when I was fresh out of South High School, had lost what little money I had over and over again trying to import a Museum of Modern Art Film Series into this area . . . had lost what little temper I had trying to get men like that tone-deaf metronome-

of-a-conductor The Denver Symphony has stuck with for years *out* of this area . . . or at least, finally, trying to dislodge from seats of *absolute* power men like Otto Bach—who *still* wields squatters rights over the by-now-oiled-over eyes of the majority of the populace . . . tried at last in sheer desperation to persuade some of the ex-sports writers of the local papers who, as the last stop before the broom closet, became the art columnists of the community—*tried* to persuade them that a painting was not to be judged *necessarily* on the basis of whether it was a 'knockout' or not, that they did *not* have to play 'umpire' to the local plays in their reviewing of them, that an orchestra was *not* a cheerleading section to be judged on the basis of its noise . . . etcetera/etcetera) . . . until I finally got tired, clear through to the social marrow of my communal bones. Charles Olson once said to me that a town, however large it becomes, always remains what it was at scratch: and I've come to believe that true . . . come to see that New York is as 'provincial' in its huge tastes as it was when it was truly 'a province'— that San Francisco is, as it was when it was established, an international city— and that Denver is, well, Denver.

I was, about three months ago, about to be convinced that all that was changing. Many energetic young people were beginning to be doing extraordinary things in and around the 'here' I once knew as home. My antenna at 9,000 feet had begun to pick up the folk-music scene coming through on the radio even. There was suddenly an 'underground' newspaper—well I hate that word, being a living room man myself: but the truth is that the news comes through the underground newspapers as straight as you'll get it in a prison pipeline system, I mean tapped out of the sheer frustration which the authorized prison newspapers will never reveal—. And there were light shows and poets coming through, and painters putting together a little gallery here and there, etcetera. The Vogue Theatre discovered Andy Warhol and pulled a few works of film art into midnight shows on Andy's coat tails. Some old enemies called up and congratulated me on this and that.

Ah, well, but it *was* nice to be smiled at on the streets for a change: though my wife, Jane, warned: "We don't know who our friends are anymore—it used to take courage to be friends of ours." All the same, I had a soft spot in my head for all the goings-on, was growing tender hopefuls down by backbone and out to my finger tips and toes, imagining very real hand shakes and dances in the air—until 'The Bust' began and all the pieces fell into archtypical placement. First the S. F. Mime Troup was pulled in for a use of language that is becoming common in even Hollywood movies, in a time when the so-called "sexual revolution" is a topic of panel discussion once a week on Educational TV even. Then Clancy's Bookstore—the only place in the state I know of where you can buy the works of the younger poets with any regularity—was raided for selling buttons! and his windows have since been busted twice by unknown members of the Boulder community. The Boulder Bardo-Matrix light shows were twice raided for "disturbance of the peace," a complaint that must have amazed the residents who live near the fraternities of that town. Local detectives attended the Experimental Cinema Group showings on CU campus and confiscated what they referred to as "pornography" off the desk of a CU art instructor. Now the editor of the "Mile-High Underground" is up before the Denver courts on a charge of "pornography" and "possession of illegal implements" (a syringe, etc., he'd had hanging on his wall). My favorite radio announcer is 'on the lam,' so they tell me. Etcetera.

A week or so ago, I spent the whole day in The Boulder Police Bldg. asking, simply: "Why are you harrassing the cultural community of this town?" and reading "The Little Flowers of Saint Francis" between interviews to help me hold my temper. I was told what I already knew: that 'narcotics' was the 'illegality' they were honing-in on: but I was essentially there to try to convince any attendant ear (and there were a couple) that art, dope, long-hair/sandals, etc., light-shows, riots-in-the-streets, etcetera, were not *necessarily* synonymous. I am here to try to tell you essentially the same thing: for the 'bust' has revealed to me that it is a 'peanuts Berkeley' many of the people want here rather than a 'Denver Art Community': it is kicks they're after and the police are, of course, the authorized kickers, the communally accepted representatives of Cain: and The Able are Abel, as always: and the pieces of this 'bust' fall into the oldest standard arch-type of this Judeo-Christian civilization. The able young lie to themselves when they scream they're "lambs led to the slaughter" as surely as the police do when they use "sex" or "narcotics" as their excuse for the Shem/Shaun game they play with all those who wear "kick me" expressions on the public streets. The Boulder Irish cop who troubled himself to admit to me that Christ probably would have been a draft card burner, has come a lot farther along a road of some thoughtfulness than most of my hippie friends have on the quest-shuns of the moment . . . I wonder, for instance, if my editor friend knows he was nailing himself to The Judeo-Christian wall when he hung up that syringe as surely as if he'd knocked himself to a cross for the occasion? Maya Deren once said to me that in a society (such as ours), lacking art, thus contemporary myth, the young seek to define themselves by breaking the laws, simply because 'law-breaker' becomes the only specific definition left to them.

I don't know how many tonight are here for 'kicks,' for the 'experiment' these films are supposed, as advertised, to be . . . how many are 'slumming' tonight, as the word 'underground' would seem to suggest as an eventuality of the evening? . . . how many want to see some SIN, some 'over-exposure,' so to speak? . . . how many are secretly hoping the place will be raided?—I don't know . . . maybe none . . . maybe I wrong you all: but it has been a rough couple of weeks for me: I would like to suggest in the midst of this current cultural bursting and busting enthusiasm—I would like to suggest some simplicities of experience: that, say, the local burlesque is a greater 'camp' than anything you're likely to see here tonight, despite the advertising—that the local streets are, for that matter, more campy . . . that the local cathouses are greater for kicks than the cops are, etc.

Let my speech be titillation enough for the evening's scandal-dogs—and if it hasn't been enough, I'll meet with anyone afterward and run through all the dirty words I know, okay? I take each of these films to be *at least* an attempt at a work of art: and I judge several of them successful in that attempt, though I won't tell you which ones because I know that judgment blinds (that is why Justice is always represented thus) and I would like to take this as one of those few occasions in Denver when the eyes have it! . . . know, anyway, that art is finally a very personal matter . . . and I would not, therefore, intrude upon anyone's private vision. Art *is* public in *this* sense: that its availability to anyone is a necessarily shared responsibility of everyone—like life itself. A work of art requires a very fragile landscape in which to exist . . . a cough, let alone a riot, can disturb its continuities . . . a *suppressed* cough, or rioting imagination, even more so—for the subtlest feelings become attenuated while experiencing aesthetics: and I have known the impatience of a very few people (who had not the sense to leave an auditorium where they were unhappy) to spread like a plague throughout an entire audience simply because it was more attention-getting, as being easier to attend to, than the complexities of an aesthetic experience. But the strength of art is that it is somehow so much needed by people that often and again they will provide the fragile landscape it requires for its existence and will even, *tho' very rarely,* attend that growth to shape the community at large, I have no such large-scale hopes for Denver environs tonight, but I will wish for the magic of that special occasion this might be: that it might be the eye of the social hurricane I've experienced lately and, as such, be focused upon something beyond all that.

ON *23RD PSALM BRANCH*

This is part of a lecture given at the film-makers' Cinematheque on April 22, 1967 at the premiere of the "23 Psalm Branch, Parts I & II & Coda," and "Songs 24 & 25."

BRAKHAGE: I think that this ("23rd Psalm") is a peculiar film, a kind of home movie war film. It really is an attempt to deal with war in the way that it was forwarded into the environment of our home.

Jane and I and the children live in a log cabin in the mountains. We don't get newspapers. We'd occasionally listen to the news on the radio. Nonetheless, about two years ago, we took into the house a television set. Primarily it was used as a form of 'going out.' The expenses and travel necessary to get to a movie of any kind were prohibitive. Because of these factors, we would almost dress up and 'go out' to the TV. We'd turn it on and view a particular program, then turn it off and go back downstairs. And in that form, I think we accomplished the most blessed use of television. Nevertheless, despite all those precautions, it (the television) finally began to affect our lives. I have been working all these years on a series of 8mm film "Songs," as much as possible out of the inspiration of "amateur," in the true sense of the word. It came to a point where it seemed that I could make a film about anything in the house, except I couldn't deal with the television set. It wasn't just the object itself, but rather that it was our only specific connection with society, with a capital "S." It was something which we were expected to be responsible for. Watching the news programs, commercials, or dramas, I saw their whole assumption was that war was being actually presented to us, and

we were directly responsible for dealing with it. I knew that the composition on the screen made quite clear the fact that it was 19th century drama or staged war, photographed flatly and projected through this incredibly hypnotic device. In effect it was hooking us to that proclivity. I don't know how this came about, except that it developed so much paranoia and disturbance in the house that my wife and I began to have a kind of quarrel such as the previous nine years of marriage hadn't produced. It was a long, lingering, building-up quarrel, that required laws and counter laws to balance it and check it. Meanwhile, I had taken a lecture tour to West Germany and had spent several hours in East Berlin and some time in Vienna, and I came back very disturbed about seeing the actual plight of things that up until then I had only experienced through Hollywood movies. I found that I couldn't deal at all with Vietnam. I had never been there. As yet, I haven't seen any imagery that presents it in any way that's even close to what Vietnam might be. Nevertheless, when you have a machine that comes on in the form that television does, where the images are carried by the light directly to the eyes (that is, not reflected), and where the images are composed of moving dots and particles (as emphasized by American TV), the effect psychologically was the same as in so-called memory recalls. That is, when an image is remembered from a person's own experience it comes as if carried by the light, and is made up of moving dots, some of them being very similar to the scan on television. I began to feel that what was causing the hypnosis of the set, itself, was simply that it presented an image in a way so

NY Film-Makers' Newsletter *1*(2), **December 1967**

[**A transcript of the complete remarks are published in** *Film Culture* **67-69, 1979**]

similar to the act of memory that the effect was as if my brain was in the television set. While I was viewing TV's experience of data, I would automatically feel like acting on it as I would on my own experience. And as my experiences aren't primarily 19th century drama, this created a crisis in myself that I couldn't deal with directly. I felt the only chance I had, was to go to the crux of my memory of the Second World War through the movies and the newsreels as a child, and then acting on that material to shoot it out with the rest of the kids in the neighborhood. I began wondering what to do in the face of having been hooked into that proclivity at so young an age. I believed that the war transmitted to me, was a real one—as a child does believe what's given him. Under such circumstances, how could I possibly make it my own war, then, or now? And it seemed to me that the hope lay in remembering, accurately enough, the order of those images as they arose in the mind's eye in the act of intensive memory, and the patterns and shapes that arose with them.

For some years, I have been painting in my films. For this film, I tried to remember the order of the color flashes. In the act of intensive memory, I saw that every image that arose arrived in banks or flashes of certain tones of colors that became very complex and so forth. I began working with a set of simple colors that I could create with. We have this idea in the language, that most people aren't aware of it consciously, that in memory (or just in looking) the eyes are putting-out (emitting) a color. We do say that a man sees "red" when he's angry. And I found that a true term, a very blunt and general one, that in anger there are various shades of red 'seen' by the angry

one, and then other colors that don't even have names. All of which come primarly through the mind's eye, each with different rhythms. We also say "Green with jealousy," or "sickly green" or "green as a go signal." And these all turned out to be true of certain aspects of green. Then we say "yellow" for cowardice, and "blue" for certain forms of sadness, particularly in relation to nostalgia. I began intensively remembering this war of my childhood and then making the film out of only those images that I could remember having seen as a child. I was directly inspired by the order in which I remembered them, and the rhythms in which they were flashed forth. This whole work-in-itself was very inspired by the films of Peter Kubelka, and particularly by his firm "Arnulf Rainier" which made me realize something of my own physiology. This is Part I. Then in Part II, I couldn't end it, yet. Even more than any film I've ever made, I wanted to make this one an "incompleted work," and at one point stated: "I can't go on," (in the film), and really meant that. Then I found that just as in the world at large, when man as a society screams: "We can't go on. We must have peace," that's when the war is really beginning to take hold. And that was true here too. I had to go beyond that point, there was no getting out of it. And then finally I got to the point where it wasn't enough to have made *that* clear to myself in a positive manner, but I had to go on to a Part II to search out the sources of why I might possibly have to make this film. I think "Part II" is even more complex than the first—as seeking out the source of anything is more complex. "Part II" seems to me to fall into a series of short films that go together and are rather like sonnets, for a lack of a better term.

You'll see that there are *Peter Kubelka's Vienna, My Vienna, Nietzsche's Lamb,* and also a *Tribute to Freud.* Well finally the work was finished.

Throughout the editing of the film Jane and I had an almost continuous number of quarrels. They reached such a pitch that I moved out of the house for three days into a motel and ran up a $30 phone bill screaming at my wife over the telephone. We had gotten to the point that we were solacing ourselves by looking around and seeing how many divorces there were occurring in this year of war, and searching out all the statistics of divorce. We also took notes of how many forms of disease were spreading in this society.

During this period, I made very careful and involved studies of the Second World War. As a result, the editing of this film has the most structured thought behind it of any film that I've made.

My hope simply is that it relates to the physiology of everyone. Anyone that leads off with drama, even in the most avant-garde expectancy, and opens up to his nerve-endings singing, and the ringing of ears, and the possible flashing of the eyes and the *idea* of death, is within his own memory of that war and his own experiences thereof this film's subject matter. For me, the film has been very helpful, and my hope is that in this time, whatever anyone may feel about the war, this film can inform anyone of how their very bones and marrow and their physiology act in the face of controlled media that try to destroy all possible individual thought. Well, thank you . . .

EIGHT QUESTIONS

Question: How do you finance films if not by a foundation?

Brakhage: The first intimation I had that I was going to make a film some fifteen years ago was when some friends and I were talking about how sad it was that an artist couldn't work with the film medium; that it was so prohibitively expensive that no artist could work with it. I remembered that when I was a child I was put in a boy's home called Harmony Hall—which was anything but that—and forced to hold my hands above my head for two hours because I had said to some other kid that anything was possible, and he reported that I had said that you could cut off somebody's head and that it would sprout wings and fly away. And when that was thrown at me, when they said: "Is that possible too?" I said: "Yes, it's possible." So I was punished for having said this. And as I stood there, every time my hands touched the wall they would hit them with a ruler. So I came at that time to believe very strongly that anything was possible; I was either going to be broken at that moment or believe what I had said. So when my friend said that it was prohibitive for an artist to use the medium, I didn't believe him. With that clarity that is real presumption in the young, I said: "Well, I'm an artist and I'm going to make a film." But that sounds too noble, because I was terribly shy, and there was this girl that I wanted to go with, and I was too shy to ask her straight out. So I cast her in the lead in this film. Essentially, I began to make film in order to disprove this statement and to make out with this girl.

And here's the financial side of it: we got some war-surplus out-dated Dupont gun-camera film in fifty foot spools. And we had to sit in the dark with pencils and unreel it onto spools and make a splice in the dark so we could get hundred foot rolls. And we then borrowed several cameras; also, we rented a camera for a couple of weekends. By the time, two years later, we got a sound track on it, I suppose *Interim* had cost something like five hundred dollars. This is how I made that first film; it seemed to me too expensive.

The second film was sponsored: *Unglassed Windows Cast a Terrible Reflection*. It turned out to be something like a sponsored film. After that I began making my own films.

When I began my third film I had no money at all. I still wasn't convinced that I was a filmmaker. Like Jean Cocteau, I was a poet who also made films. That was how I thought of myself: I was Denver's Jean Cocteau. And this third film had been promised to the public: we had been trying to import Museum of Modern Art film classics into Denver, and we had promised the public three films, and couldn't afford to rent the third one. Someone had some outdated black and white footage and since it was cheaper to pay just the processing I shot the film to fulfill that third slot. It was a biting satire on what we used jokingly to call "desistentialism." Long before the Beats, this film (*Desistfilm*) prophesied the whole concept of the Beat generation. I used jokingly to say "We've got beyond the stage of existentialism, we've got to the stage of desistentialism." So I made this satire on that form of life which is destructive to the self. It had a sound track and cost something like a hundred and twenty dollars to an answer print.

So you see, each film comes in a dif-

April 1967 remarks after a screening at University of Cincinnati; *Cinema Now*, 1968

ferent way. *Dog Star Man* (of which you'll see the *Prelude* tonight) was made while I had a job at a lab that agreed to process my film at cost while I was on the job. They never realized that I was to put through six thousand feet in two months' time. Also at this studio we had high speed cameras. So we had super equipment, and all that footage at a very minimal cost. And so it goes.

When I need to do something I somehow find the means to do it. And somehow, like magic, incredible coincidences occur that make it possible. Then all kinds of possibilities open. For instance, when some sixteen mm equipment was stolen, I had only enough money to buy eight mm equipment to replace it. So for three years now I've been making eight mm films I probably never would have made had it not been for this thief. For this I'm grateful: it's opened up a whole new area in my work.

Question: Is your intent in making a film to communicate?
Brakhage: I get this question everywhere; and the big hangup is the word "communication." It's like this: let me explain by way of a story, a true story.

A man falls in love. The girl doesn't love him. She hurts him; she wants somebody to hurt and he wants somebody to hurt him, but he doesn't know that yet. He's downcast. Then he meets another girl and he loves her and she loves him. He no longer needs to try to communicate with her: they just take walks together, and make love, and talk. Then he has it: some expression of his love is out there in the world.

Then he takes her to introduce her to his parents, and he is involved in communicating again, and this is very difficult. Well, this is like when a man

works out of love and the work is out there; and then he takes this work into society, and that's always very difficult. I mean no one truly understands it, just as no one's parents truly understand one's true love. Yet a work of art must have a life in society; once the artist has finished making it, it belongs to others. But he never made it with the idea of taking it into society. Any man that sets out to find a girl to introduce to his parents is never likely to fall in love. Any man that sets out to make a work for audiences is never going to make a work of art. A work of art is made for the most personal reasons— as an expression of love.

Question: Could you tell us what you feel about eight mm?
Brakhage: First of all, it's cheaper than sixteen mm. Next— just picking up one of those little cameras relates me to the whole sense of amateur. It's an amateur medium. I have a growing conviction that something crucial to the development of the art of the film will come from amateur home-movie making, as well as from study of the classics: Eisenstein, Griffith, Melies, and so forth. It's so small and lightweight—I stick it in my pocket, carry it everywhere— and so cheap: used eight mm cameras usually go for about fifteen dollars. Some, when they're used, are broken down and do extraordinary things, like failing to catch the film just right so it makes a particular pattern and flutter. One I had broke down utterly when I was doing an ocean film. Its spring broke permitting me to grind it at different speeds; so I would let the wave rush up very fast by grinding slowly, and then I'd suddenly zoom up so that the wave reached its peak in slow motion, and then I'd slow my hand down so that the wave would break up in an incredible order.

Then eight mm film is given such a blow-up on the screen that you can see the grain of the film stock much more clearly than in sixteen mm high speed film. The crystals that make blue look quite different from those making red and green. For years I've baked film, used high speed film and sprayed Clorox on it so as to bring out grain clusters. You might say it's inspired by impressionism, but it's a great deal more contemporary than that. I have been trying for years to bring out that quality of sight, of closed-eye vision. I see pictures in memory by the dots and moving patterns of closed-eye vision—those explosions you can see by rubbing your eyes, and even without rubbing; there's a whole world of moving patterns. It's a manifestation of the optic nerve, and God knows what else.

There are endless advantages to working with eight. Creative advantages. It's an entirely different medium from sixteen. It imposes a different kind of discipline because there isn't a way of easily working with A and B rolls and changing lights in the lab— some labs do it but it's pretty expensive. Editing, when there is editing, is on the order of the splice. Eight mm has freed me to work freely, much as an artist is freed in sketching.

Question: If an angel were to give you money to work with 35 mm, would you want to?

Brakhage: It doesn't work that way with me. To answer your question about an angel who would give me 35 mm: usually it's the other fellow who gives us things like that. If you were to say: "We must have 35 mm!" —poof, the telephone would ring and there he'd be, right out of *Faust*. For me, once, it did just that: I had been working on a lip-sync film. There I was with the dialogue on magnetic tape,

and I had no equipment to do this, so there I was trying to iron the film, and it went "wreak-wrock," like this, and then trying to drop these accurately into the picture area where the lips (*mimes lip action*) (*Laughter*). Well, three hours of this and I'm out of my mind. Before I had a chance to cool off, the telephone rang. It was long distance and a voice on the other end said: "How would you like a million dollars worth of motion picture equipment to work with?" I should have hung up immediately or crossed myself or put some garlic on the phone (*laughter*) but like a fool I said, "Who is this?" As it turned out it was some guy who wanted something on his own who was pretending he could connect me with a college that actually had a million dollars worth of equipment and he claimed he could get me a job there. And we suffered for two months as a result of this phone call. Since then I've been very careful—you know, it's like the monkey's paw or Alladin's lamp: you get three wishes, yet no matter what you wish, it's stacked against you.

If I absolutely *had* to work in 35 mm, I would simply find a way to do it. For instance, right now I need 35 mm in my work in hand painting the image. I get 35 mm film stock from the back of lab editing baskets, stock that would otherwise be thrown out. I've been working two years now and have three seconds done.

Question: As I understand it, you feel that money and affluence are not a good climate for artistic endeavors?

Brakhage: It's a personal matter. Imagine Wallace Stevens as anything but a banker, the banker he was, moving in that world of dark shadows and thick rugs and mahogany staircases and rubber plants and semi-stained glass windows, moving down to the bank and its vaults and resounding echoes. All that's part of his milieu and he's incomprehensible without it. Some artists feel they need to move through this shadow world of the rich. It's very hard to talk about affluence and art because it's so much an individual matter. There's a kind of artist who will flourish and flower under a great cultural explosion, and Andy Warhol is an excellent example; and there are other artists who make a work that will not flower under that climate. Their art must be infinitely attended. The trouble with the cultural explosion is that it tends to engender a kind of interest in an art that can be viewed quickly, or a piece that can be viewed once, or a play that can be seen and comprehend once over television, or on the stage, or a paperback that you read once and then throw away or give to a friend. This may be exciting, but it is anti-art, as I understand it. I think one finally comes back to those things that are meaningful in one's life. Films are just beginning to provide this possibility where one can have them in their homes, in libraries where they can be come back to again and again in meaningful film viewings. I look forward to this very much, because it takes film off the stage, off the public occasion scene and out of the competitive arena. Such library facilities will provide for the necessity a viewer may feel to see a particular film. It's necessity that causes a work of art to come into being, and it is necessity that makes a viewer commit a work of visual art to memory. Such preservation constitutes the true continuity of culture.

I look at a work over and over, and then thoughts come. I think art is the expression of the internal physiology of the artist. It's that at scratch: the individual expression that can be attended by a person hearing himself sing and feeling his heart beat. And always it begins with and comes to this: a man attending his physiology and making an expression out of it. I think the first expression was some creature beating his chest to give out with the heart beat, and then the feet danced, so the feet were expressing the heart beat, and then the heart beat was heard more complexly, and that made possible a greater variety of rhythms. Anyone who attends his own heart beat can find the source of all rhythmic structures. And then there were pictures in the eyes. There was experience and there were memories and the memories came up and made a picture and there were things crucial to the picture, and they made of it a hieroglyph, and writing started there. And I think, at heart, that all art is today as it was then: man is supposed to be a billion years old.

Question: And the great artist is more aware of this, of these life cycles?
Brakhage: I don't know. The great artist may be less aware of it. "Great" and "aware" are two words.

Question: This would relate to the statement you made in a letter to Jonas Mekas: "Plant this seed deep in the underground. Let it draw nourishment from uprising of spirits channeled by gods."
Brakhage: You know what this is like? It's like . . . this is strange because I kind of remember those words. Scientists tell me that short of the molecular structure in my brain there's not an atom left in me that wrote that, or very few. This is as if I presented you with a statement that you wrote eight, nine years ago. I don't know; I would say something different now. That sounds to me a little too rhetorical.

Question: I'm intrigued though at the

mention of the word "god" in connection with the earth. Was it chthonic deities you had in mind at that time?
Brakhage: God knows, as they say, what I had in mind at that time. This afternoon we were talking, and the phrase came up, "the powers that be," how timorous people were about "the powers that be," powers which are, really—non-existent; powers which have so dominated the American business world: powers which can be very beautifully defined as "the non-existent powers that be." And I said: "Take that to the nth power, and that's a power concept," but not *my* concept of god. My god is existence. My god is manifest in everything; not through power but through being, through an unfolding of being, through a willingness to dance with life and existence. All religions, however different, grant preeminently to man the power of the will. So that is my idea of "the powers that be"—the will of the dancer, open and willing, the will of the dancer.

WITH LOVE

There is no contemporary place for woman in art, if art be considered
a form in history the shape of which is determined by inventions which
have shaped it and each invention of which answers the previous inventions which are crucial to it (as is clear in the medium of mathematics,
etc.), because the form is male (as most historical forms are) and even
overtly exclusive of woman (as even the subject matter of most, say,
poems in the English language are premised thus—thus as content thus—
thus as "form is never more than an extension of content" thus,— etc.)
while yet each source of inspiration, creatrix of impulse throughout, is
woman—the muse is female . . . the beginning of any form is woman
(as, say, contemporary medicine finds its roots in the natural activities
of witches), as the first rite is rooted rightly in the imagination in a
matriarchy. Each bull dike and each effeminate man extend bridges to
and from, respectively, the world of the arts—these hang in space now,
whatever the greatness of technicality which keeps them, those bridges,
afloat (and you know what I mean when you temper this with the
knowledge of, say, Gertrude Stein's importance) make side pockets on
the trousers of historical art, that hierarchitectitiptiteploftical of men's
doing, the UNdoing of which is always at the fly-open ("side pockets"
makes me think of the story of Elizabeth Barrett Browning, more famous
for her verse than her husband all the while she was living, breaking
the rule they'd agreed upon: that they would not show each other's
work to each other, working in separate rooms, hers the study directly
above his, etc.: and coming down one day, coming up behind him as
he was looking out the window, holding his head so he would not turn
around, and slipping "Sonnets From The Portuguese" into his coat
pocket, saying something like: "Read these later—if they do not please
you, please destroy them," etc.) . . . her coming to that most clear gesture
as she became his wife, he her husband, came to understand the form
of poetry thereby, and how the inability to see she might have created
a new form, a woman's form, from scratch, so to speak, thus the loss
of the old form, the knowledge of what she never had had, came possibly
to kill her, caused the tragedy of her death in work at least despite
both her fame and Robert's rightful awareness of the greater [than his]
potential of her work, his continuous praise, etc. of the misleading terms
of his praise, her room above [more removed from the earth] his, etc.).
Ah, well . . . anyway, I see the possibilities of a woman's form or forms
growing to a maturity, being a dress, bell open at bottom to all earth

impulse, which answers at first to the needs of that sex woman is, and internally *her* organs, and becoming in time a form independent of male shape enough to permit each woman's invention to answer woman's invents in history *until* such time as male and female art may answer each other, via sex at first, I imagine, and furtively as in a lift of the skirt and some unzipping, but wherein the bridge is as extension of penis, as inspired at source, the opening of the form of woman as structured as her body, as sourced as her needs, and then, in time, as in love, the side-pockets will fall away, the hands of the masterbating man-shape of his medium be freed for embrace, their clothes in historical tatters from the workings of lust, be simply taken off and some art be reared in marriage, after all these poor bastards set adrift in the spaces of the imagination, some thus housed and finally homed, in love, growth of the union of these old arts inform them both thru its coming into maturity of their pasts, as do children always, for a being present of each in all. Okay, this is perhaps too metaphorical in my present writings here: but I sense this idea as center of beautiful possibilities, tho' it be only see/metaphor in the moment . . . "see" for "seed" there encouraging me it is more real a sight in my imagination than I had imagined—must now hope to some time Freudslip "real" to "re all" and thus inform myself it is rooting solidly viz: spect to past.

TO A CANADIAN FILM-MAKER

From a letter to Sam Perry about his description of and exercises for experiencing closed-eye vision.

Now I'd like to get on with some really important matters—those NOT promised on any specious "what's the"... I would very much like to see the Tantras of yours in a finished (in the sense of: as you would like printed form) tho' I take them to be of such a nature that they will NEVER, hopefully, be finished in the sense of complete. Apropos that: what you call "the dot plane" seems to me to be MUCH more of a complex field than your language would suggest, tho' I DO find the term "The Dot Plane" to be a clear english demarcation of first approach to that "grainy field," as I call it, that area most take to be "background" of closed eyes vision when they impose death upon it, attempt to distinguish it from the free-floating irregularly shaped forms which appear, thru imposition of Rennaissance perspective upon the whole field, as forward of grain and as, indeed, moving nearer and farther, or vice versa, upon or in a space imagined existing between grain and nothing, so to speak. At first, for instance, I thought that the individual grains were fairly fixed, and of a like nature, and moved only slowly, in a "crawl-ing" fashion,* likened them thus ALL to some capillary action, thought of them as being, in some sense, a "seeing" of self's optic nerve-endings, possibly as being erythrocytes—I was aware of the spot phenomenon scientists sometimes attribute to a seeing of laucocytes, usually perceived in chains of same, etc. I sprayed paint, off a tooth brush, onto film to approximate this field, but of course received flickering patterns only occasionally, as only luck would have it at first, approximating anything like a "crawl" in the representation. Despite my despair, at the time (time of editing *Prelude* and *Thigh Line Lyre Triangular*), my study of these flickering paint patterns MADE ME AWARE of a similarly flickering level of "the dot plane," as you call it... made me aware, in time, of several differing flicker dots—made me then aware of the, at first infinitesimally, differing SHAPES of these differently MOVING dots or grains: and I came to see varieties of shapes SOME of which were related (finally seen to be exactly related) SOME of which were NOT: and of the former of the last two areas I came to call ONE type "Reich's grains" and/or, when I saw them MAGNIFIED thru a glass placed before CLOSED eyes, came to honor Reich's vision by accepting his term for the phenomenon: "Orgone": and to accept, temporarily at least, his term for the path of movement: "Orgonic energy pattern": as I found his description of the move-ment fairly accurate—tho' I find these moving shapes coming onto my closed eye vision in blue, gold, and even red, and very occasionally green, rather than only in the "blue" Reich designated to them. My continued study of the WHOLE field inclines me to believe that there are NO exactly round grains thereIN it, that we tend to call "round" that which has *not* been seen inTO distinctly enough, that, thus "The Dot Plane" is ONLY an introductory term, so to speak, and COULD thus constitute a verbal (to the expense of the visual) hang-up if hung onto.

---

* *This* approximated most exactly in film by the use of "grainy" film, by emulsion grain.

FILM:DANCE

Film is the oldest art of our time (in the sense Gertrude Stein finds America the oldest contemporary country).

Film as film is essentially undiscovered (in the sense D. H. Lawrence defines America undiscovered), and traditional aesthetics interfere with this discovery (essentially as Lawrence finds "democracy" impeding the discovery of America as America).

Film aesthetics take shape historically (as William Carlos Williams finds American history taking some European shape aesthetically).

Whereas:

Films shape themselves with reference to very much less sense of history and very much more reverence for history than any other possible art.

Films *take* shape most truly there from some immediate sense of presence.

Film *as* film shapes itself most usually in The Present *as* Gift.

Film is, thus, premised on physiological sense—*takes* Sense as Muse . . . is oldest art to center itself on that source of inspiration.

The technological means of moving pictures come into being to satisfy the need of (particularly Western) Man for an immediately (moving) permanent (picture) impress-extensability of (visual) sense.

The art of this is, simply, the making of these means full.

The art of this, complexly, is as and according to the needs of the man making.

The art of this, historically, is the individual's impress-extense of himself to the historical forms of art.

That is a chance.

It, as all chance, is physiologically centered.

It is, as un-rehearsed dance, determined by the immediately-present *sense*-ability of the individual dancer.

Film, as this dance, is particularly American:

Its central fact is space (as Charles Olson finds: "Space to be the central fact to man born in America");

Its permital abstract is pure energy (as Buckminster Fuller defines "efficiency," American-wise, as: "ephemeralizing *toward* pure energy").

Its internal limitation is individual physiology—lack of touch, sense-thereof/with geography . . . lack of ground—for energy, lack of direction, sense-ability-thereof,/for geometry . . . lack of attitude—in space, (or as Gertrude Stein refines American definitions: "when they make the boundary of a State they have to make it with a straight line," contrary to European boundaries, *and*: "A sky is a thing seen when you look up, when you look up in America you see up. That is all.")

When, as mythed, Méliès made the first film splice, he created the possibility of a mind's eye art—its momentum subject to the dance of the intellect—its outer limitation the optic nerve endings of any individual.

As the splice became generally accepted, the motion picture medium ceased to be a flattened box stage of light into which something could be put—it became sight's gesture . . . the eyes had it.

American necessity, culminating in the genius of D. W. Griffith, gave it time/shape for memory's articulation—an optic nerve-end feed-back formality . . . the mind's eye's sway over any input.

As the Griffith grammar became generally accepted, the motion picture ceased to need to continue itself by classic cause-and-effect laws—it became sight's self searcher physio-logical.

Human animal necessity now moves most individually new world over to fulfill these means forth with more than gesture and never (the) less than search.

This is a dance.

As a dance, it is: as the body moves, the eye moves with it . . . as the eye moves, the body is in movement.

But the dance, at worst, is premised pre-Méliès and, at best,

has come along a line of internal physiological self-awareness only to sense of gesture.

The cine-dance, thus, is at worst an attempt of one medium to put itself into another medium which will not meaningfully be put upon. At best, it is a gesture art lacking grammar.

(An *almost* exception: Maya Deren, in *Choreography for Camera,* kicks casual-effectuals out in the edit of backgrounds, making them cinematic in-scapes, time-and-otherwise, but left the dance in-classic-tact.)

(An almost traditional *sort of* outgrowth: others, most notably Shirley Clarke and Ed Emshwiller, have followed Deren's suit and followed it up to various re-actions of dancers *to* cinematic shift-of-scene, superimpositions, etc.: but these are of technical necessity, *re*-acts, even re-en-act-ments, of no more immediate necessity than any seen-scene's accommodation of a dancer—no more than through-true to cinema's dance . . . no more necessarily, centered on film-maker's sense of seeing shaped by memory's eye.)

But the Dance is as one, *any*-one, exercises one's body, any part thereof, at large (Robert Duncan says he writes poetry: "To exercise my faculties at large").

And the Art of Dance is as someone is able to, and does, extend himself, thus, through all his means to the World of Dancing.

Cine-dance, truly, would seem to me to occur only as those "means" might, of necessity, include a camera in dancer's hand —(and it should be noted that both Deren and Clarke *were* dancers before coming to film . . . and that Emshwiller, like Sidney Peterson, another significant dance-film-maker, is married to a dancer—approaches the form, thus, through personal necessity).

But cinematic dancing might be said to occur as any film-maker is moved to include his whole physiological awareness in any film movement—the movement of any part of *his* body in the film making . . . the movement of his eyes.

I practice every conceivable body movement with camera-in-hand almost every day. I do *not* do this in order to formalize the motions of moving picture taking *but rather* to explore the possibilities of exercise, to awaken my senses, and to prepare my muscles and joints with the weight of the camera and the necessary postures of holding it so that I can carry that weight in the balance of these postures through my physiological *re*action during picture taking and *to* some meaningful *act* of edit. I would like to think I share something of some-such with dancers: and I do, of course, simply . . . but rather more complexly, I find that this Art of

Dance, its premise in physiology most historically (of all arts) granted, has taken itself too foregranted.

Dance sits with all other "three-dimensional arts"—Drama/ Sculpture/Architecture — having one hell of a time getting off the stage . . . it, like Drama, has forgotten its "continuity self" or else the "dis" any contemporary sense of "Space/Time" kicks "Cause/ Effect" with.

(An *almost* exception: "Events /Happenings" — but they, like "Op/Pop" depend/locate on audience, ergo *re*-act, and make gesture *out,* ergo premise themselves outside individual physiology . . . take an *imagined* sense as Muse, tend to woo it through to audience.)

I do not believe the "3-D" arts have taken all the possible contemporary means and/or found them in any individual hand.

I do not think there is, as of now, any cine-dance worth mentioning as such.

I *do* imagine that there might some day, through some dancer's necessity, be something of some-such: and I imagine the means of cinematography will be as simply taken as music now is and that the work of the dancer will, therefore, simply be called: Dance.

TO JONAS MEKAS

Late Sept., 1967

Dear Jonas,

Now that I have had some time since making my statement of dissociation from Film-Makers' Cooperative and Cinematheque, and now that my films have actually begun to arrive back from The Coop, I think I am in the position wherein (hopefully herein this letter) to examine my motives in detail and to extend to you (for whatever use you can make of them) the warnings of a, by now, 'outside' person who is, all the same (and now *primarily*) moved by friendship's concern for you and others still associated with the above mentioned organizations.

I have, as you know, spent almost two years studying the phenomenon of War—with primary emphasis upon that vast mass of written and photographed material the Nazis left us, out of that German proclivity to save every scrap of paper, piece of bone, etcetera—and have made "23rd Psalm Branch" out of the necessity to comprehend that studied material, particularly those images, which has been shoved at me in every conceivable distortion of 'mass media' since I was a child. The film "23rd Psalm Branch" does speak for itself (and much of whatever wisdom of this letter comes from my viewing it again and again since its making): but there is a particular area of researched material which did not take shape in that work (because the film centered itself upon those pictures and ideology I had been subject to since I began attending newsreels regularly in 1938, when I was five years old); and that area is usually neglected in all studies of War, histories of same, etcetera, *precisely* because it is of a quality of feeling *pre*-War, previous to historical data, and is thus as difficult to expose or posit as the intuitive faculty that prompts any action or to deal with as, say, the emotional source of any human expression. Nevertheless, I shall attempt, in this letter, to write about what I think did really begin my necessity to make "23rd Psalm Branch" as well as my need to dissociate myself and my work from Film-Makers' Cooperative/Cinematheque policies: the similarities between the popular social movements late '20s, pre-Nazi, Germany and the United States today.

Twenties Germany found itself in midst of a youth-originated Wanderlust Movement similar in some respects to several that had occurred previously in that country's history (and similar in some ways, one might say, to every person in his teens beginning to have some sense of his or her "generation" as "New," etcetera) but specifically emphatic with respect to the following 'catchwords', and the ideologies clustered loosely around them, as being "Good": (1) "Free Love"/"Sexual Freedom"; (2) "Brotherhood" ('between ALL men') / "Brother-Sisterhood" ('between men and women' . . . happily there is no martialed "Sisterhood" that women have ever really fallen for outside that specific one which exists within the family); (3) "Nature Worship"; (4) "Anti-('Academic')-Art" (I am referring specifically to the neo-"Dada" movement of that time . . . we might call it the "2nd Dada" movement, France's being the "First" and our current "Fluxus"-etc. being the "Third"); (5) "Drugs" (the taking of same as 'Religion' . . . I make that specific qualification because, after all, humans have always been drugging: and those who primarily do so have always been telling the others that it "felt GOOD," etc.: but there are particular times in history when the use of drugs has sought to sanctify itself thru its human 'pushers' by taking on 'airs' of "Religion"—such as the period of the introduction of Alcohol to Europe, at which time the advertisements claimed "Visions of God," and the like . . . that's, for instance, how Christian monasteries got into the liquor business, and so forth); (6) and "Peace"!

I think the similarities between that time-and-place and this, between the "Wanderlust" and the "Hippie" movements, are apparent on the page: thus I won't belabor the comparison of these "Liberalities" more than as is necessary to point out how the Nazis used these proclivities of "German YOUTH" (as it soon came to be capped) and to suggest how I intend to try to prevent (in whatever American version of fascism) some similar usage of myself, the films that have come into being thru me, and the ideas engendered by those films *in me:* (and I particularize "myself," with respect to these matters, because my first avoidance, with regard to fascistic dangers, would be to negate that usage that can be made of *any* man, and any man's ideas or works, pretending to 'speak' for others or to 'represent' in-and-thru himself a group or mass of peoples).

(1) "Free Love"/"Sexual Freedom"

I do *think* you know that there are very few people who have been
as outspokenly *against* sex censorship, in *any* form, as I have been—
and that very few have taken as many risks showing forth photographed nudity and sexual acts, showing films I had made and showing those of others, in times when it was *very* contrary to 'public
opinion' and (in some cases) then existant sex laws, as I have over
the last 17 years . . . : (anyway—I remind you of these activities in
my personal history, at this time, because since I have withdrawn my
films from The Coop, and have stated some moral reasons ((among
others)) for doing so, it has been convenient for many members of
that organization to misinterpret my statements and to charge me as
"Censor!" and as being "a moral bigot," etcetera . . . ; and I wish to
make absolutely clear, therefore, that I do "censor" *only myself*—
and there*from* those institutions Film-Makers' Cooperative/Cine-
matheque have come primarily to be and the policies they've come to
represent: and I emphatically do *not* seek to *impose* censorship in any
way upon any other . . . have not, for instance, sought to boycott those
institutions in any way other than by my own withdrawal) . . . : and
yet I have not ever sought to impose "Sexual Freedom" *either* upon
anybody and have never really known what "Free Love" (love free
from *what?*) was supposed to mean—except as I experienced it from
the mouths of those who shunned their ability-to-respond to loving
(thus their 'responsibilities') and therefore sought to sanctify this
loss of personal freedom by martialing others under some banner,
like "Sexual Freedom", and in the manner/militancy of every hooked
'pusher'. I express out of individual need and strive to shape film
expressions aesthetically out of the desire to make a work of art: and
I extend those expressions, *when requested,* to hopefully meet the
needs of others, and extend those film expressions to persons or gather-
ings of persons hopefully centered upon the variously shared/social
concept of "Art." Art becomes arguable, socially, to the extent any
concept of it is cut-off from historical perspective / sense of it as a
medium moving and growing formally thru history—; but it is one
of the blessings of it, as concept, that it encourages a wide latitude of
individual interpretation . . . will sustain a good deal of 'anybody's
opinion' without that destroying the basic idea of art and/or interfering much with anybody's experience of a work of art. What aesthetics can*not* easily tolerate, without distortion of all its values, is
propagandistic use of works of art for, say, "proofs" of something,

say, "political", etc., for or against which the work is supposed to
stand. Works of art tend to be most *particularly* about themselves,
each about *it*self, and each about the 'themselves' that constitutes the
'world of the arts' that any particular work is in relationship to, has
grown formally 'organically' out of, and (as Malraux puts it) con-
verses with. Therefore, any usage of a work of art to prove anything
outside Aesthetics, or even much outside each its particular aesthetic,
is as disastrous as, say, using Mathmatic's "$2 + 2 = 4$" to prove that
every family *must* have two children. Film-Makers' Cooperative
and Cinematheque have used the term "Art" and what I believe to
be works of art in film to promote social movements irrespective of
aesthetics. Their 'sexploitation' advertisement has, obviously, out-
done Hollywood's. The court defense of "Flaming Creatures" as 'a
work of art' was both cowardly and ridiculous: (and I'm not, herein,
questioning whether it is or isn't—if it, by any chance, IS an aesthetic
masterpiece, then the court defense is even more disgraceful . . . for
that is most certainly NOT a question that can be entertained in court:
and any mix-up of such consideration with the sexual rights of an
individual is bound to distort the values of all involved with it no
matter what the decision). But I, too, have too much championed
that usage of art (which assumes for works-of-such an inherent ob-
jectivity) to remain guiltless of the above disgrace. I had meant something quite different than the dominance of the considerations of one
field (aesthetics) upon another (legality): I had meant (and still
believe) that a work of art could inspire (rather than influence) an
individual to his own (most UNinfluenced) considerations of any
experience. I have always thought that one of the main reasons the
American public has always rejected living artists and their works
(and continues to do so in any but the most superficial, actually anti-
art, sense of, say, the "Pop" movement) is because the whole idea
of aesthetics becomes naturally loathsome to most persons *forced* to
it in the public schools, actually forced to memorize long rhymned
couplets (called "poems") most of which would hardly pass under
the loose term "verse," actually forced to hum and drum their way
thru what is mostly the worst trash music a rythmically crippled and,
thus, harmonically constipated civilization has produced or, worse
yet, to learn the great music of it according to those musical laws that
have sprung up in the wake of insensitivity, forced to paint, to puke
colors in lines according to Renn. perspectacles, etcetera: and, therefore, I thought it was *wrong* when you, Jonas, forced European
museums (as a condition for getting all the other films being dis-

tributed in Europe) to show "Flaming Creatures": and all of your "forces," by ploys and pulls, as well as outright coercion, seem to me part and parcel with the public school system and all institutions which (as all institutions do) operate under any belief of knowing what is better for others. I do *not* know what is better for others: but I do wish, for my own love's sake, that art were not taught in public schools—tho' I would never move to prevent such teaching, to thus become an institution myself . . . All the above considerations apply equally to sex instruction as to art instruction. Anybody who gives un-asked-for sexual advice to anyone else is 'on the make' in a most unloving and utterly hypocritical manner possible. The Hippies sought to avoid the neuroses of the 'previous generations' by a studied indifference to heterosex and a championing of homosexuality as 'a cause celebre': these negatives and positives struck off previous attitudes are, obviously, as neurotic as those of their parents—plus this: like all radical social changes, they carry the weight of conviction in young mass psychology that they are "Right!": and this sense of Righteousness moves as a force of ideology that shapes all senses-of-self to mass consideration in a way far more effectively repressive than sex laws or ancient moralistic codes could ever accomplish. "Indifference to heterosex" is, perhaps, not any more the correct descriptive phrase than "Freedom of Sex" (perhaps the latter is, in its pun subtlety, the aptest after all): young people appear to play *at* sex more openly, fuck more easily—perhaps one should say: "more readily"—but each to maintain his and her "cool," as its called, so that sex does never *appear* to arise *as a problem*. This "cool" is a 'dodge', a 'tough-guy' stance, an 'in-the-know' girl stance—as anyone who has known a number of younger, particularly "Hippie," people will be aware: and it doesn't take more than a quick review of Freud's ML Giant (or any psychiatrist's writings—including Wilhelm Reich's) to make one aware of the latent dangers of such a dodge. The faults, lacks, of sex-problem admit-ability have hatched, natch, a strong propagandistic cover-up. The primary office of film propaganda has become The Film-Makers' Cooperative—the main showcase: Film-Makers' Cinematheque. On the one hand: "Freedom from—" 'problems,' responsibilities," etcetera . . . on the other: "Homosexuality" . . . 'as a CAUSE'. The Nazis created secret internal cadres of the latter—dependably bound by "The Cause . . . the CAUSE"—and created boy and girl youth camps side by side to attract the latter kids who, at first, probably only wanted to fuck, and then channeled sexual energies into gymnastics, work projects, military training, all in a clever distracting play upon:

(2) "Brotherhood" ('between ALL men') / "Brother-Sister-hood" (etc.)

Every "Brotherhood" banner I've ever seen waved *had* to have its scapegoat—in the case of Germany, it was "The Jews" . . . there's always *got* to be 'somebody out there' in order for any group to cohere. With you, Jonas, it has always been "The Establishment": and this particular 'scapegoat' has always made you a little subconsciously suspicious of "Aesthetics"—it being so obviously an established term, a historical form, an antiquity . . . and a term much dependent upon what has been established of it. I have finally managed to reconcile some of your inconsistancies by comprehending this particular 'scapegoat' of yours—for instance, I understand now how you tolerate Fluxus, a belligerently anti-art element, when you are so very much against criticism as you truly are: Art is, after all, somewhat closely associated in your mind with The Establishment: and The Establishment is something you, yourself, feel free to criticise without restraint or the inhibition of your own feelings against criticism: you do, thus also, criticise critics freely—*if* they are anyway Established. It is the inconsistancies that make a man seem most human (lovable, in that sense) : and it is the inconsistancies of politics that seem most political, nations seem most national, masses massey, etcetera. Truly, of course, a man is always alone: every one and every thing else IS 'outside'; and his inner consistancy is self evident—tho' terrifying because he may be prey to anything and will forever know nothing about it: but it is the particular forte of The Herd that it sustains an imaginary defense against lonely self-consistancy and the very idea of the preda-tor (as being more than The Enemy.) Thus any grouping develops thru individual inconsistancies and must have its knowledgable 'scapegoat'. Your idea that Film-Makers' Cooperative/Cinema-theque escapes "Censorship" by "accepting everything" is false: for finally I must "censor myself" therefrom it; and while I may be the first to actually withdraw, I am by no means the first to have been "censored" by that institution: it has operated for years to the expense of many things I do most believe in (and even "Art" did always seem to me to be the first thing overboard in any New American Cinema crisis—tho' the term of it was always much mouthed for sanctity sym-bolism). The Hippie cracker-barrel philosophies, such as "Every-thing is Good" do only operate as Charles Olson warned they would, viz: "I Chingness. Chance Operations. All IS interesting / Nothing is" . . . that is, they wash out to a residue of easy nihilism (masked as New Hope), evasions of responsibility (masked as Freedom for All, or some such) and the pretense of friendship or love for All ("Brotherhood") EXCEPT The Enemy ("The Establishment"). Everyone in a group or 'movement' is supposed to assume he and everyone else absolutely agree as to who The Enemy IS: but the truth of such a situation, by its very nature, is that everybody is more and more (as the assumption becomes less and less explicit among the inconsistancies of group-and-, thus, mass psychology) vulnerable to being told by any particular person WHO The Enemy is and believing it, whom*ever* it may at any moment turn out to be. One of the particularly difficult inconsistencies that has moved thru you and thru the "Hippie" movement in general and thus much dominated Film Makers' Cooperative is, in addition to the assumption that everybody knows who the Enemy is, the added panacea: "There is no Enemy." The Nazis made horrible use of this similar inconsistancy in the Youthood movement of their times: The Jews became such *assumed* enemies, when there were "NO enemies," that nobody even felt bothered to find out what was happening to them. They were essentially treated as UN-natural—a ghost 'scapegoat' . . . a much more group-psychologically satisfactory Enemy than any tangible predator. I think they were essentially exterminated as a direct result of:

(3)   "Nature Worship"

The whole idea of "Nature Worship" is strictly a City-Dweller's concept. I don't know anyone who really LIVES in the country who would ever dream of using the phrase. "Nature" is, as a term, mostly a City-Dweller's depository for all that idealism which he can't possibly make functional in his primary environment. It is, thus, a 'dodge' at scratch. When it gets attached to it the word "Worship," the very hills do begin to "skip" and "tremble": and when the two terms take on a social, then national, cluster of ideologies, it usually leads to a slaughter of the animals and, eventually, of whole peoples as well. The very premise of "Nature" as a distinction—thus to be "Worshiped"—is that the very human beings who believe in it think themselves to be Un-natural, feel they must be made *more* NATURAL, etcetera, and must thus define something else as hopelessly un-natural for ultimate scape-goat. "Survival of the fittest" is the easiest catch-phrase along which this line of thought travels: and thus we soon have men stomping every non-belligerent creature in his path into the ground and worshiping the prowess of himself, the technological materials of his culture, and the "Nature Worship" ideology of his group which makes this possible. The American "Nature Worship" movement centers itself about "Health Food Stores," "Macrobiotic Diets," and the like, large scale city-park picnics and weekend trips to the country: and the filmic expressions of these, so far, have been of the order of goofing off in the woods, fucking among the flowers, and the like—all quite harmless seeming and sometimes rather charming. But it is a short step from this bucolicness to Wagnerian heroics such as manifested in Leni Reifenstahl's pre-Nazi movies (particularly those she 'starred' in). The "Nature Worship" proclivity coupled with 'Hippies' "anything goes," "all is interesting," etc., makes for a dangerous social force because of the in-group's pretense there won't ever be needed any scape-goat to sustain it—and because it is a form of worship created by a group of people claiming to be interested in something (rural countryside) they are not really (in terms of living in it *and off of it)* interested in at all . . . just as those who espouse:

(4)   "Anti-(Academic)-Art"

Each step removed from the original Dada Movement, each neo-Dadaism, has had less and less to do with aesthetics: what started as a protest by artists against Academic Artists has, thus, become the protest of those disinterested in aesthetics against artists—it is a typical pattern in the world of human affairs . . . it feeds on jealousy. However, the roots of the proclivity are solidly located in the "First Dada" which did, finally, hatch nothing more permanent than food for teen-age polemics, etc. One must remember that the phrase of the Nazi Art Minister: "Everytime I hear the word 'Art' I want to reach for my revolver!": could just as well have sprung from the lips of Tristan Tzara or Andre Breton. Many such polemical jokes took on nightmarish proportions in 30s Germany. All "Cultural Explosions" have had their political equivilants and, thus, ultimate realization in bombs: for the very idea of changing even a historical medium *by force* is a barbarian concept seeking its *sack*. It begins with *suck:* all those who would ask endless questions of artists, investigate their home life, etc., looking for some short-cut to culture—rather than attending the works of artists with any diligence required for comprehension. Masses of people whisking past paintings in museums, listening to their Hi-Fi's while talking on the telephone, and thumbing thru poetry books produce a semblence of culture while effecting its destruction in themselves and as a concept, even, in the nation: they will all, finally, prefer to be *told* what art is: and an anti-art movement is the best clearing-grounds ("Explosion") a future dictator has for defining "Art" as *any*thing BUT what it is. The New American Cinema movement has, finally, backed the theatrical (one-time showing) experience of films above (and to the expense of) any consideration that would make it possible to view a film as a work of art. This has played into the hands of ALL those who can best deaden the sensibilities of people, thus use them, by defining art as "Escape" and aesthetics as another form of:

(5) "Drugs"

The Nazis supplied drugs 'openly' to their secret cadres and 'secretly' to the kiddies in the camps, etc. (later the soldiers, etc.)—for it was found that a small amount of most of the 'ine-ending' drugs running in the bloodstream makes it easy to channel energies militarily. It is evident that the extent to which anyone is 'hooked' by anything is the extent to which he is vulnerable to *any* kind of 'hooker'. It is my experience that the finest sensibilities kill themselves under drugs: and the least sensitive humans desire to kill *others*. When any society really manages to couple "Art" with drugging and drugs with "Religion", the result is, inevitably a 'Holy'/WHOLLY WAR of one kind or another. And no one has ever made a bomb, in actuality (or of human sensibility), that they did not intend at some time or other to explode (or exploit, thus). And those who plan these things do usually do so in the name of:

(6) "PEACE"

Most people tend to forget, these days, that Hitler spoke primarily for "PEACE" right up thru 1938—when that tack became too ridiculous to continue . . . tho' he still tried it sporadically with the U. S. into the early 40s. I have always, intuitively, been against The Peace Movement as such—have always found it as martialed as any military parade: and I am as opposed to those films that propagandize for Peace as I am against ALL forms of propaganda. I'm no ivory towerer; and I had hoped to have made clear, thru speech and "23rd Psalm Branch" itself ONE idea, at least: that war is a natural disaster and that the most promising hope of alleviating the misery thereof it is by taking the most practical measures with regard to it—and that these be in the area of those measures taken with regard to other natural disasters . . . the evacuation of civilians from the path thereof it, the provision of economic means to rebuild the areas of destruction its havoc has wrecked, etcetera. I see prayer as practical only insofar as it engenders humans to be instruments of the kind of miracles which can pass thru their benevolence: but I envision no more practicality in shaking fists at blank or thundering skies—or presidents of governments—than in the indifference of "God-save-me"/ or-"The-King" supplications which are not attended by inspiration-to-action . . . thru, say, lending one's benevolence to the means at hand. Thus, I'm as indifferent to peace marches (as is Pres. Johnson, obviously) as I am to all religious ceremonies that end in themselves and/or the smug or raging contentment of the congregation. Finally, it is only art that seems to inspire individuals to actuality and, thus, acts of meaning: and that is altogether an individual matter.

TO ROBERT KELLY

Late Oct., 1967

Dear Robert,

": . . . a close detailed study of psycho-physiological response to all available frequencies of light emission; . . ."— YES! . . .: and your whole letter to Barbara Rubin FULL of specifications of specific need (that that's so personal it is uni-versal) . . . bump-pa-ty-bump (why do I always sound such German-ness early in the morning —doth coffee and the sun combat it, as the day draws on?—on light?)—Oh my!, I'm shy with you, dear Robert . . . even in a letter . . .

I'll just write you about what I'm doing and leave it to the Irish in you to draw charmed conclusions:

I think the mind's eye's electrical out-put to the backsides of its optic nerves does express itself in rhythm shifts, many clusters of same per the second, much as the ears hearing-of-innards is, if attended carefully enough and in relative 'silence'◄ outside, audible as clusters of tiny beeps that are at first heard as smears of har-monies that, if not heard well at all, sum-up in the listener's in-attention as tones (the dominant fifth Cage heard in the sound-proof chamber: but when I asked him about this recently in Cincin-nati, he changed the wording from "tones" to "noise," himself now hearing much more than 'scales even): the com-parable light-beeps of eye's out-put do tend, *thru colors* (order of colors, in rapid flashes), to make the shapes of closed-eye-vision which resolve into the specific details of memory's pictures; but, at first, these multiple colored flashes do smear (for the inattentive) into over-whelming color tones, (viz: red for anger, green for jealousy, blue for nos-talgic sadness, and yellow as basic but also reflective of its psychological cow-ardly connotation, increasing with fear, by being even in its basicness a reflective of passivity): and the memory pictures do seem to most to be "coming from elsewhere," etcetera.

I found, while editing "23rd Psalm Branch," that if I pictured myself in a scene I remembered, a scene in which I was but had not actually seen myself mirrored when there, that that image of myself was always 'remembered' in a pulse relative to my overall heart-beat of the moment of remembering—usually the 'figure-of-myself' flashed on and faded out at about equally spaced inter-vals (usually a little shy of a second apart); and on questioning others (pre-vious to stating my own experience), I found this rhythm of picturing-oneself-in-a-remembered-scene to be basically the same for all persons so-questioned. Then, a few nights ago, while editing "Scenes From Under Childhood," I found this 'law' of rhythmic picturing of self to be no more applicable when I pictured myself as a child, *nor* applica-ble to memories more than a decade past; but I *also* found that in picturing many friends of childhood (whom I had seen in the scene remembered) the pulse-'law' applied to my re-membering of *them*—astonishing, yes? . . . (is it that the act of memory creates 'identification' with others to such an extent that the self becomes a stranger?—wow!)

I think there is some 'short-circuit' of the light pouring into any eye, as it 'meets' that person's out-put/memory's-discharge, and that we SEE in midst of a smoldering fire of cross-currents.

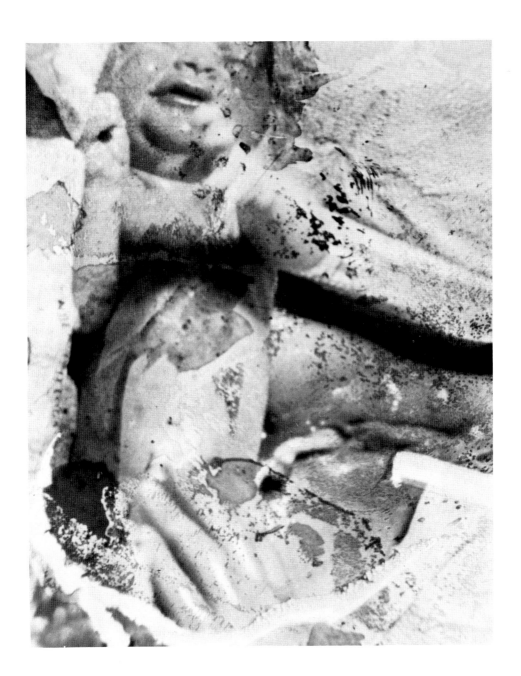

Thigh Line Lyre Triangular

Clockwise:
circa 1967, photo Arnold Gassan;
1971, photo David Aschkenas;
1980, photographer unknown.

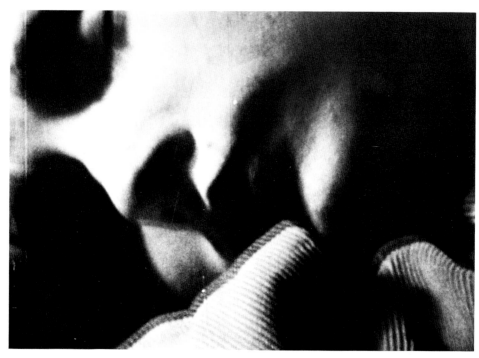

Joann Tenney in **Daybreak & Whiteye**

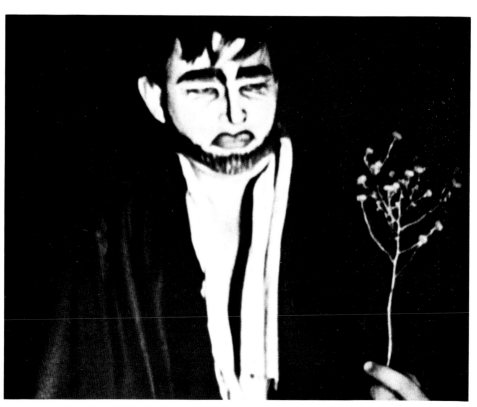

Robert Benson in **Blue Moses**

Windy Newcomb in The Way to Shadow Garden

23rd Psalm Branch

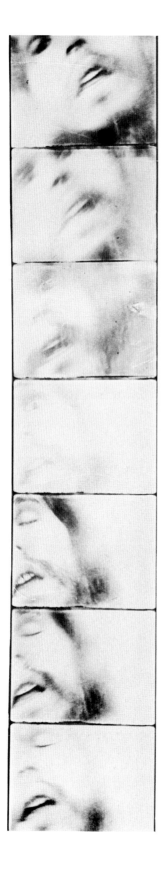

Prelude: Dog Star Man

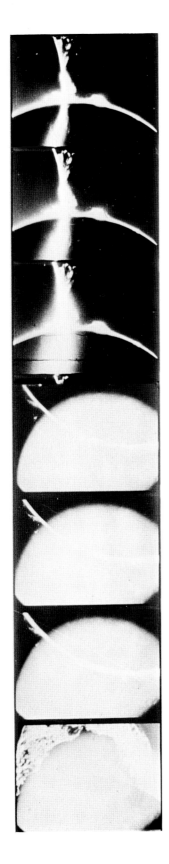

Prelude: Dog Star Man

Short Films 1975

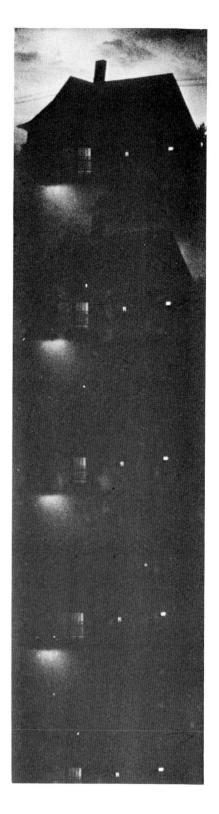

Fire of Water

TO ED DORN

Mid. Oct. 1967

I go out of this house sometimes with an awful desperation-un-(to me)-namable—and I drive as much, sometimes, as 20 miles to find a bar where I can sit really alone in midst of strangers who'll leave me alone there in their midst (I keep exhausting bars in this respect—in hopes of gaining this respect); and I sit there, then (in this unfamiliar bar) and order always very much the same thing: a cheese burger with french fries and a brandy alexander, or B & B, or just plain brandy: (*that* attracts too much notice already at scratch); and in midst of often juke-box AND T.V. both blaring I eat and drink while reading something like (as now) "The Education of Henry Adams": and I swear I don't know *why*: but after an hour or so of this, I'm steady enough, nerves and muscles all one solid/plastic piece, to go home again . . . and, Ed, I never went to bars before in my entire life—I mean . . . not ever as a continuum, like that. Finally, inevitably, I get intruded upon in each bar (and I think always, for me, *that's* the moment secretly hoped for): but it does always turn out to be by way of some curious bastard who's going to pump up his own ego at my expense, however devious the trail he takes to that accomplishment: (however far afield in conversation, or actuality—as I went with one and his wife and friend to the local pool hall for some games the other night—, he does always seem to have in mind the arrival at some suitably lonely place for secret murder . . . all justified, in his mind, I see, because I affronted him with "Brandy Alexander" or book-reading, or my shyness, or some-such): John Houston's a really BIG Time Killer, is he not —I mean . . . actual shoot-'em-up death figure plus politics plus heroics, etcetera . . . and all so much a part of American history/heritage (one can easily imagine identifying with him played by John Wayne). —The pool hall episode has not played itself out, yet: and one difference in it IS that I, this time, went up to the man I knew was about to speak to me and spoke to him first; bought him and his wife a drink, etc. (was I just buying Time: I remember that when I was a kid, the little fat boy with glasses whom everybody else was beating up on—and whose ugliness did deserve that—, I finally learned to steal in order to buy candies and what-not for the bullies in order to hire them, thereby, to protect me from others . . . soon, thus, became the leader of an organized gang in North Denver—actually cased joints/dime-stores, etc.—taught other kids how to shop-lift—took my cut—and the whole bit . . . till suddenly I dropped it, all of it, in one instant of accumulated boredom, and began putting on plays in backyards and making comic books to sell, newspapers, etcetera): but the other night, in the pool hall, any ball I'd sink was roundly treated as the miracle it WAS: and yet I could see that three weeks' diligence at the game would put me par with those guys (tho' not the wife who deliberately loses, is obviously encouraged to lose by her husband, who even cheats, even obviously, to make his point somehow: and I remembered when, as a kid, I learned the marble game in order to win friends—soon won all the marbles—I've never been somehow able to deliberately lose and have not, either, the natural ability of a loser —and lost all friends thereby . . .) . . .: you'll forgive the confusion of punctuation in all this, please—but then that's symptomatic of my actual state of confusion in this out-pouring . . .: that I don't somehow know how to make *my point* socially whatsoever—and can't seem anywhichway to give up trying: I'm due to go back to the pool hall with Jane, one of these nights: maybe she'll manage to make the scene tangible, or blow it sky-high if not.—I'd been thinking a lot about a gun, lately—wanting one, like a '45 . . . I mean, a very powerful pistol, Luger or somesuch—(with a lot of excuses, such as, well I remember *you* pointing at that ex-army truck across the street and telling me about the Pocatello Minute Men: "If that son-of-a-bitch has access to armaments you better . . ." etc.: and Colo. is, you know, a gathering place for those troops: the Minute Men have an actual machine gun *factory*—where they make them—not 20 miles from our cabin up Coal Creek Canyon, etc.: and then it is the hunting season here (and our dog is missing two weeks—tho' in the pool hall they told me many local dogs had been got by the increased predator population, coyotes, wolverines, bob-cat, even bear, and that the hunters-human were all that would "save us" from "a very dangerous winter," etc. . . . . all *that* confusion— what to fell paranois about—etc.) : and The Times, The Times (sad as always when capped, sadder yet when FULLY capped as THE TIMES) . . . The other day I took my six-months old camera which was already breaking down and my utterly un-running Victor projector into a sporting goods store where I'd bought the former; and I was utterly determined to get my rights in trade-in and come home with two workable pieces of machinery or to walk out of there with a gun; and I argued for FOUR HOURS, collected an enormous crowd of curious customers, *forced* my way upstairs to the almost impregnable office of The Boss, stormed back downstairs, called the camera company in New Jersey while they kept trying to take the

phone away from me—I WAS magnificent— . . . and every time I began to lose in the trade I'd switch the whole transaction to include swap of projector for gun . . .: and finally, Ed, I walked out of there with a brand new projector and a brand new camera ($1400.00 worth of equipment, retail, for which I'd swapped the two broken equipments and $400.00 —the last of all we had in the bank—) . . . it was FANTASTIC: (and I know they only let me get away with it because I was fucking up their whole "Hunting Season Sale" and had finally tied up and exhausted salesmen and customers alike, including The Boss ((whom I had to respect as the only other *living* man I there encountered: I mean I saw him alive like a snake, absolutely dedicated to what he was doing/business but with all the coils in coils of him LIVING in the crazy life of that endeavor))): (and I came away with the sense I could have done *that* too: been a business-man/gangster, etc.; I mean, I re-experienced in myself how-it-is-done/piling-up-millions, etc.; ((and I know they *still* probably made a hundred bucks' profit out of me, etc.))).

I have no real sense of Nat'l: I meet nation as an -ality working its way thru the killers of the local bars or stores, or those more subtle killers of the public schools that keep operating on my kids—cutting them up anaesthetically. But in our house, here, we raise a 6-foot tomato plant, with real reddening tomatoes on it, a 4-foot peach tree at the head of Jane's split-logtable, a lemon tree that smells more essence of lemon than all those I've bought in stores in my whole life, an apple tree, coleus, parsley, mint, and a terrarium with tiny mountain orchids: and the kids do dance and sing (when they've un-bent from school) and roll naked on the floor and play with their shit and pots and pans (and toys, all the same) and talk a blue streak of lightning imagination: and I do photograph all of it I can and pour the strips of it into "Scenes From Under Childhood": and Jane's thumb-greenness and tapestries and table and stain-glass window and recorder playing and loving altogether make it all, herein, somehow possible.

Blessings,

THE STARS ARE BEAUTIFUL

1) There's a wall there, a great dark wall with holes in it; and behind the wall is an enormous fire of white flame.

2) The stars are entirely in the eyes of those who look at the sky. If no one is looking at the sky, it is utterly dark. But the stars in the eyes are very much the same in all eyes; and those looking at the sky at the same time are all participating in the kinds of communication that have to do with stars.

3) It's a great roof studded with sequins. The movement of the stars is in relationship to the movement of the sun, giving the impression that the stars are moving across the sky.

4) The stars are optical nerve endings of the eye which the universe is.

5) Sparks from a train of God's thought.

   (I have one big toe in bronze and the other in eternity.)

6) There is such an intense brightness that we can't really see it. The sky is really burning white and the stars are black. The daytime is less bright and therefore the yellow, that is really there in daytime, we see as blue. The sun we see as yellow: I'ts really blue-black. *That* that we see as blue sky is burning away the black spot of the sun; and the sky at night is burning away at the black stars.

   (Novalis has seen the sun as black, and so has everyone who has closed his or her eyes on it. Retention colors are the only true colors.)

7) The stars are sparks from lightning.

8) The stars are the loopholes into 256 dimensions.

9) The fact is, the earth is falling into a well. The sun is the top of the well, the blue sky the walls. The stars are reflections of the real stars behind the sun.

10) It is a furry animal. The stars are silver hairs.

11) The sky is a cylinder to the moon.

12) The sky is all together, not composed in such great distances as we

suppose. In truth, it is an old fire. The stars are small sparks, the sun a burning coal. The black of the sky at night is ashes, the moon a bubbling drop of water. This is the same with us, i.e.: as the universe burns, so do we. Our heads contain water very much like the sky holds moons. The burning in us keeps the water in our heads boiling and sputtering.

13) The sky is the dead decaying body of God; the stars are glittering maggots.

14) It is the back of a blue dragon; and we are the eye of the dragon, watching him die. The sun is the blood-hole.

15) The sky is a cup of tea which the earth drinks every day, then at night inverts the cup to read the leaves.

16) The sky is a lens of air magnifying a single atom of itself.

17) [There was one of these stories that I liked but didn't believe; so neither Jane nor I could remember it.]

18) [This one's fairly traditional]: The sun is the ejaculation of the penis in the vagina of the universe. The stars are the sperm searching for the eggs of moons.

19) The universe is part of a vast brain, the stars the firing of brain cells — each a visualization of the bark of a dog, i.e.: when a dog barks, the response in the ear of the sky is a star; when a dog howls, the response is the moon. The sun is where everything else goes to a further place or places; and we really don't know what happens there.

20) The stars are trembling silver strings to everyone's brains. The sun and moon are the eyes of the great puppeteer…Once a month he smiles and winks: He has control of our fates.

21) The day-sky is a pool of all our tears: the world is getting smaller and smaller. The night-sky is a blotter to all our black thoughts: there is very little space left.

22) The sky is the low-water beach on which are left phosphorescent plankton which will grow to be enormous beasts.

23) Light is everywhere; and the sky draws everything to it that we

make. For instance, it draws our air and condenses it, 'till it becomes black with our breathing; and it draws water in gigantic drops, which we see as stars. It draws the earth in streams till it blazes golden; and finally it draws all our fire into the ash of the moon.

24)   The earth is a pool of brown watery waves in a forest of trees we see as stars near a golden bird flying after its white mate.

25)   The stars are clear sounds; the sun a magnificent silence; the moon? . . . whispers that are almost sounds in the undulating wave of noise the universe is.

26)   The sky is the solid state of time; the sun? . . . its emergence; the moon, the tube it all falls into. The stars are the fragments that never move on.

27)   God, taking pity on those who stop smoking, made the stars to look like so many cigarettes burning, the clouds to look like smoke, the sun to remind them of the striking of a match, and the moon in the shape of a filter tip.

28)   The night sky is a fold-over-pattern of the sun. The moon is a visual echo.

29)   The stars are a flock of hummingbirds. If you look closely, you can see their wings flickering. The sun and moon are their flowers.

30)   The sun, moon, and stars are the footprints of God (we are his head) as he walks currently in a circle.

31)   Everything's happening at once; but the sky is a clock and makes it look like things are happening one at a time.

32)   The stars and the moon are reflections of the sun which can't be seen.

33)   Once upon a time, long long ago there was in the sky at night only the moon — as even now in the day there is only the sun. Then some wise men projected into the night sky hieroglyphs of their thoughts so that everyone who looked, after that, would know those thoughts and be wise also.

34)   The stars are the places where snowflakes are made; each star has a

different shape and makes a different shaped snowflake. When the snowflakes fall from the stars, they shrink and become changed in shape; and thus every snowflake also is a different shape.

35) The stars are the broken fragments of the mirror that reflects reality.

36) Big dust motes.

37) The nets are boiling.

Narrative script circa 1967 (as transcribed by Jane Brakhage, night after night of their telling).

ANGELS

. . . move thru the qualities of shadow in a diffraction of the light—
   the doors of illumination / home of angelical forces (as George
MacDonald would have it: ". . . home . . . is the only place where
you can go out and in.") . . .
. . . and the shadows of shadows are the shadows of angels . . .
. . . and the fixed instants of constantly changing shapes are the pictures they take of themselves:
                                        a smoke pattern in the hearth's wall,
                                        a cloud held in the mind's eye,
                                        a face in tree leaves . . .
. . . all that we call psychological projections are the movies of the
angels—
   the home movies of angels are qualities of light held as if in mid
air—
   any gathering of dust motes in the light records the passage of
angels:
                                        for they do itch in the lungs when the
                                        soul is troubled;
                                        and they scour the hideout of the soul's
                                        enclosure;
                                        and they seize the brain in the body's
                                        fitfullness:
                                        and we do sneeze them out—
                                        cough up whole angels—
                                        sweat ephemeral motes—
                                        bite off tongues for blood speech—
                                        roll upon the ground and die for them,
                                                   make mirrors,
                                                   fresh motes,
                                                   maps of passage . . .
. . . and the angels, thus, feed upon decay and are the leeches of all
that we call "evil" . . .
. . . and they occur to the mind as a rising in the bake of any thought
cake—
      physical fevers do levitate them surely—
      thoughts of/in repetition attempt to trap them,
                                        for we would feed upon angel food
                                        cake

(the barococo of sweet Bach's awful
hunger) /
(gentle Gertrude Stein having her cake
and eating it too—

the residue:
"There is no
repetition.". . .)

. . . *In* which—the angels move . . . up and down the ladders of language . . . with*out* moving—

out of *which*—comes the nervous endings . . . *this:* is it Asmodei,
as H. D. would have it? :

"the second of the genies zodiacaux,
to whom one may cry,
exhaussez mon incantation, ma prière . . .
raise up, lift up, receive my recognition,
and this at last, with no reservation," :
(and is this that Asmodeus I came to know? . . .
angel of asthma?—
and is that why I cried reading "Hermetic Definitions"?/
could not, in my whole life, go beyond :
"what has the word done?
you include but in small grandeur,
the whole circle of the sun.") . . .

. . . *with*in which: the beg in beginnings / the thrown up pun—
all of undigestible language the angels feed upon: these *distinctions*
of vision:

that / thus:

the dimension of angels is a tensor—
the reality of angels is a surety—
the grasping of angels is as a disjointed leg and a blessing for.
poor Jacob—
the handling of angels is as the hand feels itself,

in transformation,
surely moving,
to its ends . . .

. . . and the angels of fingers can be seen in the bend of light when
the tips almost touch and wherein (aura?) they seem to be touching . . .
. . . and the angel of auras (the guardian angel?) can be seen after
staring at a yellow sheet of paper and then looking to the naked body
of another . . .

. . . and the guardian angel of self (angels of eyes? / angle of ego? / anguish of soul?) can be the actor of seeing itself,

> as I impersonates each eye
> (to see the moving yellow
> of all angels of the sky as
> some stilled blue),
> as I'll an isle become
> (to bend the rays of sun's
> set into renaissance perspective
> for ego's grasp of the angel
> of the dying of the light),
> annihilation . . .

. . . and the angel at the gate of Eden is viz-ability itself . . .

. . . and its sword is the word of God—is the word of sword—
is the knowledge of shape that makes a circle of the sun . . .

. . . and the flames thereof it are that stolen light whereby the mind's eye projects its pictures—its flickerings those rhythms of thought itself—its fuel the decay of vision into the smoke of memory . . .

> and:

angels move thru the qualities of smoke in a diffraction of the shadow of light—

the doors of darkness / home of angelical forces (as my wife Jane has shown me, in my mind's eye, the strands of light that stream from the shadow cast by her head) . . .

. . . and the halos of halos are the halos of angels . . .

TO SIDNEY PETERSON

Feb. 15, 1968

Dear Sidney Peterson,

I'm writing very much out-of-the-blue/grey here—it's been 6 or 7 years since we've had a good talk—and very much INto remembrance: I did always very much depend upon the past-wise of those few meetings we had . . . your critical faculty (certainly in viewing *my* work) unsurpassed!—some few comments of yore(s) serving for years.

I'm living now in an 1890 cabin in a 'ghost' town on the slopes of The Continental Divide—an almost embarassingly symbolic place to be in times like these—: but the advantages of this placement far outweigh the dis-ads (tho' the weight of such is mostly upon my back, viz: I am forced to deal with all old socs., the race war, the raze, the war, etceterrrrr, as is-YOUS?, i.e.—in terms of the proclivities raised in *me,* since child hood . . . that is, I have no convenient scape-goat to kick OUT at, no sets of externalizations peopling my streets, nothing more tangibly outside me than natural catastrophy: broken trees, avalanches, snow-drifts, thunder/lightning and the like.

I am working on a long color and sound film called SCENES FROM UNDER CHILDHOOD: and your exposition on "Blanks" in my work (black/white leader in "Dog Star Man," etc.) and your statement that "there are essentially two kinds of sound, mood-music and lip-sync" are still sharp cutting tools in the endeavor . . . problem IS: the actual statics of childhood memory (the essential 'stillness' of childhood scenes remembered—all movement, true to the *act* of memory,—very limited, as if a set of scrapbook pics. were seen thru

heat waves) does condition the editing in such a way as to throw all film aesthetics back on painting, aesthetics of painting . . . something like: slightly moving pictures emerging from and dissolving into "blanks" of colored 'leader.' Then there are, in concentrated memory act, interruptive flashes of various colors that seem to come in rhythmic 'blocks' which seem to denote specific emotion responses. To be general about it—red/anger, blue/sadness (blue-grey/nostalgic-sadness), green/jealousy, yellow/cowardice, etc. . . . the degrees of color, color mixture etc., shifting these emotions into their subtleties while the rhythms of their flashings seem to qualify their means (meanings) in relation to each other and to the image being invoked (envisioned): all of which throws film aesthetics back on music, aesthetics of music. As I begin to into-it, there's a felt-*trap,* for film, in all such deep-*end*ency upon t'other arts: but I can't seem to intellect it nor quite (physiologically speaking) put my finger upon it!

The question IS: what are the generalized dangers of one art's as lapped on another's? To be specific: where do you find the ice thin on Pound's pro-ing: "Music rots when it gets *too far* from the dance. Poetry atrophies when it gets too far from music."? I realize I'm asking you to shoot in the dark; and, to alleviate that a little, I'll include a strip from an earlier 8mm film ("The Kids" section of 15 SONG TRAITS) trusting you can read a strip of film still as well as any musician a sheet of music. Therein (that strip) you have interruptive flashes of shaking-static images: make a theme and variations of it in your good mind's eye and, also, imagine long spanches of these colors fading in and out. What's the catch could lock film in?: spring this -thetic if you can!   Blessings,

TO BRUCE BAILLIE

1st week Jan., 1969

Dear Bruce,

For years I have been planning to use the footage of yr. newsreel film of "Brakhage leaving S.F." in my autobiographical work "The Book of The Film." Yesterday morning, while searching out material for the '1st chapter' ("Scenes From Under Childhood") of that work, I came across yr. film — looked at it carefully...; later I said to Jane: "You know, I think I'll leave Baillie's film intact in 'The Book'... even when Baillie fails to — well, achieve clear balance (what you might call 'Art'), he DOES manage such a forcefully clear statement... statement of visual-fact language, say... that it seems impossible, to me, to break it up — even verbally, let alone to re-order/translate his images: I'll just have to find my most meaningful setting for his whole piece within 'The Book', and let it go at that."

Well, it'll probably be years before I get to the chapter of "The Book of The Film" where this decision will apply, if it does; but by that evening, yesterday evening, I was up against *another* visual fact-state of yours, that film gift you sent in a can marked "Show Leader" (also marked "Poison," with a scattering of other markings, numbers, etc.) and shaken to the very roots of my being by the overwhelming power of this filmice (yes, the pun is right — cold crystalline surety that prompted my unconscious to add an "e" to filmic... and the other pun, too, "mice," hones in as express of those scurrying greys within which yr. frost-scapes — Apollo, the mouse-god, dominates my mind's reception of this theme in yr. work). I had not been in any hurry to look at it, as the marking on the can made me think it was the "Show Leader" of yrself bathing happily naked in a stream, turning to the camera and saying "Hi," "Hello!", whatever as you wave to the lens, the picture-take; and thus, thinking I had seen the film many times, I was simply waiting for a good opportunity to show it to Jane. Can you imagine my surprise when the film you *did* send unrolled before my eyes? I almost passed out. Well, this film piece of yrs. — one of the most powerful visual statements I've ever seen — prompts this letter from me... *moves* me to give you back *literally*, in my most UNhesitant language, some express of all those feelings I've been having, in my worrying, abt. you, yr. illness, yr. total living situation (since I visited you a couple months ago) — and to risk this outpouring of language even tho' I may be utterly mistaken: (I *have* been mistaken abt. you, yr. work, before, you know: and I have refused to ever judge a film contest again principally beCAUSE I mis-judged yr. "To Parsifal" in that L.A. film fest. years ago... wrote you a letter at the time, if you remember, torturing the question of its aesthetics — that beautiful film which means more and more to me, now, every viewing: timidity because of this gross error years ago has caused me to bite-my-tongue, and typewriter keys, in addressing you these many months now): but *now* I *must* write you what I feel/think . . . only hoping to be helpful to you—and trusting your strength to resist whatever, of this, may be stupidity on my part:

At beginning of this film-piece—which, I assume, is from "Feet Fear," as the total image-feeling is kin to those previous sections I saw in Kalamazoo— . . . at beginning, then, you assume the mask of that lordly drunk, weather and alcohol seam/sear-scarred face, near end of "Quixote" . . . you stare into the lens, which becomes your mirror, in a series of gestures and movements which almost exactly parody those of, say, a young woman preening before her glass to assure self of the appropriateness of a new hat, mask, dress, whatever—it is a terrifying series of metaphorical movements: the glass (the camera's wide angle image) is snuffed out (and I immediately recalled how you would, did constantly, avert your eyes from mine in our last meeting); but the continuity metaphor is that the glass breaks up into a series of sea-waves, dissolve then of foam into what is surely your totem animal (all thru yr. work): the sea-gull . . . flights of sea-gulls, then singular gull, then falling star (spot of street light, actually) which evokes the quarter moon in its passage—the clouds tearing at even this rind of some full circular moon: and the following series of shots carries this metaphor thru in terms of shadow block between/twixt the camera lens and its imaging the sea . . . shadows of houses (or house-like structures) and then finally the sharply clear, indifferent-(seeming) profile of a man/ (woman?)—no, most surely a man (is this Paul Tully?) eating, drinking then— the spot of light on his glasses fixing the (previously felled) star at moon's (previous) place . . . his total profile blocking view's passage to the sea: (is it that Tully, or someONE, then, both blocks your sea-life, your gull-flight, while yet serving to stop your Fall at moon's phase?:   :and, if so, consider— does he save you from death (or that loneliness/death's-life-symptom your singular gull evokes)? . . . or does he keep you from going THRU some death-consciousness (acceptance of loneliness) to/re(newed) LIFE, your resurrection (as is the blessing of Totem Worship, when followed THRU)?

My first terror at your situation came from a comment on the tape (sent to Kalamazoo) suggesting your desire—and I quote—"to go beyond Art" . . . : this, for an artist, is tantamount to saying: "I want to die!" Religion (ANY Religion in this century's time) does act on Western sensibility ALWAYS in terms of "Beyond": (and, as such, is as clear a blasphemy of the tradition of god worship as is, for instance, "Xmas"—spelled every year more & more that way—a black mass of the celebration of Christ's birth): AND, as such, "Religion" has proved THE most destructive force against artist sensibility—has, in all my experience, tended to tear The Artist schizophrenically apart (schizo-phrenic: :broken hearted)...Maya Deren, her Voodoon 'beyond-ness'...Vanderbeek, his god *of* technology—the 'beyondness' the term 'com-munication' can ONLY mean to an artist sensibility—: perhaps the clearest track of this destruct-impulse in contemporary western art sensibility is mapped in Parker Tyler's magnificent biography of the painter Tchelitchew: "The Divine Comedy of Pavel Tchelitchew"; Tchelitchew up against Heaven 'beyond' geometry, beyond the spaces between geometrical creativity, beyond creative evocation...and THAT after having slogged his way masterfully thru Hell AND Purgatory—most only manage Hell, even as 'beyondness' (say, Artaud) in our time.

   And I am, in all honesty, fiercely ANGRY at the wastage these Romanti-cisms (this 19th century "neuresthenic dark of the Circe-world and its Hell-like cul-de-sac," as Davenport puts it)—the wastage these devil's tricks of the romance of madness, illness, drugs...the wastages this trap effects in 20th century sense-ability/response-ability to Life—: and I am angry too at the particulars of the form of it you, Bruce, seem to me to be inflicting upon yourself—the Tibetanzen-Orient-a-shun drift be-yon-(east)-der TACK yr. tape comments seem to suggest you are taking...: and I am angry at the UNreality-(Be-seeming to me) of your Ducks, the neurosis of your Dogs—the fact that I can't even remember whether you have a cat or not (and Cat is *my* Totem animal, you know)...and that your horses (which DO seem to me, from that visit, to have real touch with you, your ground, etc.) move in the mind as, and ONLY as, in a Dream Of, etc. —: and I am even annoyed at yours/Tullys weighted/(EMphasized) Southwestern drawl (and I *have* an ear for that lingo *at source*)...: am angry because I could NOT seem to get in even brief eye touch with any tangibility of you on your farm during that visit—all as if in a shift of eyes, scenes, animal stances, verbal postures (and I *do*, you know, live on something like a farm myself, surrounded by winds-of-the-sea, sea sounding right now, animals, spaces fixing some distances, etc. and whatever verbal provincialism blows my way...am not, thus, at odds with the air of country retreat, etc.)—: and I am mostly angry that I cannot even determine whether or not illness weakens the believability of your being, whether your sickness is the major mover of your scenic environs, or whether it is the other way round...whether, perhaps, the Set-to of your circumstances does force (con-tinuing) illness upon you—does force you to assume the mask of (thus prop-agating the very real) illness.

   The triumph of your ART, as *I* see it, does convince me of the latter of the two above possibilities: and, thus, the film piece you sent convinces me to risk the terrible presumptuousness of this letter in spilling out all my worst fears since our last meeting—the WORST fear being...: fear of that most danger-ous self-indulgence which love-of-death IS: I fear it in myself and thus abhor it in others: (I, too, did toy with the suicide of myself in the make of "Anticipation of the Night"— and insistence on the actual Dream thereof, that self-indulgence of Posture, making presently a Past Statuesque of oneself, did mar the ending of that film... as you should know; and I did again perform such colossal selfishness during one whole summer in midst of editing "The Dead"—tho', thankfully, didn't edit until I was fully well again and could, therefore, salvage out-going/growing sensibility from the experience):... well—try to cut thru all this verbiage, the garbled struggles against my timidity (my *other* fear of misunderstand/interfering with your life, your work), to the simplest meaning of this letter: it is a GET WELL card... albeit fraught with the perils of advice—advice which is fashioned out of my own limited experiences (inadequate, thus, to even meet the contingencies of my coming life, let alone yours, dear friend—ah, how I wish you were more my friend, that I knew you better, that I did not have to so-much guess at your being in this attempt to help you—I do not know if you even need, let alone want, my advice...: yet, surely, you DO want at least *my views* —what more direct appeal could there BE, to me, than that of the incredible film-piece you sent? —: and, as *film-maker* then (where I'm surely on firmer ground for response), I can state that film-piece—magnificent as it is in its terrifying power—does absolutely need a counter-balance measure... of some equal power prompted by life-giving forces... to qualify its *part,* of whatever *whole,* as being something more than Posure—that particularity of Drama which, say, Selfish-Play/Masterbation is: (Orpheus *must not* believe in the Games of Hell... let him, rather like Gluck's Orfeo turn to Amor to restore his wife/life—or at least let him seek Persephone rather than Circe in those dark regions): let the 'verse' of my GET WELL card be Wittgenstein's:

"In brief, the world must thereby become quite another. It must so to speak wax or wane as a whole.

"The world of the happy is quite another than that of the unhappy.

"As in death, too, the world does not change, but ceases.

"Death is not an event of life. Death is not lived through.

"If by eternity is understood not endless temporal duration but timelessness, then he lives eternally who lives in the present.

"Our life is endless in the way that our visual field is without limit."

(from "Tractatus Logico-Philosophicus")

Even in writing 'as film-maker,' I can be quite wrong (as I once was, as judge, of your "To Parsifal")—my danger is, perhaps, some tendency to make a god... a 'beyond'... of Art...: if I have misunderstood—please forgive me these, then, presumptions; and correct me apropos the following:

the simplest part of your message seems to be that this "Anthology Cinema" is too much for you to take on at this time — that you have accepted that position only out of your willingness, as always, to do everything you can to be of help to others... your counter-balancing self*less*ness that, often with you, over-extends yourself to meet the needs of whomever: I think you have your hands and your FEET-FEAR *FULL,* at the moment; and I am going to move to 'let you off the hook' of this coming N. Y. stress-session (as I would have at Kalamazoo, too, if I'd known how difficult that trip was for you to consider). As I suggested you, in the first place (thus got you into this additional strain on your capac-ities), I'll take the responsibility of insisting that Broughton be the "west coast representative" until such time as you ASK to be consulted and included in these matters; and I'll risk this (perhaps further presumption) because I'm afraid your reluctance to disappoint anyone's request — that beautiful graci-ousness of yours — is among your worst enemies at the moment... in that thoughtfulness of the needs of others may act to distract you from some much-needed kindness-to-self (quite an opposite from self-indulgence). Anyway, you can let me know if I err here by simply insisting on being included in that Feb. gathering: thus I, who did the first insisting that you BE the "west coast representative" now veto that recommendation and, thereby, leave the matter more surely in your hands, in the future.

Jan. 15, 1969

Dear Bruce,

What a relief / yr. letter of assurances: I feel 'in touch' with you again; and, more importantly, I feel yr. clear sensitivity to yrSELF: in midst reading the letter, Jane said: "Oh!... I *like* him!"; and, as we talked about it later, she specified her admiration thus: "...that Bruce does get to 'the heart of the matter' immediately — and that he takes what he can USE of your letter and, then, leaves you free of any responsibility for the rest of it."

Okay — so...: I'm honored to be yr. "theatre": and it is of great help to me, too. I'm *right now* in midst one heaven-of-a period of transition — MUST articulate!... thus cut all possible 'cackle' out of the work process: sharing with you something of your developing vision (which is SURPRISINGLY yet naturally/of-course along the same lines) suddenly like having TWO eyes for scanning the landshape instead of one: and I'll keep coming back at you as flat/blunt as I'm able — so that we don't run any danger, in this exchange, of a depth-cage, INflu, and/or the complexities of perspectacles (i.e.: so that you don't come to think of me as your glasses into The Renaissance, western cultch-klatch or somesuch...I mean, I do wax a little wan/aesthetical sometimes — but By Zantium!, I'll try to keep the talk flat as a movie screen and straight as a beam of light, spreading OUT/TO focus!)

Okay, THEN/now: your latest section appears transitional—beautifully thus...as in daily living (you know: :like eating, walking: but, more specifi cally, the hesitancies of the finger, the hand poised as thought's tool over something other than the food, or as stomach's extension then to crack a nut, the foot pause, etc.); but it also unreels like a drum roll—at first a muffled beat, drawn from these hesitant movements, and then with the solidity of the walking: this underscores the whole with an ominous feeling...at first eerie, in contradiction to the catch of colored light on food, the quietude of the table top, and then later fortified by the grays and blacks and molten shapes of rock and the more absolute rythmn of walking and working thru to a martialed, almost rat-tat-tat-tat (as the rythmns at frames' edge begin to show, as they DO when the central image looses clutter of rock, and its heaviness of beat, in the overall texture of sand), as you walk onto the beach): (I wonder why I add "n" to "rythm" in my spell of it above?...: maybe I'm trying, thereby, to add some semblance of a quality of the pulse you've got into this section—some dragging hummmmm, maybe?—ah, yes!, something like the quality of smoothness of, say, the photographed walking: how DID you achieve that technical vir- tuosity?...: it is, yes, walking; but it is as if a thousand pounds of, yes, organism were ambulating across the surface of the moon). Dramatically, this (Sec. #43) creates that kind of tension which often haunts human living—all is well, bathed in a good light (sun, in this case, but sometimes of a quality of cozy electric or contained fire light)...the happenstance and occurences calm and common to daily experience—yet over all a quality of foreboding dread begins to build inexorably (and inexplicably in these circumstances) thru each moment of living, making seconds merge into some momentum as small waves do into the whole pull of the river approaching Falls: the most frightening (and lastingly memorable) haunts, of this type, in my living are those which pass away as mysteriously as they came (thus giving no climax/sense, thereby, of what was fore-boded): I await eagerly your next reel—in a way like I used to await next Saturday's chapter of the movie serial...only MORE thus beCAUSE the adventure of your film is of the world as I daily experience it— rather than that world of the imagination as I fancy it.

I'll return your two rolls today (with some reluctance selfishly, I might add— it's so good to have something specific of you in this house...and I'll repeat my request we swap some film prints for keeps—tho' maybe this film-in-progress is, by the so-far looks of it, the one I ought to wait-for). I wish I could send you some of my work-in-progress, of the moment; but it is all tangled up in ABC rolls: once each string of it weaves its way into the total basket, even I can't see it until it is printed. Wait!...maybe I can send you the completed section of "Scenes From Under Childhood" (it is Section #2 I'm now working on)—I'll let you know in a couple days. Anyway, it is close to your work (& now, & from now on, as 'in touch' as I am): and one of the most exciting approximations in this involvement with the-scene-*as-photographed*, relatively free of Edit's Intellect and/or the SUPERimposition of the process of memory upon each instant of living: you, as I, seem to be taking strong advantage of film's most unique possibility—preservation of the track of light in the field of vision (thus the each move of the visionary) at the/each instant of photographing: I now find myself solidly see-er of my photography, rather than Editor thereOF it: but this inspiration—in the work process—exists in the incredible tension of my feeling an equal need to let Memory COLOR each unedited light track... via "B" and "C" rolls generally... and SHAPE both objects and spaces... by way of compounding pics./spaces, rather than superimposing upon them—again BC stuffing mostly: sometimes I even compress, by additives; and I do, then, tremble on the edge of superimposition: and, let's face it, sometimes I still just-plain-superimpose, as always, also: but the general DRIVE is one in honor of the moment of photography, so that there's very little shifting of the orders of shots within a sequence, and very little cutting of lengths of shot either. Actually, I've worked (more subconsciously) in this area of direction many times before ("Desistfilm"—THAT far back—"Daybreak & Whiteye," "Films by S. B.," the "T.V. Concretes," many "Songs" and many sequences of 'Scenes From Under Childhood," Sec. #1): and it's coming to seem to me that "Scenes From Under Childhood" on its primary visual level IS a track of the evolution of SIGHT: thus its images flash out of blanks of color, thru fantastic distorts/twists of forms and orders (those fantasies wherein one *imagines* oneself: even suggesting those "pre-natal fantasies" wherein Freud, to his dispair, finally found that unanalysable nest hatching all basic neurosis), space/shape absolutely dominated by the rhythms of inner physiology, then shaking like jellied masses at first encounters with outers, the beginning of The Dance, shattering OUT of even memory's grip thru TO some exactitude of sight/light... FROM, as Pound puts it: "Eyeless that was, a shade, that is in hell": thru: "Light lights in the air": TO, at least: "'as the sculptor sees the form in the air... /'as glass seen under water'":

> and saw the waves taking form as crystal,
> notes as facets of air,
> and the mind there, before them, moving,
> so that notes needed not move.
>
> (from *The Cantos*)

... and evoking Pound minds me of "The Anthology Cinema," which does very directly tie-in with all these my currents of creation... (I mean aside from your being in N.Y. in Feb.—since Broughton forwarded your note, I've decided to take your original word for it, viz: that you want to come: and that I may or may not see you there in Feb... okay?): that this "tension" is part and parboil of the whole Western soup—that "realism" (rounding of shapes in space) which Giotto gets blue ribbon for and/or versus that flat-hatch of history/memory-'s compounds the Sienese (Sassetta at best, first, for me) carry on out of the so-called "Dark" (pre-natal) "Ages," etc.: those who seem (within this tradition) to solve and resolve it within themselves/their work, like Fra Filippo Lippi, DON'T seem to get noticed for that accomplishment (the world wouldn't probably remember him if he hadn't been such a naughty monk and got writ-up by Browning): it's as if The West, insistent upon some joust or continual box match, hadn't time for The Dance: and the U. S., all See-uneasy bent, at the moment (right-wingers abt. to fling Wyeth at Warhol, or West Coast at East ONLY via "The Figure," etc.), overlooks the whole Dance of American Art, betting on Ryder out of all proportion, on the one hand, and Currier and Ives on the other: (this drive in U. S. —to have art as a sport in the European sense—once drove Washington Allston into Frenhofer's corner...: he worked 35 years on one painting unfinished at death which, when unveiled, was proclaimed a mass of nothing... drove Morse—who had a BEAUTIFUL resolve in his painting—OUT of art and into invention of the telegraph... and drove the whole Hudson River School into that same obscurity of social regard P. Adams would like to dump D. W. Griffith into—and for the same reasons: :the feeling of "cornballness" American viewers associate when confronted with their own grandeur—each ring of provincialism terrifying U.S.ns we've strayed too far from Mamma, Europa, DaDa, etc...: thus lower east N.Y. provincialism passes this prejudice as smartly as any import will—it having been brought over almost piecemeal from DaDa's turn-of-the-cent dinner table): well, (aside from this Atlantic spat... and no wonder the west coast wants to drift off and join The Orient), we've got the "agenbite of inwit" schemmmmin' & schaunnnnnen' within U. S., too: and the line grows thick" (degenerate, as Pound sees it) out of the 13th century push of, say, Winslow Homer, beyond all proportion, un*til* you get to the fragments of the line—what the line is, finally, made-up-OF/pointillism-crystalline-space-tracks, the interior world where lines are—as IS their only existence—imagined: but what holds true (to physiology) there to, say, Jackson Pollock does ALSO hold true for any several-inch section of Andrew Wyeth...: HooRAH!, as I see it, we've, U.S.ns, taken on the whole thick line at source—and naturally, thru the whole history... (heaven, hell too, help me SEE that whole Main—betwixt the X-streams—Street; and help me be Seer of it as tracked naturally with camera so that it can be/MOVE across my work table thoughtfully): and may we at least Purgate our way thru SOME sense of film's history of it and, thereby, better shape The Anthology Cinema.

With that prayer I'll end this (perhaps too much historial/terical) fuss... and extend—

Blessings

Feb. 2, 1969

Dear Bruce,

Well!... the 25 ft. of yr. roll 46 and the full 47 contain as perfect a weave of metaphorical harmony and supportive color tonality I've ever seen in film— and they *have* to, in order to carry the dramatic weight of yr. Uncle-Sam-like mask against the textures of the beach: you'd *never* 'get away with' that Bandmaster, this side of Surrealism, unless he operated in as tight a knit as you've composed for him...: but he(you?) is *not* Surreal—that's the miracle— nor the metaphors dramatically obvious, either.

First, you've an over-exposed—yet carrying yellow—beach piece upper left frame, answered/echoed by the dark blue rock-patch lower right... and in between?: a black chasm *which* seems to be seen thru white mist—the 'bleed' of beachlight, yet also evokes, or visses, green in some eye-expectancy tension between the yellow & blue. A man shadow begins its move across the beach piece: and into this *prepared space* you thrust the ghost white mask of Unc Sam in red band-master costume complete with gold braids, etc: (so prepared IS this space that I took the 'entrance' as a dissolve first several times viewing): the ephemeral white-over-black has reached, thus, and solidified over blue-black rock: the red coat answers green-under-black of chasm in a harmonic clash comparable to over-yellow & under-blue: and the gold braids & buttons shift us to the glints of textured sand just as the whiteface leads to the following foam-wash in a by-play still of the opening theme... over-yellow & under-blue—now played out as sand whitened over with sea foam AND dark-blue of water emerging in each backwash of foam: and the footprints are, of course, the beach at its most yellowish, echoing both the pizzicato of buttons AND some drift of the original diagonal chasm: and all finally moves, then, into a shimmer of grains, as in 'closed-eye-vision' and cuts with a chunk of over-yellow and, then yes, under-blue rock-drop. But Sam still 'sticks OUT,' does he not?—tho the mind has to rack back over the events to catch him...

...you resolve that, next roll, beautifully, starting with an electrick sunset (a bulb so photographed—in reflection?)—as to stand for electric-light/sunset synonymously... then a pan up the features of the mask transformed by the yellow bulb light and close-up textures as to echo the sand shots—but *more,* at least at first, to be-seem a landscape painting (for such a sun to set in), past lips (which settle it as mask but also, wonderfully, echo-in-shape the sun-bulb-set AND give us the red of some-such, as wld the sun—were it such), then settle on mask's eye (in a shot exactly evoking Mt. Rushmore's Lincoln): then you shift along a line of yet deeper-red lines... still sinking yr. sun, as I take it... until block-white, echoing Sam's hat, fills frame except for the tiny grey idol, all backed by white sky, of a lovely girl—the full haunt of remembrance-photo grips all thought here... would pitch over into sentimentality except that you move, then, along a line of silver verticals (utensils) intersperced with, yes, red verticals and an echo-of-pix white-block (measuring cup): this shift to verticals roots the gray upstanding figure of the girl almost subliminally in mind: yellow-brown and wood-waved wall backs this continuing pan of kitchen utensils, carrying on the sand-and-water theme as surely as the white window-block you come to carries on pic./cup theme... (other colors coming in, now: but even outsides green, thru window, ONLY after introduced by a flower*pot*, etc: finally you *stop* this pan when you get a resolve of horizontal and vertical reds in an egg shaped fuzzy mass of red yarn *backed* by the dried rain-drops of the window—shift diagonally over yellow and then down wood's wavy grain to (what looks like) the remains of the supper you'd been having earlier (1st roll you sent me), picking up silver verticals, now, wherever you can, all the way... even leaving in a light-struck frame—as it fell, magically for you, in vert-streaks over first picture of yourself in mirror, wherein yr. ruddish face becomes the sunset (in a near perfect balance of red & yellow) struggling against the encroaching dark of yr. own movements.

TO P. ADAMS SITNEY

mid Jan., 1969

Dear P. Adams,

I simply don't know what to make of the world this morning—woke up in the middle of last night with tears streaming down my face . . . hiccoughed myself to sleep, then, finally: one can't seem to be anything but ridiculous as a middle-aged man in this culture—I think YOUTH-Propaganda is undermining me . . . and I'm not old enough yet to ignore it: I feel myself behaving in a most confused manner (all of a piece with, say, the confusions of my withdrawal from Film-Makers' Co-Op and the two years' quarrelsome thrashingabout with Jane during making of *23rd Psalm Branch*)—and yet I KNOW I know more than when I was younger and that I act with more thoughtfulness and clarity upon any given matter: but nothing seems to work ordinant with that 'sense of magic' I once, sometimes, had. I cannot help but think The Times will not permit any coming to Claritas—that if "the line grows thick," as Pound puts it, NO man shall be enabled to thin it of himself: for, if he does work with needle-fine mind-point, he shall find himself mid-age making a million needle-fine parallels altogether into thick-approximate . . . trapped beyond individual deliniation by the magnetics of his social Time (as Pound escaping Circe's hell does make a hell for others in the grotesqueries of his prejudice . . . a hell which does, then, snap back over himself in old age—leaving a trail of thick black industrial smoke between him and any vision of Persephone which he, younger, willed to lead The Cantos/himself OUT of hell/Idaho, etc. I, who 'took arms' against The Tree, as surely as any man in these Times find myself mid-point my life thrashing "In cold Hell/In Thicket" as

surely as Olson, his generation—find myself with something as ridiculous as Hamlet's problems, lacking Hamlet's youthful/ignorant surety wherewith to dagger them down: imagine a Hamlet who doesn't die young but rather ends up surrounded by ALL those ghosts inCLUDING his Father's still twittering/bitching, say, abt. the sloppiness wherewith Hamlet had effected Justice, etc.

Take the matter of Baillie, for instance: in the same day, yesterday, I get a letter from Vigil stating he'd seen Baillie recently, that he was worried about him, that he seemed definitely to be "on some death kick"; and then I also get the enclosed from Baillie himself: and I don't know what to make out of either—every clear-seeming wash of inspiration I have (as that which prompted my last letter to Baillie) seems to leave me stranded in some backwash Gordian weed, some "Backlash" as Nelson metaphors it.

I, who've turned down good money offered me to judge competitions because I was so absolutely clear abt. the evils of judging Art, find myself now part of the greatest film judge-klatch of all time—find that all the limitations of competition-judging are as surely manifesting tendencies as in any film festival.

I, who JUST had a clear inspiration abt. the limitations of Editing, find myself entangled in A B & C rolls—in a tapes-Tree weave that often makes Dog Star Man seem like a Ute basket in comparison . . .: the only residue of that splicer-crisis I recently had does seem to be the inclination to honor the orders and specifics of the photographic inspiration on the A Roll—on the other rolls only in the sense they 'take their cues' from that A Roll.

And I'm DAMN tired of having to

take on the defense of D. W. Griffith: BUT—here's my home-work on the subject . . . (and I feel absolutely certain we HAVE to deal with at least the following films of his, consideration of him, ESPECIALLY if—as it looks to be turning out—he's excluded entirely from the Anthology Cinema):

In 1907 it is certain he STARRED in "Rescued From The Eagle's Nest"; but it is by no means certain he directed that film: in 1908 he made 49 films of abt. 700′ apiece (FOR which, incidentally, he was paid 14¢ a foot) ; and "The Adventures of Dolly" does seem to be the film most remarked-upon (I hesitate to say "remarkable") : in 1909 he made 146 similarly short films ; and his "Edgar Allen Poe" and "The Renunciation" seem to be those most necessary for us to look at: in 1910 he made 102 short films ; and "Ramona" gets critical mention, along with "Corner In Wheat" (which is, I think, of this year) : 1911— 93 films; and "Enoch Arden"—Parts 1 & 2—is among his outstandingly noticed early longer films: in 1912 he makes 52 films, as he's making longer films now ; and "Musketeers of Pig Alley" is a 4 reeler must-see of this year: in 1913—47 films; the 4 reelers "Two Men of The Desert" and "Judith of Bethulia" stand out . . .: no—in 1914 he went over to Reliance Majestic Co., THEN made "Judith"; and, also of this year, his "Battle of The Sexes" (4 reels), "Escape" (7 reels), "Home Sweet Home" (6 reels), "Avenging Conscience" (6 reels) and, of course "Birth of A Nation": 1915 then gets us "Intolerance" (his AND yours, apparently): 1918—"Hearts of The World" and "The Greatest Thing In Life" (which Lillian Gish said was his greatest work, whatever that's worth) and "Broken Blossoms" (somewhere in there): 1919 —"True Heart Suzy": 1920—"Way Down East": 1921—"Orphans of The

Storm": '22—"One Exciting Night": in 1923 he went to Germany and made a seldom seen film made with the assistant direction of Eric Von Stroheim, released in 1924; "Isn't Life Wonderful" (an ironic title, natch) : somewhere mid-20s he made "America": in 1929 he made a film starring W. C. Fields— "Sally of The Sawdust": in 1930 he made a film starring Walter Houston; "Abraham Lincoln": in 1931 a '10-nights-in-barroom' piece called "The Struggle" (which was SO unpopular in prohibitionist America it ended his career once and for all). Most of this info. is dug up by Ed Diamond (THE film enthusiast of Denver) : and he and I have come up with this list after dozens of phone conversations. And as Griffith is, at least, MY 'Hamlet's Father,' all these films gotta be viewed one time or t'other. Forrest Williams and I are also working over the old Doc. school-of-thought (Oh, the IRONY that *I* should feel obligated to help this old hoss of the M. Of M. Ahrt, this Fuseli nightmare that did trample me again & again in my green years!)—and thus . . .: "Pluie" (I don't know WHO made this: but Forrest's enthusiasm prompts me to include it), Ruttmann's "Berlin," Ivens' "Borinage," (and a film highly recommended by Kubelka when he was here—an anthropology film, called) : "Dead Birds." Also, then, Abel Gance's "La Roue," to put his best film-foot forward (tho' "Napoleon" also should, probably, be seen) and, of Epstein "Coeur *(something/something)*" and "Les Tempestaire," of course.

$#%!+*+#$!!!&!*$#+"@, etc.: and I KNOW you're groaning, P. Adams: but god-dammit!, yr rejection of Griffith (or mine of ol' Doc.) IS, really, like say Pound's of "Paradise Lost," ". . . Regained," etc.—is a youthful folly, at best . . . IS compounded out of intolerance of the whole world of

Milton or whatsoever: and it all falls into such a recognizable historical *pattern: THAT,* say, we can pass easily on Méliès (and, incidentally, while passing 'easily' on it we'd better see ALL of it— i.e. you better just take Kubelka's catalogue on Méliès as a 'List' . . . and let's have it) because he's past THRU yr./ my generations Culture-Dropout period, whereas Griffith is right smack in the middle of that period-of-rejection which does, say in painting, have it that Gustave Moreau is just beginning to be visible again, Franz Liszt just barely listenable-to again, George Cabot Lodge still out-of-print, etcetera.

I dunno . . .: I'm tending to feel like I oughta resign from The Anthology Cinema—I'm too old and not old/ (wise) enough for it! I'm too 'middle aged' to just "Have FUN"/have at it (as I insisted was necessity of blessing OF it, in earlier letters) . . . : every single original demand I made upon it (like "unanimous decision" and "west coast representative") does seem to hatch evil tendencies and utter confusion— (even my decision to "vote as if buying films for my home" has shaped itself into some damn-blasted Ideological straightjacket of "The Cabinet of Dr. Caligari") . . .: and I was only tempted to go on with this letter to try to avoid its secret title being: "I simply . . . Dr. Caligari."

TO DONALD SUTHERLAND

January 16, 1969

Dear Donald,

I am quite fussed by your article on local culture: (I don't know what the mag. "Cultural Affairs" really tries to be: but, as they begin by quoting Kay Boyle's wish to say too little rather than too much, *I'll* wish them/it the ultimate luck that they say nothing at all).

The first page of your article (the Kootchie-Koo section) is very funny, in your best 'letter' style: and I found your thread of perception apropos the discontinuities of regional culture very excitingly clear: but your defense of this art apathy, even tho' couched on tongue-in-cheek, is galling to me—it does seem to be at the expense of (what *I* take to be) your own magnificence . . . all wisecracks backlash on you, me, Thomas Hornsby Ferril, even, *and* (thereby) the whole possibility (—no! . . . I should say, absolute NECESSITY) of aesthetic continuity in this region. I'm not "flip"-ing when I say "There is no audience in Denver": I'm taking a STANCE against the audioly deaf who supported a puppet—absolutely attached to a metronome—as conductor of The Denver Symphony for years, who set up "the blind leading the blind" with Otto Bach as head of The Denver Art Museum, etcetera—or those in Aspen who import N. Y.'s import of old Dada (and never once did ask Henry James Jr., who lived there, to exhibit, never once asked Mina Loy to read) . . . those who set up Art as a Church of Lip Service and thereby blight the natural growth of sensibility in the whole area: the VERY real "audience" hereabouts is always OF Denver, etc.—runs to either coast . . . or each person backs up into his/her living room (run OUT of public occa-

sion by the fakery of such as are locally sponsored by the most UNregional rich) —or backs up into the hills, as I have, Angelo has. While it *is* true I'm "better known" in "Brussels than at home in Denver," it is perhaps more to the point that I'm better known in Salt Lake City (or in, say, Oslo) than anywhere in the whole state of Colorado—and rather *simply* because my films are more often shown in Utah (and even in some "Iron Curtain" countries) than here . . .: and that has *nothing* what-so-ever to do with the peculiarities of geography here shaping special sense-abilities: it is the result of an active force against any continuity of good sense, even, which might unsettle the exploitation possibilities of these environs—(this is, in the minds of those who rule it, a cow pasture for Texas rangers . . . a shale-oil pot—or, on the other hand, a Marie Antoinette farm for tired eastern business men).

I think the whole "regional" question, as you've handled it in that article, is rathed "dated" anyhow. Ed Dorn recently said: "I can't accept any sense of 'region' smaller than The Earth": and I agree with that. I saw the dress rehearsal for your "Requiem For A Rich Young Man": and *I* remember it as regional TO G. Stein's Spain rather than to any local Mexicanism. Your Greek translations, as they exist so MUCH in the present, inhabit the whole space/time of The West, in the *full* sense of that term: I can't accept anything less than that consideration of you, your work; but I do understand that the local clutch of culture does tend to prejudice ALL of us against such consideration—that we do tend, thru neglect, to wither into some local-yokelism ourselves . . . wax fatuous and wan folksy—: and THAT'S why I just can't let this article pass without blasting the whole premise of it: I don't take that premise to be naturally yours, but rather take it to be some corner which you are at least determined to inhabit wittily: I (fortunately, I think) lack all sense of humor in this respect.

I think a good deal of whatever rancour* in my reaction to your article is due to the coincidence that, shortly after reading it, Forrest Williams—with some Univ. of Colo. funds to spend on films—called and *actually* consulted me seriously as to whether he should purchase "Frankenstein," "The Bride of Frankenstein" or "Frankenstein Meets The Wolf Man," etc. . . . : and that I was, that morning, so *regionally SUNK* as to discuss this matter as-if-rationally with him, *is unbearable*—IS, worse, frightening—means (to me) I've been undermined, somehow, in the relationship with him who has been, obviously, undermined by the bureaucratic drift . . . if not utter stagnation . . . of C. U. *I* see I've got to become either some absolute hermit crab, here, or else some tough and raging old bastard (rather than some Colo. "grand old man") if my very sanity is to survive 'madhouse' encounters such as I'm having these days; or I could take the wit tack, call Forrest back, and dicuss 'seriously' with him the philosophy of Will Rogers.

Continuity is exactly what The Arts need in order to weave way into community experience: men will, wisely, attend that which is available as a continuity . . . (I say "wisely" because "The Special Event" will always—no matter what it innately IS—affect living experiences out-of-proportion, thus, finally, superficially . . . much as the 'religious'

experience, and aftermath, of traveling "Soul Saver" tent-meeting conversions to Christianity: the local church, no matter how unspectacular and/or even utterly stupid, remained the only really possible touch with religion in the collective experience of the community): thus, even I go to "the movies," fall back on that norm of public event, rather than search out those few "Specials" that occur hereabouts—there is a dependability-of-experience in, even, undiscriminate movie attendance which has not been achieved in any other series (indeed there are NO other continuities really) offered in this state: and this state of affairs DAMN blasts us ALL aesthetically, except as each and any one of us creates those continuities of art he's able to maintain in his home: if there IS anything you might call 'an art audience' in Denver—then that's no cause for rejoicing either: it would be better if there were nothing of the sort (just as it would be better for me if they closed down all Hollywood movie theatres in the state) . . . until such time as some continually open and utterly alive art center were created to sustain aesthetic sensibility as simply and naturally as the movie theatres sustain the Holy Drift Wood of penny-dreadfulism.

My "STANCE" is against a false church; and it should be equally against the poisonous escapism of pop culture (which does, I see/hear ((Forrest Williams)) insinuate itself into the colleges for serious consideration—the religious fanaticism of comic strip worshippers is just the other side of the coin of orthorox pomposity . . . : and I'm newly fortified, since reading your article, in my determination to rid myself of the influ of BOTH these X-streams of culture.

---

* (the "u" is there maybe to express the actual agitation of my heart)

late June, 1969

Dear Donald,

It's okay—: I was not seeking to change your attitude . . . but, rather, to given VENT to mine—which does, otherwise, smolder and fume too much around me in this lonely place. Actually, I *didn't* know that you can "take . . . or leave" civilization—had/have that indifference to it, as a concept—: a perfect demonstration of the unimportance of "concepts," anyway, is existent in comparison of your letter with mine: your prose shows forth more civility than mine which, while championing at the bit of "civilization," does growl (if not bite) rather primitively. Nazism, of course, grew in just such grounds of broken-heartedness (schizophrenia): and, while we're not yet gassing anybody in Gilpin, you *are* right to warn me of such facism as any simplistic world view (mine, Dorn's, or Margaret Mead's, say) does engender—tho' I'd add that "regionalism" amounts to the same thing (viz., Olson's Gloucester, etcetera) . . . certainly Pound has taken his toll—right off the Ida-(westward)-HO!-(American)-heart; yet as he grows old, and speechless, in Italy now his life-shape takes on the proportions of a great sadness (if not tragedy) not primarily his personal fault—U.S.ence has been cracking pots in infancy of each out-reaching member since the Declaration of Independence started off that whole terror of separation from Mama Europe: and then along came Dada, the happy alcoholic, at the turn of the century adding fuel to the fear all over again. Ah, well . . . *I* don't want to end up speechless: (and isn't it strange that all three of those New Jersey, a-Philly-ated budding poet buddies—H. D., Pound, & Williams—did come, at the last, to some complete inability to speak): *nor* do I want to end up the raging ghost of

Gilpin . . .: (nor am I likely to ever manage some salon in Europe wherewith to by-pass either of these two usual fates for American artists).

I think the center of my fuss in relation to any localism is best exemplified by the quality of feeling of the occasion of your introducing me to some(any)one in your bar. You usually say something like: "This is Stan Brakhage, our greatest film-maker" . . . or "one of America's greatest" . . . etc.: this factual introduction does, always, pass in feeling tone for some kind of 'put-on' or joke in the local circumstances: "This is Stan Brakhage" would suffice in New York whether I was, thereby, known for anything more than my strange name or not: I think that in either locality I would rather pass as 'the mysterious stranger' ('mysterious' to give me a *little* elbow room for drama) rather than as *any*thing that has to be *explained*. My difficulty sociolocally is that I seem to be always some subject to be tossed into the cultural gap —and that I cannot manage to fill such a chasm in the lute nor even to temporarily bridge it . . . nor do I even have any real (personal) desire to do so (wouldn't really dream of making Aspen "my business," "properly" or otherwise): my constant Colo. nightmare might be parodied, thus: . . .

. . . I've tried to slip sideways into this 19th century cowboy drawing room, to get warm and snitch a bit of food and take in the sights, etc.: they've caught me at the door and have even, inexplicably, found my name on the list of invited guests; but they won't let me pass on into the anonymity of the drawing room until they've found the proper announcement card and proclaimed my presence with the usual pomp and ceremony: I stand with increasing embarrassment and frustration, shivering in the doorway and/or raging to keep warm, while they endlessly shuffle the cards.

IN DEFENSE OF AMATEUR

I have been making films for over 15 years now. I have contributed to many commercial films as "director," "photographer," "editor," "writer," "actor" even, "grip," etcetera, and sometimes in combinations of all of these. But mostly I have worked without title, in *no* collaberation with others—I have worked alone and at home, on films of seemingly *no* commercial value . . . 'at home' with a medium I love, making films I care for as surely as I have as a father cared for my children. As these home movies have come to be valued, have grown into a public life, I, as the maker of them, have come to be called a "professional," an "artist," and an "amateur." Of those three terms, the last one—"amateur"—is the one I am truly most honored by . . . even tho' it is most often used in criticism of the work I have done by those who don't understand it.

The 'professional' is always much admired in the public life of any time. He is the Don Juan whose techniques (of sex or whatever), whose conquests in terms of number, speed, duration or mathematical-whatever, whose stance for perfection (whatever can be intellectually measured to determine a competitional 'winner') does dazzle any man at any time he relates to the mass of people, does count himself as of a number, and does thus have a public life: but when that man is alone, or with those few, or that one other, he loves, his admiration of Don Juan, and of all such technicians as "professors"/"professionals" are, disappears from any consciousness he may have—except, alas, his consciousness of himself . . . and if he is then tempted to 'lord' it with those he loves, if his "home is his castle" and he "The King" thereof it, he will soon cease to have any private life whatsoever; and he may even come to be the Don Juan himself, forever in 'the hell' of the admiration of other people's public life. He will, as such, tend to always think of himself as 'on display': and if he makes movies, even if only in his home, he will be known for making a great 'show' of it and will imitate the trappings of the commercial cinema (usually with no success whatsoever, as he will attempt the grandiose of visual *and* audio with penny-whistle means); and he will buy equipment beyond any need or real joy in it (usually penny-dreadful junk-stage-props for the 'production' of his imaginary profession . . . rather than for any loving *re*-production of the movements of his living): and his wife and/or impatient friends will be expected to take his egocentric directions, to labor under his delusions, to come

Written circa 1967; *Filmmakers Newsletter 4* (9-10), Summer 1971 to "grips" *for* him (as laziness is usually a sign of professional ego-centricity which would have some servant to follow its every aspiration with a director's chair to sit in) ; and his children or whomever will be expected to 'grin and bear' his every pompous set-up and staged dramatics (to the expense, as usual, of any real play) . . . ah, well—we all do really know him, this would-be professional, who does in his imitation of 'productions' give us a very real symbol of the limitations of commercial cinema without any of the accomplishments thereof that endeavor: the best we can hope for such a man is that either he goes on into commercial film-making and takes all such professionalism out of his home (where he might become amateur again) or else that he makes an obvious fool of himself (whereupon he becomes lovable again to those who love him).

Now, as to the term: "artist": I've come to the conclusion, after years of struggling to determine the meaning of this word, that anyone becomes an artist the instant he *feels* he is—perhaps even the instant he *thinks* he is—and that, therefore, almost everyone, some time or other in his living, is an artist. A public Artist, with capitol "A," is as much admired by many, and of as little value to an individual life, as any professional. It is a word, in our current usage, very like the word "love." When Love is capped, it applies to Mother, Father, Sister, Brother, Wife, Children, Lover and—as also capped and usually prefaced by a "possessive" word—"your" country, "my" dog (even "yours," "love me, love my dog," etc.), "his" favorite food, "our" friendship, club, etc.—and, thus, the word comes to have very little public meaning . . . just as the word "Art" applied to craftsmanship, cleverness, or facility of any competitive kind ceases to have any special meaning what-so-ever: but both words continue to move with the deepest meaning that individual intonation can give them in the privacy of every single living utterance of each of them with personal meaning . . . that is the beauty of both these words—and that is why I do no more care to be called an artist, except by my friends and those who love me than I would care to be called a lover, publically.

"Amateur" is a word which, in the Latin, meant "lover": but today it has become a term like "Yankee" ("Amateur—Go Home"), hatched in criticism, by professionals who so little understand the value of the word or its meaning that they do honor it, and those of us who identify with it, *most* where they think to shame and disgrace in their usage of it.

An amateur works according to his own necessity (a Yankee-enough proclivity) and is, in that sense, 'at home' anywhere he works: and if he takes pictures, he photographs what he loves or needs in some-such sense—surely a more real, and thus honorable, activity than work which is performed for some gain or other than what the work itself gives . . . surely more personally meaningful than work only accomplished for money, or fame, power, etc. . . . and *most* assuredly more individually meaningful than commercial employment —for the true amateur, even when in consort with other amateurs, is always working alone, gauging his success according to his care for the work rather than according to the accomplishments or recognitions of others.

Why then have critics, teachers, and other guardians of the public life come to use the term derogatorily? Why have they come to make "amateur" mean: "inexperienced," "clumsy," "dull," or even "dangerous"? It is because an amateur is one who really lives his life— not one who simply "performs his duty"—and as such he experiences his work while he's working—rather than going to school to learn his work so he can spend the rest of his life just doing it dutifully—; and the amateur, thus, is forever learning and growing thru his work into all his living in a "clumsiness" of continual discovery that is as beautiful to see, if you have lived it and *can* see it, as to watch young lovers in the "clumsiness" of their lack of knowing and the joy of their continual discovery of eachother, if you have ever loved and can appreciate young lovers without jealousy. Amateurs and lovers are those who look on beauty and liken themselves to it, thus say they "like it": but professionals, and especially critics, are those who feel called-upon and duty-bound to profess, prove, improve, etc., and are therefor estranged from any simplicity of reception, acception, or open-ness at all unless they are over-whelmed by something. *Beauty* overwhelms only in the form of *drama;* and *love* overwhelms only when it has become *possessive.* It is The Critic in each man that does give credence to The Professional Critic's stance against The Amateur, for when any man feels ashamed of the lack of drama in his 'home-movies', he does put something of his shame into his making (or his talking about the pictures he's taken) and does, thus, achieve the drama of embarrassment. And when an amateur film-maker does feel vulnerable because of the open-ness of the love-expression he has made in photographing his wife and children he tends to shame himself for the simplicity of his vision of beauty and to begin to hide that simple sight thru a complexity of photographic tricks and staged cutenesses, to give his 'home movies' a veneer, a slick and impene-

trable 'hide' and/or to devise filmic jokes at the expense of himself
and his loved ones—as if to protect himself and his images from
criticism by making them *obviously* foolish . . . as if to say: "Look,
I *know* I'm a fool—I *intend* to make you laugh at me and my pictures!" Actually, this latter proclivity at its ultimate is one of the
most endearing qualities of amateurism, but also, like any self-protec-
tiveness, it prevents a deeper experiencing and knowledge of the
person and his films and, indeed, of the whole amateur film-making
medium. It makes 'home-movies' endearing like fat, jolly people
who obscure their features in flesh and their feelings in jokes and
laughter at their expense—thus protecting themselves from the in-
depth involvement with others: and, then too, the amateur film does
often beg for attention in ways that impose upon any viewer, force
him to a hypocritical 'kindness', and preclude any real attention . . .
like the stutterer who can hold a roomful of people to a constrained
silence as he struggles to come to speech. Yet the stutterer is very
often worth waiting for and attending carefully precisely because
his speech-difficulty can tend to make him think twice before struggling with utterance and can condition him to speak only when he
has something absolutely necessary to say . . . he will obviously never
'profess' and is, thus, automatically a lover of spoken language.

I suggest the conscious cultivation of an *honest* pride in all 'neu-
rotics' (rather than any therapy which would imply the ideal of some
'normalcy' or other) *and* in the 'neurotic' medium of 'home-movie'
making (rather than any professorial tutoring which might set a goal
of some 'norm' of film-making). I would like to see 'fat' films carry
their own weight of meaning and stuttery montages reflect the mean-
ingfullness of repetition, the acts of mis-take as integral steps in motion picture taking. Mistakes in filming, like Freudian 'slips' in language, 'puns' and the like, very often contain the meaning that was
covered-up thru error as well as the reason for erring. When mother-
in-law is 'accidently' superimposed over images of the family dog,
a pride in one's own wit (rather than self-conscious embarrassment)
can free both film-maker and his medium thru recognition of delightful confession and inform him and his mother-in-law of a relationship that could, as always, change for the better if both are capable
of facing the truth . . . besides, when such a *super*-imposition as that
is treated as a meaningless joke or embarrassing mistake, the deroga-
tory suggestion is the *only* one noticed ("Well . . . is *that* what you
think of me—ha! ha! ha!," mother-in-law will say) and never the
positive aspects (such as the amateur's affection for his dog, for in-

stance.) As we are all much conditioned by language, many technical errors refer to the name of the technique via visual/language 'puns' (as, for instance, a man may take a picture of his wife 'over-exposed' when she was wearing a dress with a neck-line he considered too low) and even pictures that depend primarily upon referential words for their full meaning (as, I'm convinced, most amateurs tend to photograph a tree on the far left of the film frame with an even arrangement of rocks and bushes extending horizontally from left to right to approximate the look of the word "Tree"). I find these references to language constrictive film-making (as most movie pans are left-to-right because of the habit pattern of reading) as finally rather obscure from a visual standpoint: but one must be aware of them in order to break the habit of them: and awareness actually begins in some taking pride in the accomplishments of these linguistic visions. And some film-makers will enjoy these word-oriented pictures (that *I* find "constricting") and make them consciously: but either way, shame will never end a habit or make it a conscious virtue; but it will, rather, obscure the process and pot-bind its roots beyond any possibilities of growth.

The artificial 'tricks' with which amateurs tend to hide their real feelings do, like 'mis-takes', tend to contain-thru-method the very truth they were effected to conceal; and they are, in fact, consciously contrived 'puns' or 'metaphors.' I, personally, do very much care for the whole area of technical innovation in film-making: and I am very often accused of being too "tricky" in my motion picture making. It is certainly a proclivity I am conscious of: and I only run the personal risk of taking *too great* a pride in technical trickery. To counteract this danger to my own growth, I make it a point *never to contrive* a 'trick', an effect, or a technical virtuosity, but only permit myself *to arrive* at a filmic innovation when it arises from the felt needs of the film itself in the making and as an absolute necessity of realizing my emotions in the act of motion picture making. I try very hard to be honest with myself about this; and I can usually discipline myself most clearly by making all technical explorations the direct expression of acts of seeing (rather than making an image to-be-seen). For instance, when I photographed the births of my children I saw that with their first in-takes of breath their whole bodies were suffused with rainbowing colors from head to toe: but the film stock always recorded only the spread of reddish blotches across the surface of the skin: and so, by the time I had photographed the birth of my third child and in each occasion seen this incredible phenomenon, I felt compelled to paint some approximation of it directly on the surface of the 16 mm film and superimposed, as it were, over the photographed images of birth. As I had no way to prove whether this vision of skin rainbows at birth was a hallucination of mine or an extent reality too subtle for photographic recording, I felt free while editing this third birth film to also paint, on each 16 mm frame at a time, all the visions of my mind's eye and to inter-cut with the birth pictures some images I had remembered while watching the birth— some pictures of a Greek temple, polar bears, and flamingos (from a previous film of mine) . . . images which had, of course, no real existence at the time of the birth except in my 'imagination' (a word from the Greek meaning: 'image birth') but were, all the same, *seen* by *me* as surely as was the birth of the baby (were, in fact, given-birth-to- by me in an interior act of mimetic magic as old as the recorded history of Man.)

All of which brings us to the question of symbolism and subject matter in 'home-movie' making. When an amateur photographs scenes of a trip he's taking, a party or other special occasion, and especially when he's photographing his children, he's primarily seeking a *hold on time* and, as such, is ultimately attempting to defeat death. The entire act of motion picture making, thus, can be considered as an *exteriorization* of the process *of memory*. 'Hollywood', sometimes known as 'the dream-factory', makes ritualistic-dramas in celebration of mass memory—very like the rituals of tribal people— and wishful-thinking movies which seek to control the national destiny . . . as sure as primitive tribes throw water on the ground to bring rain . . . and they make 'social' or 'serious' dramas, at great commercial risk to the industry, as a corporate act of 'sacrifice'—not unlike the practices of self-torture priests undergo in order to 'appease the gods': and the whole commercial industry has created a pseudo church whose 'god' is 'mass psychology' and whose anthropomorphism consists of praying *to* ("Buy this—NOW!"), and preying *upon* (polling, etc.) 'the-greatest-number-of-people' as if, thereby, the human destiny were predictable and/or could be controlled thru mimecry. But the amateur photographs the persons, places, and objects of his love and the events of his happiness and personal importance in a gesture that *can* act directly and solely according to the needs of memory. He does not have to invent a god *of* memory, as does the professional: nor does the amateur have to appease any personification of God in his making. He is free, if he but accept the responsibility of his freedom, to work as the spirit of his god, or his memory, or his particular needs, move him. It is for this reason that I believe any art of the cinema must inevitably arise from the amateur, 'home-movie' making medium. And I believe that the so-called 'commercial', or ritual, cinema must inevitably take its cues from the films of amateurs rather than, as is too often the case these days, the other way round.

I now work equally in 8 and 16 millimeter making mostly silent films (and am even making a 35 mm film at home); I am guided primarily in all creative dimensions by the spirit of the home in which I'm living, by my own very living room. I have bought some 8 and 16 mm films which sit alongside books and LP records on my library shelf and I have sold many of my 8 mm films to both private homes and public libraries—thus by-passing the theatrical limitations of film viewing entirely . . . thus creating a circumstance wherein films may be lived-with and studied in depth—returned-to again and again like poetry and recorded music.

I am currently working on a long 'home-movie' war film in 8 mm: I discovered that the television set was as crucial a part of my living-, therefor working-room as the walls of it and its various other furnishings, and that T.V. could present me with as necessary an involvement as the activities of my children: ergo, I finally had to deal with its primary impulse at present—The War—as surely, as an amateur, as I would with any and every important occasion of our living. I carry a camera (usually 8 mm) with me on almost every trip away from the house (even to the grocery store) and thus become camera-laden 'tourist' of my own immediate environment as well as in those distant places I travel to—(many 8 mm cameras fit easily into a coat pocket or purse and are, thus, no more of a burden than a transistorized radio) . . . and I call these home and travel movies "SONGS," as they are to me the recorded visual music of my inner and exterior life—the 'fixed' melodies of, the filmic memory of, my living.

STAN AND JANE BRAKHAGE
(AND HOLLIS FRAMPTON) TALKING

Frampton: Last night you said you would like to make something beautiful . . . and get away with it.

Brakhage: What does one mean by "get away with it?"

Frampton: Things that are beautiful are seductive, are they not?

Brakhage: Ah, yes, you've worried me for some time by saying that *The Riddle of Lumen* was the least seductive film I'd ever made . . . until I realized that you meant I'd gotten away with it. Seduction is what the people who steal beauty use it for. What I mean in getting away with it is that I want to be able to get all the excitement, the absolute ecstacy at times . . . and I feel confronted by anything that I've photographed or even been moved to begin to think of photgraphing . . . get all that excitement and intensity all the way over into whatever I make. That's what I meant by getting away with it.

Maybe that's too simple. Let's think of it a minute in terms of something somebody else got away with. Sergei Eisenstein got away with the short cut. He used every trick in the bag to get away with it. For instance, the machine-gunner. There was a reason for the short-cut: it was approximating the machine-gun. Bullshit. That was the excuse whereby he could get away with a quality of vision that was closer to the ecstacy of what his own eyesight must normally have been. Similarly, in that same shot, not only did he have the machine-gun as a context to lean on, but he was intercutting two or three distinct scenes. He kept repeating—I can't even remember exactly—do they repeat exactly: 1, 2, 3; 1, 2, 3 or do they go 1, 3, 2; 1, 3, 2?

Frampton: No, there's a transposition.

Brakhage: If there is, then he's really getting away with something. Because there is no reason there should be. So he was confuting reason. What he was relying on was that the normal sequence of pictures is 1, 2, 3—a scene following a scene and so on. He was relying on repetition, and relying on that to make motion, the trickery of motion. We have a repetition of cuts, every single 16th of a second; and every shot encounters something almost like itself. All he did was to space two or three scenes apart from each other. So he got away with expressing something that was normal to his vision. And how do we know it was normal to his vision? Because of the *persistence* with which he expressed this thing, and because of the lengths he went to to make it acceptable. Even socially acceptable: look at all the words he wrote about it.

With every artist it's a case of trying to get something of what's really

Artforum, January 1973

intrinsic to his being, and separable from all social senses of what other human beings are, out into the general air. I can't beat, as a basic maxim, Robert Duncan's statement: I exercise my faculties at large. In the same way other men make war, some make love; I make poetry—to exercise my faculties at large. It's like hoity-toity the way it's put. Really what it means is that young men and women are faced with an impossible contradiction between their own intrinsic loneliness, and their own absolute dependence upon others. To make themselves *imaginable* within the general airs of all the other imaginations that others have accepted of themselves—they're forced to accept an equivalent. It's either that, or madness, or death, or total withdrawal, or a bitter eccentricity... and all the various other alternatives every artist toys with.

When I was a certain age, and when the glasses and the fat of me were a solid manifestation of my own removal from everything around me that I was so dependent on, I lost weight and threw away the glasses. When I threw away the glasses I literally could not see to cross the street safely. That meant I had accepted other persons' sense of sight—it didn't mean I couldn't see. I mean the ways in which I was seeing weren't acceptable, and therefore they weren't acceptable to me. I had no other equivalent for any of them in any of the books or pictures. Everyone else had an easy referential relationship with Renaissance perspective.

Frampton: You're saying that the spectacles designed to give you corrected perspective were, as we say, rose-colored glasses?

Brakhage: If they had *worked*, they would have been. But they didn't work. The assumption that anything mechanical like that will work, is based on the idea that seeing is mechanical and other people are trying to see according to those glasses. Why I couldn't cross the street safely, was that no on had given me the idea that there were ways in which I could make myself safe in crossing the street, just as surely as that shared, 'acceptable' form of making yourself safe.

Frampton: That you could see with the eyes you had?

Brakhage: Yes, perfectly well. The one place where I did see in relationship to all other people's seeing was the movie house, from the beginning, glasses or no.

Frampton: Did you take off your glasses when you went to the movies?

Brakhage: Yes, but when I first took them off, the screen was just muggy shapes and blurs. I was struggling to re-see. But people in the movie house, with or without glasses, are on a much closer plane than in the general phenomenal world, because there is a system for sight that even with glasses, apparently, I could accept. In fact, it's a system that's more suited to someone with glasses than not because it's a system that passes through lenses.

Frampton: Now, you're at this end of 20 years of work which pretty well does

establish the primacy of a vision of your own. You have survived the necessity
to get something out...

Jane: There's the need to make more, each year...

Brakhage: Well, people have also made a large case for beauty as terror.
Assuredly the dragon must look beautiful to St. George when he finds it,
because he's there to do it in. And he dances with it in so doing. But he can
only dance with it if he kills it... and that sense of beauty hangs like a very
dark shadow over at least the first half of the 20th century. And I think my
growing disinterest in that sense of beauty has a lot to do with why I'm
embracing so many aspects of the 19th century, over the last several years. In
the 19th century there was a much more direct relationship with beauty, and it
became *fearful*. One wonders why. Certainly we understand why, socially. It's
just as simple as this: no honest, decent, socially involved man is going to sit
around painting roses while an obvious misery is destroying the world in front
of his eyes. It's impossible. He either puts on blinders, or removes himself to a
garden; or he becomes essentially a social artist. And to the extent that he's
unable, because of his obsession and his own primary needs, to become a
social artist, he immediately opts for discovering the beauty of the monster that
confronts him. Not an unworthy task, in fact one of the more favored in
Western history, is the confrontation with the dragon—to be slain. But what
interests me now is that I envision a way in which that dragon can be confronted, and danced with, without killing it. Everybody deeply involved in the
social scene jumps all over me (and everybody else that says any such thing)
because they think that we mean to get along with the Devil, or to help the
dragon slay people, and that's not what I mean at all.

Jane: What's the dragon?

Brakhage: Well, the dragon is the ashcan of the Ashcan School of painting.
The dragon is the tortured and screaming faces of Germans in German Expressionist painting. The dragon is the waste of city landscape.

Jane: So you're not doing in the dragon?

Brakhage: Well, I think in a way I am. I think going to Pittsburgh was
confronting the dragon in his den. I didn't go to Pittsburgh to photograph the
city as the Emerald City of Oz, or to make a cathedral of it like Feininger. I
walked straight into a police car, and then a hospital, and then a morgue. And
this had to do with the city as an image of death, or as a vast graveyard of
sensibility.

Frampton: The dragon has often been emblematic of what is unwarranted and
surprising, and thus undesirable, in perception and in imagination.

Brakhage: Every artist, in some way, is trying to get around this dilemma,
which really is a 19th century dilemma. What did Eisenstein have to start
with, to celebrate? Heroics! He was confronted by a mass of people, which for

most of the history of the world is a pretty ugly apparition in any form in which it occurs. He made *this* the hero. He strung people out in the most incredible patterns, across vast landscapes and around city streets, in order to create an image of the heroic mass. *There's* a contradiction!

Another question the artist runs up against—the prime one—is to find a way to make manifest to the general air his own socially unacceptable particularities. Then the artist starts confronting ways in which his culture is unacceptable. By 'his' culture, I mean, say, the culture of Lump Gulch, which I have so far found no way to transport to New York or San Francisco. And by this I'm not just meaning to be able to give that vision to others, or not even primarily that. I've found no way yet to reconcile my living *here*, in relationship to my dreams of the city; not those dreams in relationship to the cities as they *are*, those specific cities I've known in New York, San Francisco, and, of late, Pittsburgh.

So there's Eisenstein (who presumably, if you look at those young pictures of him, had a normal bourgeois upbringing) confronted with the ordinary 19th-century leanings toward the dramatic-heroic, forced to use as his material, first of all by his own decision and then later by the decision of the Politburo, the ordinary mass. That's something he had to reconcile. He had irreconcilable elements enough to tear a man apart, if he can't forget them. His only means of having both these elements in the same air with himself and his proclivities was to *make an image*. That was probably, on his part, very much a *conscious* collective image. So there actually *is* the artist working for the state. But obviously he couldn't do it if he wasn't on the goddamn spot himself.

Frampton: The spot being the problem of reconciling his own particularities with what had been presented to him as how one was supposed to be?

Brakhage: It's *two* how you are supposed to be's. One, the primary one, is from his childhood. Then there's his own personal revolt, which puts him in the way of being representative of the other.

I think anytime any artist is working, he's working with material that's so disturbing to him, it's just like a scientist picking up pieces one of which might be distilled radium. Haven't you had that sense when you're putting two pieces of film together, that it might burn you to a crisp?

Frampton: Absolutely.

Brakhage: That sounds too much, though, like the condition is heroic.

I'm always in terror that I'll never be permitted to make another film. You know, the *real* danger is that I'll start believing the role I've created for myself, or that others have created for me, and that this will become such a viable and totally acceptable role in the world that I'll start living it, and then there'll be no need to create anymore. Why should there? I mean then I'll have a place in the world, like everybody else. The trouble is that if that had happened to me just naturally between the ages of one and six, or even by the time I was 18, I probably wouldn't be an artist. I'd be going around in the world fulfilling my role. But it *didn't*. The film is a by-product . . . and a very useful by-product. Hopefully, if it is an art, then it's a useful by-product in the sense that I can use it again and again to re-experience.

Frampton: As a magical amulet to hang around your neck, to ward off evil?

Brakhage: I don't know. Maybe people who make objects feel that way about it. But how can you feel that way about film, which is a continuity art? In film, the closest metaphor is the *thought process*, so "remind myself" would be the most correct way to put it, because film has the ability to be closest to thought process in its continuities.

Frampton: Just by virtue of its being continuous?

Brakhage: Yes. I do think that the way people name it has a lot to do with it. I think that *kino* has a lot to do with Russian cinema.

Frampton: The name means *move*, it means movies.

Brakhage: Cinema means something a little different, it has that tendency, in the world-language, to be going on to imply *cinematographer* which means *writer* of movement. And I think that kind of distinction, while it's small, grows from its small acorn across the span of 50 years and takes a very strong effect.

Film is our word. That's how independent makers distinguish themselves from the pros, who make movies. So it's ghosts we're after, as a group, although every single one of us is changing that continually, and at some point it will be so thoroughly changed that the word 'film' won't be used anymore, or it will be changed after 25 years or we'll drop that word.

Again, it's a question of "making place." And then there's this aspect of it that I begin to be aware of. I become aware, at a very early age that I'm not sharing the world of vision that I'm supposed to in order to exist in the general air with all the people around me. What a terrifying situation! What to do? O.K. then 20 years later I begin to be perfectly aware that the place I'd made for myself, and the altering of sight that occurs absolutely contingent with that, is similarly embarrassing young kids all over the world and just those I would most sympathize with.

Well, I've brooded on this on dark nights. I can never quite bring myself to say, "Ah, fuck it, that's their problem" . . . which is the extent to which I am 'social' . . . and it worries me.

Frampton: That's because it *has been* your problem.

Brakhage: So an awful lot of this talk we do, and a lot of the writing and the teaching, and an awful lot of study, has been trying to find some way to slip this goddamn knot altogether. There is the kind of man that goes out to level all the buildings that interfere with the new landscape, that he and some few others envision. Eisenstein had a lot of that fire in him too. I feel him trembling at times, always on the edge of wanting to cut the Gordian knot. He was stubborn.

He was a good stubborn man. It all holds together once you begin to see him as human. He's also very toughened by the time the Politburo is telling him how to live. He's used to evading that since he was six or so... people were telling him how to live or fuck or whatever so he's toughened. And that's another thing all artists seem to share—something has toughened them. Usually it's that they don't accept it, so they're in a tough spot. Right from scratch. Then, something that they've embraced in their not fitting not only doesn't fit with the society around them but is obviously enough to get their heads cut off. If everyone realized what is perfectly true, that they *don't* fit... if each person realized how distinct and unique he or she is, well, then, art would become normal everyday expression. And people would swap their artifacts or works of art or their words as naturally as they now swap slogans that are handed to them by the State. Art is personal in the making and it is personal in the appreciation. All that I try to do in my lectures, and when I teach in Chicago, is demonstrate my personal appreciation. The outside social hope is that it will inspire others to demonstrate theirs, or at least to *have* theirs. That if I can do it, then anyone else can make up his own Eisenstein. I made up my Eisenstein, or at least the Eisenstein that was real to me at the time of writing that essay on Eisenstein. ["Sergei Eisenstein," *The Brakhage Lectures*, Chicago, 1972.] Having done that, anyone else can. Mine is certainly unique and personal... which is why it gets attacked. Consider the level of the argument against it— that *I* am in it, that I am visible in it. Ken Kelman said, about the essays in general, that I had done a good job of fitting into the shoes of other film makers, but that always a big Brakhage toe sticks out!

Frampton: Let's extend this a bit. If everyone is free to make up his own Eisenstein, then everyone's likewise free to make up his own Stan Brakhage.

Brakhage: Right. Absolutely right.

Frampton: In this case we have a little help from Stan Brakhage?

Brakhage: Now there's the trouble with artists being living. That's why people so much prefer for artists to be dead, because anybody free to make up his own Stan Brakhage can give me the feeling that I have not found any kind of place in the world. Having done that I will naturally explode or fight back or argue or scream or cry or do something embarrassing.

Frampton: You're saying that there are thousands of Stan Brakhages, but they're all in other people's heads... which leaves you in an embarrassing position.

Brakhage: I may be so, that's preferable to everybody agreeing on who Stan Brakhage is, and then beating Stan Brakhage over the heads of the coming generation, which is the thing normally that's done. I had my own head beaten bloody by Sergei Eisenstein, whose work I loved, and whose tradition I was working, absolutely lineally, to spring my own traps. And the horror that that is happening now, with my work, to another generation of people, really sits heavily on my sore head.

Frampton: It has also been used, for as long as I've known your work to beat you yourself over the head. After *Anticipation of the Night* you were beaten over the head with the psychodramas.

Brakhage: Well, that's always very confusing too. Here again we have Eisenstein and the Politburo. I guess he never lived down *Battleship Potemkin*. What to do about that? It happens because people have such a narrow view of person, because most people are trapped in a narrow view of themselves, which they've been forced into by social expediency. *Not* by social necessity. I do not subscribe to the despair of the old Sigmund Freud, in *Civilization and its Discontents*, for instance. But it is *expedient* to regard anything narrowly.

To put it simply: in the name of "progress," an *extensive* view of human personality has been almost destroyed as a possibility of consideration for most people. There's really no problem in seeing that the same man who made *Anticipation of the Night* then made *Dog Star Man*, then made *Scenes From Under Childhood*, and is now doing the films I'm doing. There's really no problem with that at all, because you have one absolute surety to go on, and that's *style*. I had thought to emphasize that by *signing* those works. It takes me hours to scratch on film: By Brakhage. Certainly since *Desistfilm* that's been there as a possibility for most of my films. If I can sign checks while leaning on a steering wheel, while sitting at my desk, while I'm raging, while I'm sad, while I'm happy, while I'm writing quickly, while I'm working slow... and all these checks obviously bear the signature of Stan Brakhage, which is absolutely defensible in a court of law by a handwriting analyst, and is immediately obvious to most people on sight, then why is it that most people have so much difficulty recognizing style in art?

Frampton: I think it has to do with a constricted definition of style that has arisen particularly with regard to plastic arts, in the last 20 years or so: that it is not something that can be as *various* as the signature of one person, but that it is as *fixed* as the same signature repeated exactly by a forger.

Brakhage: What you're saying is that there's such a degree of forgery in the world that it has made style suspect.

Frampton: I wrote recently that style is the adoption of a fixed perceptual distance from the object. That was in connection with 19th-century photography, and I used Julia Margaret Cameron as an example but I had very much in mind any number of painters of my own generation, who are very careful to demonstrate constantly a step-by-step continuity in their development, from one work to the next.

Brakhage: That's interesting to me because I used to know my continuities like the alphabet. I knew not only the orders of the films made, but I knew almost to the month and certainly the year when each film was completed, when the shooting was done, or editing or whatever. Since we've moved here, to this location in the mountains, that's ceased to be so. I can tell you when the first two or three films were made when we came here; and I can tell you the order and the months of the last six months. But I cannot really differentiate any of the rest. That's interesting. So I'm thinking that for a while there was that determination to hold each step in mind and build a progression, as if I were making a ladder.

Frampton: Is it something that happened in your work because you came here? Or was it simply because of the time in your life?

Brakhage: I think both. For many years I was thinking I was getting *out* of something. There were steps in the direction of finding my place in the world. This place, after all, carries the exactitude that we have lived here eight years now. That length of time I never lived anywhere else on earth or anywhere near it. So that I've found my place in the literal physical sense.

And I've become aware that I'll *never* find my place in the world . . . and that all that I can do is keep making elbow room in the general air. I can toss out some metaphor for *this* aspect of myself and some metaphor for *that*, but it's unending.

But that hasn't anything to do with the creative act. What I mean is, that I feel as if the creative powers *use* my social embarrassment, and whatever else is useful, to permit the making of the work; and I feel that in an equal degree while I'm working on something, making place for the particularities of my vision, and my thought processes, my own physiology, in the world. So that's an absolutely poised shared experience: a dance, you could say, between my sense of myself and something that I don't know anything about . . . or a mystery.

Frampton: That verb *make* comes up again and again—*make* place, *make* sense, *make* a work of art, *make* love—with two implications I think. First, as taking an active posture toward something. And second, with an implication that things that must be *made* have a kind of half-life, that unless they're continuously restored and regenerated, we run out. Why do we say *make* love for instance? Suggesting that it has to be remade . . .

Jane: Maybe it does.

Brakhage: I completely believe that.

Frampton: Like a radioactive substance that gives out energy and is diminished and needs to be augmented.

Jane: Making your image!

Brakhage: Yes, which is always very important to me; after all that's how I got into this in the first place. That's how they, if there is any they, dragged me into this.

Well, there *is* a *"they."* I just don't know if this unnameable likes to be referred to as a "they." I am very clear that I receive instructions from the outside. I have had no question about this since I was editing *Cat's Cradle*; and certainly since *Sirus Remembered* I have had no questions about it. At times I have questioned it—but I have had no questions *about* it. It's made me think about younger artists a lot; and I think the young depend very much, not only on a lot of instructions, but depend on *drama*. As I get older, I don't depend on *drama*.

In fact, I begin to have a sense that I understand something of what it is to be an old artist. And it's something so simply wonderful as being granted a responsibility for what's been given you to do . . . as distinct from being charged continually with forces you have absolutely no control over. I've seen many artists begin to make this transition. I'm watching Paul Sharits begin to make it, for instance. Actually in *S:TREAM:SS:ECTION:S:ECTION:S:SEC-TIONED*, Sharits presented us with the voices of the Muses, literally on the sound track. Having done that, he had certainly a more comfortable relationship with them. The relationship, in getting older, is a less dramatic relationship with what some men call the Muses, and much more . . .

Frampton: What we used to call intercourse, in politer days?

Brakhage: Yes, I think so. A shared responsibility, maybe. Do you know the story about Paul, and how he came to that sound track on *S:TREAM:SS:ECTION:S:ECTION:S:SECTIONED?* That was the sound he heard while working on some film—not, I believe, this one—when he was sitting late at night in his little room in Baltimore. And he couldn't *stop* the sound, it kept coming back. There are infuriating aspects to the voices of the Muses which were captured beautifully for us by Rameau in that piece called *The Conversation of the Muses*. In fact, people should really listen both to the sound track on *S:STREAM:SS:ECTION:S:ECTION:S:SECTIONED* and that piece by Rameau. There can be no question, while we may not know what it is we're talking about—'Muse' may be only a very inferior term—that there is *something* that artists share. Some refer to them as whisperings, some as outright visions, some as sounds, or ways in which sounds in the surrounding atmosphere gang up and produce effects on their nervous systems. It's a pity no one ever thought, to ask, say, Eisenstein about it.

Frampton: He would have felt constrained not to answer.

Brakhage: Yes, he probably would have. But, it's surprising. You'd think that certain men would never give any answer in relationship to anything that is the contemporary experience of something. And then they surprise you. For instance, I can believe that Eisenstein might somewhere have left some such statement, because I have seen D. W. Griffith's statement (and I am paraphrasing it, but I am very close): all that I really want to do is to make you see. Now, that's about the last statement in the world that I ever would have expected to share with Griffith. And the only change I would make in it is the obvious one: I would change the word *make*. But he was, after all, very involved with social drama . . . he wanted to *make* people see. And, look, in the very beginning we have the implication of Muses in film—in Méliès' work, in no uncertain terms, however humorous the context.

But of course people really *haven't* accepted film as an art form yet. And until that becomes a general assumption, we're certainly asking too much to expect people to consider how the Muses operate in relationship to the creative act in film. But actually, in the 20th century, it's embarrassing to mention these things, because everybody's so concerned with the social usability of art; there's nothing very usable about what most people would regard as madness. Thinking over how I work today, and how I used to work, and what slight difference there is . . . it goes along with the whole change in my life. When I was younger, I really couldn't find much significance except in a dramatic confrontation. It isn't an older person's sense of living to be dependent on drama. As you get older you see the damage that it does, for one thing, and you *feel* it more. Then, the minute you begin giving up pieces of that form of knowledge, then you discover so many others. I shouldn't say *you*, that means I'm not quite sure what I'm trying to say. I discover many other ways to be informed, and many other ways to elbow myself, my physiology, a little place in the world, than through dramatic confrontation. And as I do so my whole life changes incredibly. The work process doesn't depend on dramatic confrontation. This is why it isn't important to me anymore to know which film came when.

Again, some men were not permitted that. We were talking about style earlier, and you said there have been so many forgeries in the world that people are no longer cashing esthetic checks on the basis of style. Consider this though. Who are the forgers of Méliès? What are their names? When you say Méliès you get, right away, a sense of style. Now tell me, who's forged that style? We're not talking about the grammar he's left, or the things he's given socially; we're talking about *style*. Come on, give up! No one has!
Frampton: I do. You're right.
Brakhage: The closest you come . . . and you have to leap all the way . . . is Jean Cocteau. And I certainly wouldn't call him a forger of Méliès. He's just the only one who picked up on Méliès' style sufficiently to let it quiver in his work every now and again.
Frampton: I heard a demurrer from you, Jane.
Jane: I don't think he forged Méliès at all.
Brakhage: No, I didn't mean that he did. I only meant that he was sufficiently aware of Méliès' style.

Jane: You shouldn't have said that he did.

Brakhage: All right, let's take another one. Let's take the big chief in the line-up, Sergei Eisenstein. Who forged his stuff? Same thing: no one. Now let's cap it. Who's forged Stan Brakhage's style? O.K., a lot of names come suddenly to mind as possibilities. But I'm sure they did with each of these men, in their time, because at the time something is being made, the style is not seen or perceived clearly enough to distinguish the forgeries.

In fact, we know that there were many forgers of Méliès. And there were forgeries upon forgeries, and the forgers became much more successful than Méliès, and that's how he was beat out. We know that . . . but where are they? Nobody could ever bear to look at them 20 years later, or we'd have a few of them around.

Frampton: What a paradox this is: the Master ends up in the candy store and the forgers go into oblivion!

Brakhage: And we know people's sensibilities change incredibly. For instance, Edison lined up a string quartet on the Carnegie Hall stage, in front of a supposedly experienced audience, and had fake strings on all their instruments, and fooled the audience with a cylinder recording of a quartet played while they went through the motions. No one could pull that stuff today.

Frampton: But then it also seems unthinkable that people in France and the Soviet Union ran around behind the screen to look for the actors in the Lumière films. They were *black and white*, for God's sake.

Brakhage: And people recognized themselves in Méliès' *Dreyfus Trial* —people who'd been to the trial took it as a newsreel footage and recognized themselves among what was actually a crew of actors. That's the whole basic trick . . . which brings us to another interesting point. We *are* in a continuum. Now that we see that forgery only operates within a time-bound context, and therefore can't be anything more than a brief distraction from what an art is — or from what the style of the man who made it is — then we come to the question: what about a lineal tradition?

My big problem has been, all these years, that no one has recognized that I (and all my contemporaries) are working in a lineal tradition of Méliès, Griffith, Dreyer, Eisenstein, and all the other classically accepted film makers. Why not? Why are they unable to recognize that? I took my first cues for fast cuts from Eisenstein, and I took my first senses of parallel cutting from Griffith, and I took my first senses of the individual frame life of a film from Méliès, and so on. Why has it taken so long for anyone to recognize this as a lineal tradition? Why did we all have to go through that terrible embarrassment of the late '60s when we were presented to the world as though we sprang full-blown, completely new, from an LSD dream? Why is it that those men who studied grammar, even of Griffith and Eisenstein, were so slow in recognizing that? In fact, most of them still don't and would rather curl up like the Wicked Witch of the . . . North?

Jane: West!

Brakhage: . . . in a pool of black smoke, than acknowledge that lineal tradition.

Frampton: We live in a 'heroic' culture. We live in the midst of 'masterpieces.'

Brakhage: Do we?

Frampton: Well, we certainly don't.

Brakhage: I think maybe there's a simpler explanation: that they never were really looking at the person or the personal style of Eisenstein.

Frampton: Which is to say, they never looked at the films.

Brakhage: Exactly. They never looked at the art of the films.

Jane: What were they looking at?

Brakhage: The trickery. And the "social significance," as it's called. Well, to be graceful about it, maybe this is the only use most people have for art. In fact, one could let them have it that way, if they weren't so mean about it. I don't particularly care, for instance, if people *really* don't want to interest themselves in obsession or vision.

I used to care a lot. But I guess I was beaten in my arguments with P. Adams Sitney, years ago. He just simply did *not* want to close his eyes and see hypnagogically, so that he would have some sense why I was hand-painting film a frame at a time. Finally, I've made peace with that. Why should he, if he doesn't want to? But on the other hand, as long as he and many others busy themselves with pronouncing to the world what we are, what the artist is, then there's bound to be a continual fuss in the relationship between us.

Tape Two

Brakhage: It's my problem, at the moment, that I am once again, or let's say especially for the first time, trying to make a portrait of Jane. This is after years and years of Jane's image being central to film after film after film. And this is weighted with the problem that every now and again Jane will say, well, you've never gotten an image of *me.* So here I go for the first time — again.

Frampton: Why is it that he can't make a portrait of you Jane?

Jane: He just uses me.

Brakhage: Oh, boy, now I'm in trouble! The whole women's lib movement at this instant descends on me like a puddle of Harpies!

Jane: I've just been doing something like having a baby, or minding the kids, or standing around or something. And he just photgraphs a woman having a baby, sweeping the floor, or making a bed. It's the making of the bed or whatever *Jane* does with it.

Frampton: Jane, you have to realize that, from the outside, you are presumably the most profoundly differentiated and individuated woman in the history of film—and, probably, one of the most completely differentiated *persons* in the history of art.

Jane: Hmm. You really think so?

Frampton: You can look it up in the goddamned library, Jane. Of course you are!

Jane: Where? Who said that?

Frampton: I said it. Then you cut your long hair off and fucked it up.

Jane: There, that's just what I mean...

Brakhage: I think that's probably why she cut off her hair.

Jane: That's *right!*

Frampton: You felt, then, that you had no life outside your cinematic myth, that you were becoming a movie star, in fact, that kind of object.

Jane: Yes, an appendage.

Brakhage: I'm sure Saskia must have felt similarly, Saskia who was asked to dress in all those fancy costumes so that Rembrandt could paint her as this, that and the other. He used himself in the same sense.

Jane: I didn't resent it. I just feel that that's the case, that's how it is.

Brakhage: I'll be the first to say bullshit.

Jane: That was years ago that I did care, and now I don't, and now you can make the goddamn film because I don't give a shit.

Frampton: I'd like to remind both of you that I am the interviewer here.

Jane: What kind of rights do you have here?

Brakhage: Why don't you whip your camera out and make another film, *Bride of Critical Mass?* No, let me finish what I was going to say. I think actually what it is—I think everybody will recognize this as a truth—is that you just want *more*. And that's perfectly reasonable, and I am willing to comply...

Jane: I *don't* want anymore.

Brakhage: ...because I have that *necessity*. I have never been able to make anything for you or for anyone else, actually. I've tried to make children's films for the children. At times I've really felt I would swap everything else I've accomplished to be the Hans Christian Anderson of film. But I cannot commission a children's film from myself. I've tried to make films for Jane, and they always fail very quickly and I throw them away. In fact, they've never been seen. But she, rightfully, always wants more and more. This really is her inspiring function in the creative process.

Frampton: Do you feel this way about his portraits of other people, Jane?

Jane: Scenes From Under Childhood is maybe really a thorough thing. But that's the only thorough thing I can think of, unless the Pittsburgh films, which are documentary, and therefore more objective, so the cops can be seen as "out there." Most of his stuff is inward.

Frampton: You have always the feeling he's making a portrait of himself?

Jane: Yes.

Brakhage: I agree.

Frampton: That's why you say you're simply part of a pretext for that self-portrait. Has the case ever been otherwise for an artist?

Jane: Yes, that's a good question.

Brakhage: I can state it better than that. Has the case ever been otherwise for any human being, ever?

Jane: So I quit complaining, because I felt that that was not something that he *could* do.

Brakhage: You see, to accomplish that feeling that you designate as "out there," with relationship to the images of the police in *eyes*, the clearest way to accomplish that is in drama. And drama is where the art completely and totally lies in order to state a truth. If we'd been making drama films all these years, and you were an actress, then there would be many images of you that would seem "out there" in the sense that the police do in that film.

Frampton: You do have a film between you which very precisely mimes the Aeschylean drama, and that's *Wedlock House: an Intercourse*, in which the camera is tossed back and forth like the stichomathy in Greek argument, and the camera is the impersonal messenger that brings everybody bad news.

Jane: We did that in *Scenes From Under Childhood* too, in one of the last parts.

Brakhage: We were "acting," as all people do when they quarrel. To the extent to which we act, we give the appearance of being "out there." The Pittsburgh police were, surely, continually acting. In fact an enormous part of their job is to act; so it is with doctors, with all public servants.

Frampton: So it is with teachers. We know as teachers the classroom is a great theater.

Brakhage: Certainly. So to the extent that we have ever been acting, there's a sense of a presence "out there." But that to me is the same as what got me, and every other artist, into this in the first place. The *act*, the general shared public act, is, for some reason, not possible, to a man or a woman. And if that man or woman still chooses to attempt to relate to all these others in their social acts, he or she is then forced to make his or her *own* act, an act that will accommodate the necessities of the person. And there is a beginning of an art.

There are two interests in art. Robert Duncan is curiously always very dedicated to the theatrical act. This is why he was so fascinated with Ingmar Bergman, for instance. He was interested in that sense of making, that you "make it up," with all kinds of conscious trickery, into a vast lie which is then so removed from ordinary living experience that it serves as a truth, a truth which carries the feeling that it is "out there." I'm not against this way of creating. In fact I guess this is where I started—I started with drama. For instance Janis Hubka probably recognizes herself very much better in the first film I made, *Interim,* than you [Jane] ever have . . . because we've been so little involved in drama since we've known each other. There's no real sense of there being an "out there."

Jane: I'm no kind of an actress.

Frampton: Hear, hear, bravo, encore!

Jane: Gee, is it that bad?

Brakhage: I have tremendous necessity to keep re-seeing Jane, and all my many ways of seeing are engaged with her continually. And of course some of them have never been used. And some of them are very habit-bound. And I shudder at the thought of those artists who continue to paint and repaint their loved ones in the same fashion, in the same situation.

Frampton: As if, by some kind of magic, to freeze them in a snapshot.

Brakhage: To hold to the original vision. Yes, that's a good term for it—the snapshot approach to it. For one thing I'm fascinated right now to make a film bouncing the light off Jane, which is something I have never really done, and to make it a film that's totally about her, in the sense that all its considerations center on her. And *that* I've never done.

Frampton: Do you like to have light bouncing off you, Jane?

Jane: I'm trying, I'm trying.

Brakhage: Well, I said it wrongly. I don't bounce the light. I turn on a bulb, and don't have megalomaniac senses that I bounce the light in so doing—or I set up an elaborate lighting apparatus and aim it this way and that way. But I really *catch* the light. That's what it's all about.

Frampton: You catch what's leftover—after Jane is through with the light.

Brakhage: O.K., let's get it straight, after Jane is through with the light I catch it. That's the normal condition of my life anyway, so that should work for something magnificent.

Jane: What is your interest in light?

Brakhage: I see so many qualities of light, so many things that seem to *be* light but aren't anywhere categorized as such or spoken of as such or referred to by other people as such. I always have, and as I get older I see more and more. I see so many qualities of light continually, every day constantly new ones and new aspects of old ones, that it's become a normal condition. At this time in my life it is the variety of the quality of light that I see, and live with daily, that removes me most from feeling I share sight with other people.

Frampton: And that leads you to the necessity of making something that *will* share that sight with other people?

Brakhage: Yes.

Frampton: You've spent a lot of time attempting a very exact registration of the seeing process. But the prime condition of seeing, *at all,* is light, the carrier wave which makes everything visible, which visible things modulate, change and so forth. And that seems to be a very recent shift of focus in your interests.

Brakhage: It's not recent, because it was a long time ago that I was startled by Scotus Erigena's, 'All things that are, are light.' Along with all the many gifts of Ezra Pound, this was certainly one of the most startling and immediately meaningful to me. Because even if it were, as it first sounded to me, an absurd statement in the face of my scientific prejudices, it still expressed beautifully the natural condition of the film maker at the moment of making. And of late that phrase has come back to me again in many forms—one of the most beautiful of which is Hugh Kenner's exposition of it (and all other aspects of light in Ezra Pound's work) in his book *The Pound Era*. It comes back to me at a time when I really *need* it because slowly and gradually over the years my attention to the world in relationship to light has increased my seeing of all kinds of things that other people either don't see, or don't admit they see . . . or don't have any *way* to admit they see. So now I take that statement very much more literally. One can make scientific arguments about it. So much of everything we know—and it's hard to think of anything for which this is not so—is, in its state, because of light. Let alone *whether* we see it or not. Year after year more and more things began to seem to me to *glow*. Having been raised by Germans in Kansas, and being fussy, I troubled myself to try to figure out if I was *superimposing* this glow upon things, in my mind's eye, or if things were coming from some outside and pressing on my brain at the point where it surfaces as an eye. And finally, even through some experiments, I came to convince myself at least some of these extraordinary things were certainly coming from the outside and pressing in on me.

So far I'm just talking about an intrinsic light that seems to be emanating from all things. I wrote, when younger, about certain experiments that Jane and I made with qualities of light, like 'elfskin,' for instance, which term we got out of old Saxon by way of Michael McClure. That is, the quality of light that emanates from all beings. But that was too general a sight. Finally I found a way to make some equivalent of it by combining high contrast positive and negative film, slightly off register. That gave an approximate of that thing we were seeing, that we and Michael were calling 'elfskin,' and were presuming that maybe the Saxons did.

But now there are so many qualities, that that seems just one among hundreds. Other qualities of glow from . . . not only beings, but all objects.

Now let's take another sense of light. That light that we more normally refer to, light that comes from the sun and bounces around here on earth, by which we see. I suppose for a long time I had a normal relationship with *that* light, or thought I did. But one day I knew rain was coming. I asked myself how I knew. We get many scuttling clouds that go over and deposit nothing... but I knew rain was coming! And then I *saw* it. I saw streaks of whitish lines, almost as if drawn, or as if comic-strip drawn, very quickly coming down on a slant into the ground. There was a feeling that this was being *sucked* into the ground, that these were actually being pulled, as if by gravity. These lines were, in fact, a metaphor for rain. Very shortly thereafter rain began to fall. Because of my scientific upbringing I tested myself. Again and again, as I sat on the porch, I would ask myself, as one cloud or another looking promising passed over, is it going to rain or not? And I finally was producing a 100% record. Because before every actual rain there came this light manifestation. It looked like streaks of light, metaphors of the coming rain.

By now, I've seen so many other similar qualities of light that precede a material manifestation, that the question came to my mind: maybe everything that's taken shape on earth, had its shape defined for it by light, by some quality of light, before it came into existence. I even thought maybe that's what ghosts or spirits are, maybe that shape humans have taken was preceded by that which we call angels, or demons, or ghosts. I see them; and what am I to do with having seen them? The best that you can do, is to try to determine if you're making it up.

For instance, I have seen angels. That is, in the 20th century, a rather embarrassing sort of thing to admit. I have seen figures, usually with wings or something like wings, that are in a tradition of what we call 'angels' when referring to painting or sculpture in Western art. After I'm through the experience of seeing them, then I rummage my mind, and this whole bag of books over here, to see if I can find an angel that's like the one I saw, or a composite of angels that would have made up mine. To try to figure out if my mind has taken many parts of angels out of the history of painting and projected one in front of me. I've never found anything at all like what I *saw*. Angels are quite a tradition, you know. It doesn't begin with Christianity. Just one sculpture that shows that angels aren't Christian is the *Victory of Samothrace*. East and West there is a tradition of angels, which have been expressed in various forms of art.

These visions occur, these days, normally, and just as something passing. They don't occur in any way that would be particularly dramatic, helpful, or useful. And so with the qualities of light. I see light that appears to pool. It appears to be a glow that's as if it had weight and liquid substance. It doesn't pool in holes in the ground, necessarily, or any depression. But it pools *as if* there were some hole there. And it is of a glow that's all of what we call light, as we extend that term to phosphorescence. It happens quite normally. And there's also a quality of light that streams over the ground; and I've seen it running absolutely counter to the blow of the wind. Just streaming, in all senses as if it were a charged or phosphorescent mass of floating liquid. In fact, it looks very much like a mountain stream, only it's a slight differentiation of qualities of light coming from the sun, and bouncing in the ordinary ways that we recognize and refer to.

Now if there's no other value in all this, there is at least this specifically for me at this time—that I can't photograph it. The materials of film are too clearly attuned to some other quality of light, or too gross or too inferior or whatever to be receptive to these qualities of light. I find myself in the position of having to search out an equivalent. So I am back in the same spot I was when I realized that I couldn't photograph closed-eye vision. I could not get a camera inside my head so I painted on film to get as near an equivalent I could of things. I was, yes, seeing, but had no way to photograph. Here again I cannot photograph so I have to search for equivalents that will give something of the quality of what I'm seeing. Well, that takes me back to the absolute beginning— because, all along, all I or anybody else have been able to do, is create by whatever means—film or any other art—an *equivalent* of what we were seeing.
Frampton: That's a classic definition of the artist's problem.
Jane: It's a weird thing to do in the first place.
Brakhage: Yes, it is, isn't it? But if you think about it, it's so beautiful, because only by doing such a weird thing could you actually get involved in trying to create an equivalent for something that most people *weren't* already seeing. I mean you begin trying to get an equivalent that's rather close cousin to whatever anybody else is seeing.

And this is the value of the classics and of the other artists that the young man adores and worships. His life depends on them, because they have, through their personal needs, taken a thing so far and then here comes... myself as a young man, and I know that my eyes are doing this and that and the other and suddenly Eisenstein is giving me a beginning of an equivalent to do something that *I'm* doing. And this isn't really taking something *further*; the process here is the adjusting of my equivalents to his.
Frampton: So you find you are not, after all, so very particular, that there are needs you share with others?
Brakhage: It's more that, if nothing else that the works that I make can be close to his. If I can't live reasonably in a world of standard cliché visions, at least my films can live in a world of developing visions along with his. I don't really feel that I could actually get along with Sergei Eisenstein any easier than I might with my mother. But I can sense that the *works* can share a world. Presumably, then, later, other people will share something, such as is useful to them. I'm trying to find a way not to put down the normal decision of most

people to accept a limited vision in order to communicate with each other. That's their business, if they want to do that. I would probably do it too, if it were possible.

Jane: Why do we have to communicate with each other?

Frampton: I don't really think there's any question about having to; we simple *do* it. That's Ray Birdwhistell's paean to inevitability.

Brakhage: Let's be careful of the word communication though, to absolutely distinguish it from, say, Stan Vanderbeek's sense of the word communication. I think that's a very dangerous word. I don't really mean that I want to communicate with other people in that sense of getting my message all the way over, or I'd have maybe tried to become a polititian. That's what makes certainly a dictator—that absolute insistence on total communication. In my case it had to do with the eyes. I wanted to share a sight. That's not the same as telling "them" about that sight. I wanted to feel like I lived in the same world with other people. That's not the same as communicating. My primary necessity was not that they understand me, or obviously I'd never have become an artist. My primary need was that, at some point, I share a sight with them. Is that fair and clear? Does that make sense? I want to say it right?

Jane: It's *you* you're talking about.

Brakhage: If I had needed to show them "sights," then presumably I'd have gone to Hollywood.

Jane: You can see how that doesn't necessarily have to be a very widespread need.

Brakhage: To tell you the truth I don't even think it's very important. I don't think it has much to do with the creative act. We're back again to talking about what creative forces use, in people, to prompt a man or a woman to lend themselves to creativity. You know one of the nicest simple social definitions of an art that I have ever heard came from the brother of Robert Oppenheimer, Frank Oppenheimer. He is a very nervous scientist, who's suffered particularly because of the things that happened to his brother, and a very attentuated man. And one day he simply said, "I always think that an art just says: now see this, now hear this."

Frampton: But you imply an extended and intensified sense of 'see' and 'hear,' do you not? You have talked about seeing as a registration of the whole electromagnetic spectrum. When you speak about seeing as a metaphoric precedent for coming rain, you extend the sense of seeing to include anything that is light.

Brakhage: But would people say that you *could* call this light? What about what it is that I see as a pool? What about the streams I see move along the ground, contrary to the wind? What about those things that Wilhelm Reich suggested...that I have seen? He sees a certain quality of movement of a glowing particle in the air, billions of glowing particles, that make a little half-spiral. And he called this orgone energy, and he tried to use it to cure cancer...or at least he tried to see whatever curative effect there might be in it. He's the only person who referred in writing to something that I was seeing.

Among these particles there's another quality that looks like light, like a light particle that has a particular movement. I can see it with my eyes open, and with my eyes closed. I see it very intensely in the blue sky when I relax my eyes. It fills that blue with golden movement, and I see the sky as gold. I have performed one of his experiments, that proved to me satisfactorily that it was "out there," because it would magnify through closed eyes. Now, he refers to it as blue, I do yellow. That's no problem, blue and yellow being so inter-changeable on the optic nerve level. I'm sure, by a simple shift of attention, I could see the blue. I *prefer* to see them yellow. And at that point people can rush in and say, well, so you prefer to see them yellow, you prefer to see them. You create them, you invent them. But I was seeing them for a long time before I ever read anything by Wilhelm Reich, so here was another voice that sus-tained me. Someone else was seeing something of some such thing, to put it in a nice Gertrude Stein phrase.

What I ponder on, and what I suppose I'm going to think more about as I get older and older is, can't I just make films and stop talking about it? I would be horrified by people who would insist on this system of qualities of light, and derive it from me, and apply it to my films...I would be as horrified by that as I was by P. Adams Sitney's absolute refusal to close his eyes and see if he couldn't see something that was related to the painting on my film. He made a very strong refusal. It was Jane who put me at peace with that. She said, leave him alone, why does he have to do that? And in the long run that's safer... because the other way leads to a religion. They'll make a religion out of it.

Frampton: If your own eye insists upon your absolute right to feel different, then it must also confirm the absolute right of others to feel different.

Brakhage: That's right. Then, the minute P. Adams refused to search for his own hypnagogic vision, we had our next quarrel, which sprang up when I said I am the most thorough documentary film maker in the world because I docu-ment the act of seeing as well as everything that the light brings me. And he said nonsense, of course, because he had no fix on the extent to which I was *documenting*. He and many others are still trying to view me as an imaginative film maker, as an inventor of fantasies or metaphors.

Frampton: You are saying, along with Confucius: "I have added nothing."

Brakhage: Yes, I have added nothing. I've just been trying to see and make a place for my seeing in the world at large, that's all. And I've been permitting myself to be used by some forces that are totally mysterious to me, to accom-plish something that satisfies me more than what I *thought* I was setting out to do.

Art is the reaching out to this phenomenon or light or moving creatures around us—I don't even know what the hell to call it. I have no name for it. And the extent to which different societies at different times have decided that everyone shares this or that relationship with the world is all some social usage of art, long after the fact of its creating and usually after the fact of the artist's living. People finally decided, all of them, to see sunsets. Well, what have we left out?

Jane: All the rest.

Brakhage: There's not too much about specific films. I don't know that it's even appropriate to talk about them.

Jane: The list is too long.

Brakhage: I don't feel that way about them anymore. It doesn't seem to make much sense.

INTERVIEW WITH RICHARD GROSSINGER

Grossinger: Let me begin by asking you about the new films you're doing, especially the set of three made in Pittsburgh.

Brakhage: I mean it's such a damn long story. Actually, those Pittsburgh films . . . they really began . . . it's funny because I just wrote Creeley this morning after noticing something in his letter about document . . . he had reminded me in that letter that the Pittsburgh films actually began when I made a statement to the audience of the Carnegie Museum at my lecture-showing there that the real reason why NASA was cut back in all its expenditures is that they didn't get any image from the moon, that actually, it turned out, they were dependent on selling that as some kind of an interesting event, and they spent maybe a billion dollars on PR over the years selling that as an interesting event: that man takes his first step on the moon, which phrase itself is a piece of their propaganda; I mean they did a terrific job of selling people on that idea; but then when it came right down to it they showed them images that were . . . that did not in any sense permit people, even in the Hollywood sense, to participate in that event, have a real experience with it like you can with a work of art. And so I was commenting to the audience in rather a flip manner actually, I said the last person on earth NASA would ever think of sending to the moon would be myself, for instance, or any artist; and yet that that so clearly demonstrated the poverty of our culture, so clearly demonstrated how unable we are as a people to make use of the artist . . . because it was quite normal, I mean, for those exploratory ships out of Spain and so on, that they would include at least a very fine draughtsman, a man who had dedicated his life to drawing, whereas in this case they had the assumption that if they handed a camera to any of these astronauts that they would be able to bring back images; they would set up a t.v. on the moon, and people would see it. Of course, all that they set up, all that they got was something that looked like a second-rate very boring science fiction movie made maybe in the '20's. And the reason they got that is because you can't . . . most people can only get an image of something that they've already seen; and so they had seen science fiction movies, and they set up their cameras, and they framed their compositions, and they approached the whole thing, I mean, from that standpoint; and they weren't very good even at that, so they got just the most boring pictures on earth. In fact, these men were probably the kinds of men that, if they go on a trip with their wives to Wyoming, she takes all the pictures. So that was the actual beginning. I made that statement, and then I went on to explain to people that there, at that time if you remember, which was a year ago last September, was a lot of horrible antagonism that had built up toward the police. It had sort of reached a peak of the Pig period at that point. And I said to this group of people, I said, for example we have no real image of the police; we have none. And I for several years have been trying to get permission to ride in a patrol car to make a film about police, for God knows whatever reasons of my own, that when I was a child I toyed with the idea of being a policeman, so it haunts me and I've also suffered very much at the hands of police for having done no wrong whatsoever. I shouldn't say "very much"; I've never been actually arrested, but I have been beaten. So I had the policeman both as a childhood attraction and as a bogeyman, and I said, here I am with the abilities to see and arrive at some clear sight, and I want to make a film on police, and the nation desperately needs an image of police, the police need an image to be made of them, and I can't get permission, because what am I? I am the absolute bottom of the pile, I am an independent film-maker, I mean that's totally suspicious, I'm not even using that most terrifying of all terms; that is, to say you were an artist; in America that's still not something we can write comfortably on the motel register as an occupation, and so therefore it's not accepted, and therefore there's no such possibility. Well, what happened, happily, was that Mike Chikiris, a newspaper-reporter-photographer, was in the audience, and was that kind of person who took it tremendously seriously, and within two days, using his... well, not so much his prestige as his actual charm, his wonderful ability to charm people and persuade them of the necessity of something, he managed to get me into a patrol car. Now this was one of the times, not the first, but one of those times in my film-making experience when I had nothing to go on, experientially, actually, in terms of what was happening. I hadn't been in a patrol car before, and I've never known a policeman; and so suddenly the considerations of film-making, without my thinking about it at all, became concerned with something that I'm now puzzling in my mind about that I call *document*. And this is something quite distinct and different from documentary, and something quite distinct and different from home movies; I was not there to get a movie of my experience of being in a patrol car; I was there to get the most naked fix I could manage on what was transpiring. And the previous times that have come to mind when I was also thrown on this level of film-making in my life was when the first baby was being born and I was filming *Window Water Baby Moving,* and, for another example, when I was making three of those episodes that ended up as the film *Lovemaking*. So that birthed as a reversion to earlier concerns; I picked up some threads that I've stumbled into before, possibilities of seeing, and began operating. Then the thing that happened also that was very important, a crucial moment occurred.... First of all, the patrolmen drove us around for a couple of hours, and nothing happened, and they talked with us, and we talked back, and at the end of these two hours we were getting a fairly reasonably human conversation going with them. And then suddenly one of them looked at the other, and the other one winked, and then the first one turned to the back seat where Mike and I were both sitting, and said to us, "You guys seem to me to be pretty much alright"; and he said, "We've actually been told just to drive you around, and take no calls, until you get bored, and then drop you off." He said, "But you've convinced us that it's interesting, what you want to do, so we're going to call in and tell them that we've dropped you off, at which point we'll start getting calls, if it's alright with you." I said, "Sure. That was the whole idea. That's what we're here for." He said, "Well, then, you know, we have to warn you that you're . . . that you have no legal right to be in this car, for instance, and if something happens that we have to drop you off somewhere, that'll be that, you know; we'll drop you off wherever we are, in the middle of a riot, or whatever; you'll have to take that chance." I said, "Sure"; and he made that call. And the first thing that happened: almost immediately they got a call of a dead body in the street; a man who, in fact, as it turned out . . . he'd been a child molester, and the police had just questioned him, and he had walked out of one of the precincts and had crossed several streets, and then had laid down with his head under a truck wheel that was stopped at a street light. The truck started up; it ran over his head, and killed him; and I had really never in my life seen anything like that before; and it was so dramatic and terrifying that the instant the car drove up and there lay this man with his crushed head in the street I began filming in a very direct way, which is, say, opposite of directed. So that was an important moment. And then another thing happened that was very important. I had brought along with me . . . I had just bought a fifteen-inch lens, and I had brought it along with me; I don't even know why I brought all this equipment with me to Pittsburgh, but I had this fifteen-inch lens with me in the car and I had never used it, and in fact the instructions on it said: you do not use this lens without a tripod. Because a fifteen-inch lens is such a telephoto that if you stand stockstill, just your heart beating will create an earthquake in the image; it will look like the whole scene is shaking; and so I got out and started photographing this body in the street, and then the homicide department arrived and one of the homicide officers pointed at me and said, "No, no; you don't take pictures of the body." And this terrified me of course because we weren't even officially supposed to be in this car at this point, and so I went back into the back seat of the patrol car, but I had such a desperate need to confront this scene in the streets that I screwed on that fifteen-inch lens, which would give me enough telephoto to shoot from the car, and I didn't have any tripod equipment, and I didn't care, but I did have this behind me, that I had spent years, in fact all my film-making life, practicing hand-holding camera, and made many films with hand-held camera, so I knew a great deal about it, just even instinctively; and I knew that if this image was going to shake continually, from my heartbeat even if I was standing still, then I must make counteractive movements to that heartbeat, and dance with my own heart beating and with my own breathing patterns, with this huge lens, and I did that, and most people are astonished, even professionals who use this equipment all the time are astonished that a fifteen-inch lens could be hand-held and create such an articulation of movement. In fact, there are many discoveries of sight that fell out of this; I really feel now that the reason that the whole world doesn't shake in our vision as we walk along is because the muscles of the eye make counteractive movements which smooth out the passage of movement. Because, really, what we're doing, we're walking along, and this eye is a jelly, and it's quivering continually, with our heartbeat, with our walking, with our breathing, with anything that happens, any movement we make. And what I did was to make an articulate dance with that possibility, with this lens; so that was a great discovery, that it could be done. So, then I went on and filmed with them two days, two and a half days, and came back and finished the film called *eyes*. I remember that that whole last day I had running thru my mind: *Polis is eyes,* and if so, these are the public eyes, in that same sense that we speak of the detective as the private eye, and that was crucial to that film.

So at this point they asked me what I'd like to film next in Pittsburgh, and up to then I didn't really realize what I was into here, and I thought that I was really trying to get a fix on the city, and do it by strata as Ed Dorn said, and as he also said about this form of shooting, he said, *yes, shoot first, ask questions later:* what seemed to be the premise of what I was currently doing, and to get a fix on the city, but it didn't really turn out to be that I was trying to get a fix on the city. I mean, I said, "Oh well, I'd like to do a hospital, I'd like to do lawyers, politicians, gangsters even if possible," a kind of simple-minded notion, but I did emphasize hospitals because that was something I had had a lot of experience with, and I wanted to see what this form of shooting that was evolving in me would do in a confrontation with a place that I had spent a lot of time in; I've been sick a lot in hospitals, almost died several times in hospitals. This turned out to be very very difficult to arrange. Hospitals are very uptight about having anybody photograph anything in them, but finally, after months of negotiation through the Carnegie Museum and through Mike Chikiris' efforts through the newspaper and so on, they managed to arrange that I could film in West Penn. Hospital. So I flew back there at that time and I made that film; that took about ten days, and it went right through many different rooms and aspects of the hospital, including open heart surgery, and very often in this I used the fifteen-inch lens, though not always, but the biggest, the greatest moments occurred again . . . and thus a further miracle occurred, what seems miraculous to me . . . when I was filming the open heart surgery for instance, I was using the fifteen-inch lens, but I was backed up and I was standing on a ladder to get back as far from the actual surgery as possible, so I could get focused, because you can't focus . . . particularly with the thing shut down you need, oh, twenty, thirty feet to focus a fifteen-inch lens; it doesn't come into focus unless you're that far back; so I couldn't get back quite far enough to use the lens, and I wanted that kind of articulation, of the hand-held telephoto lens, in that open heart surgery; and so I found myself unscrewing the lens, and when you unscrew the lens, with each fraction of an inch you get more and more focal length, or it gets closer and closer to you; so finally the lens was off of the camera. I was not only hand-holding the camera with a fifteen-inch lens; I was hand-holding the lens by itself, anywhere from a quarter inch to an inch-and-a-half away from the gate, depending on that part of the surgery I was shooting, with that much space between the lens and the camera, the camera in one hand, the lens in the other. Fortunately I was in a dark corner; otherwise light would have poured in from the side; and so that gave me another mobility; to focus it by moving my hand ever so slightly forward and back and around I had a tremendous control of focus. But I was using almost the strength of what they say a madman has; I was so disturbed by the heart surgery that I had a strength I couldn't repeat for you now unless I had some similar urgency; but it was possible to do it, and the best footage came from that, really, what anyone would say is a totally impossible photographic situation. And once again I learned very much about the eyes from this footage, how they move muscularly, what permits our sight muscularly; and that film was called *Deus Ex*, most especially because I knew . . . again I quoted Charles Olson in my statements on the film because one thing that went thru my mind very often while shooting *Deus Ex* was Charles' poem on meeting death; you know that poem, how he confronts the figure of death; a man came around a bush on an island, and for some reason this was a total image of meeting death, casually; neither man mentions it: that sense was what pervaded the hospital.

Then they asked what I'd like to do next, and I said . . . newspapers . . . or football; and somehow I couldn't develop any interest in myself about either of those subjects. I was still operating under that stupid idea that I was doing the city by strata. So they were trying to arrange with the newspapers, and the newspapers were on strike . . . there's really only one newspaper in Pittsburgh; there are two, but they are really controlled by the same interests, and they were both on strike. Then Sally Dixon, who really did most of the arranging for all this (she's the head of the film department at Carnegie Museum); she and Mike together really made all of this possible. Well, they kept trying to arrange and wondering whether the newspaper would go off strike, and thinking of football, and so on, and then it turned out that other film-makers were coming to Pittsburgh after me, and Sally had then begun to offer this same possibility to other film-makers, and Hollis Frampton came, and shot some footage in steel mills, and then he told Sally he wanted to do autopsy because he needed images of autopsy for his long work in progress *The Clouds of Magellan;* and when Sally mentioned it here in this kitchen last summer, I said, "Oh gee;

yeah, that's something I really have to do," but I said, "I'm more interested in doing, like, the funeral parlor." As it fell out, what was arranged was the coroner's office. And I mean it's so mysterious how these things fall into place; I cannot explain it; but obviously now all three of these films go together; they are a trilogy that go in a direct line toward the last film, and so much so that I have no idea if there's anything else I intend to shoot in Pittsburgh, or in cities, or even in this form. So because of these strange circumstances, it evolved because the newspapers were on strike still when I arrived in Pittsburgh, but the coroner's office had been willing that I could photograph there. And I took on the coroner's office. In fact, it bothered me so much that that's what I wanted to photograph that I sort of lied about it; I kind of kept saying, well, I'm really doing this because actually Hollis was supposed to have arrived somewhere in here, and for reasons of his own, or troubles of his own, he was delayed; so I said, I'm sort of filling in for Hollis, because he had arranged with the coroner's office, and so I would go down and fulfill that arrangement; I mean I invented outrageous lies to pretend that I was forced into filming at the . . . well, they weren't lies, in the sense that whatever internal thing was driving me certainly made the rest of me feel quite forced into a situation that I would never choose to enter without a camera. And so, there I was, in the coroner's office. I began filming what's called an external autopsy, that is, where they don't cut anybody open. And so that day that's all I did, and that was hard enough for me to take; I'd never been that close to a dead human being before. Then the next morning turned out to be Saturday morning, I mean Sunday morning, and they had told me, you should come down Sunday morning because there's so many people that die on Saturday night. So I was more or less obligated; that's the way I felt about it; actually I was driven, for my own desperate reasons, to go down that Sunday morning, early, and suddenly walk into a room where there are several murder victims, some suicides, people who died by violent accident; I walked into this room where the day before I had only photographed a . . . and everywhere I turned . . . suddenly I was surrounded by . . . slaughter! And so I just began photographing desperately. I really overshot because I was so desperate to keep always the camera going; every moment I stopped photographing I really felt like I might faint, or burst into tears, or come apart, or something like that.

Grossinger: Was it like filming *Window Water Baby Moving?*

Brakhage: Well, with *Window Water Baby Moving* also, well, in the first place I was by strange circumstances forced into it; Jane wanted me to be in attendance to photograph the birth; well, she wanted me to be in attendance first of all, and that, in those days, was very hard to arrange anywhere. They did not want husbands watching the birth, for the reason that many husbands faint at that moment, or they interfere, and they come apart, and they faint and fall down and crack their head and then sue the hospital; very often, if there's a bad relationship between the man and woman, the woman will, in the midst of childbirth, curse the husband in a way that she never would otherwise. So, for these simple reasons, plus the hospital policies throughout the land at that time, they did not permit husbands to watch births. So Jane's tack for getting this permission was suggesting that I photograph it. Well, she went to the doctor with the idea of photographing it, and again a strange coincidence, when the doctor learned that I was a photographer, before Jane had even said anything, he said, "Say, I've always wanted a film made of a birth. Do you think he would be interested in photographing it?" Then we tried to work it out with the hospital; they wouldn't permit it, so finally this doctor was intent enough on having a film made that he agreed to deliver the baby at home.

Well, it sort of looks like . . . in these cases it looks like fate had arranged, or circumstances external to myself had arranged, but in fact, as one now knows from my almost desperate attention to birth, and the many birth films I've made, that I'm obsessed with childbirth . . . perhaps for reasons of something of my own birth; I don't know. I'm an adopted child; there might have been some tragedy, death of the mother, or who knows what; I'll never know what my birth was like, and that in itself may be the center of the obsession. Anyway, it's like the other circumstances in that way. Also, I remember that when they told me about the police car, that I could go into the police car, I was suddenly terrified. I didn't want to. I felt that by opening my big mouth and asking to be sent to the moon, I was getting my comeuppance. And here I was being forced into a patrol car, which was scary enough for me. Also, with the hospital. I remember day after day, as Mike would take me down to that hospital, I would say things like, "Oh God, let's go back; I'm going to pack and go home." I didn't want to face that hospital anymore. Again, feeling forced into something by external machinery that you yourself have set in motion. But, of course, in all cases the films themselves say that it was desperately necessary, and in the case of *Window Water Baby Moving*, then once I started photographing, I knew for that first birth I could never have stood it in that room, without passing out or something, if I hadn't had a camera. I'm not so constituted to be able to take an experience like that, at least the first time, without camera in hand, which is the major reason why I have a camera in hand, what my life's work is. In fact, there's very little that's understandable to me about life, or even bearable, except the seeing of it. I have managed my whole sight by making films.

Grossinger: Let me just cut in to ask how you would relate the possible film of the moon to the films made in Pittsburgh? Is that part of an imaginable sequence?

Brakhage: Actually, Jane and I were talking about it this morning because of Creeley's letter. He had mentioned this business that here we had set men on the moon, and the real image we have of the moon in the movies is Melies'.

Melies will dominate everyone's thought of the moon until what the hell...
until we actually send an artist there. Because his desperation to go to the
moon was real enough that he built the moon to go to, and the machinery to
photograph going to it, and the invented rocket ship that goes there, and the
imaginary creatures that are there, and everything. I mean he had that
urgency, and that is, in fact, what art is. And then all the science fiction
movies watered down Melies' vision of the moon, until finally Neil Armstrong,
as a kid, saw it somewhere in some serial or Saturday afternoon theatre, and
then he got out his camera and made yet another watered-down version when
he was there. So we got that watered-down version, and everyone sat and
watched on the television. I mean Jane was saying, "my mother said of course,
with tears in her eyes, how great it was that man was walking on the moon." I
said, "yes, yes," but the truth is that everyone said that, but obviously they
didn't mean it... because NASA didn't get the money. The whole thing fell flat
as a pancake, which *even* Norman Mailer knows... and so everyone knows it in
fact. Her sense of it was: well, yes, but think of all the problems of sending an
artist to the moon. So we argued about that a little bit; and I mean Jane knows
about the problems of living with an artist, so she knows very well what she's
talking about when you say, like, you're going to bottle up an artist with an
astronaut in a capsule and they're going to move two-and-a-half days away
from the earth and...

Grossinger: In that kind of police car!

Brakhage: Yes. Well, you know, it's a dangerous situation; I mean of course.
But the point is, I mean, if he has the urgency to get to the moon, I mean he will
certainly behave himself, and I'm the living proof of it, you know. She said:
Well, you might have asthma you know. What if you had asthma? There's
moondust to affect your sinuses. Or you'll get up there and you won't want to
come back. All these things are true, but they're true because the artist,
particularly when he's working, is really the prime example of human concentration. He would be real there. And, of course, anything that's real is considered a problem by NASA, or the United States government, or any government, or all these powers that be. But, sure, just as well as any dog or creature
in the forest confronted with a necessity... any creature will hold itself in
check to accomplish that necessity, and so an artist can go to the moon, could
be put in, and would try very hard to do everything he could to accomplish
getting there and getting images of it, and getting back. Otherwise the animal
gets cheated. And they *are animals*. That's all they are. I don't mean that
there's something else that is getting its. The minute the animal human is
cheated, that's it. We are animals. And the artist can only work on this level.
This is what the work comes out of. If I was forced into it, if they took me up on
it, it would be the same as going to the hospital, I'd be scared to death, but I'd
do it. It would be a chance to actually give people an image, a new image, and I

don't mean because of the subject matter, but because, I mean, a man would be going there, behaving personally, and therefore we would get an image. The trouble is: artists are the only ones that are forced, while working, to behave personally. And that's apropos how I named the third film. I named it *The Act of Seeing with One's Own Eyes*; and the reasons for that name are: that I looked up "autopsy" and discovered much to my amazement and delight that it comes from the Greek word "autopsis," which translates out most specifically as: "the act of seeing with one's own eyes." And that was exactly the reason that I went through that experience. I had to go through, mind you, the *act* of seeing, something different than just seeing, in fact something, I wouldn't say opposite, but quite other than *The Art of Vision*. I very consciously took that very dictionary term because I knew that it would stand as a . . . again, not a polar opposite, but an extreme other than *The Art of Vision*. Gee, it's hard to say. The word "act". . . . Again, I'm reverting with my slow mind to when I was a little quicker this morning writing to Creeley. After that conversation on the moon with Jane I went to the phonograph and I put on Schubert's 6th Quartet. And it begins with a beautiful base: mmmmmmmmm. It isn't the deepest base note he could give us; it isn't even the fullest; it isn't a Russian basso's base, but a base note beginning that's for maximum vibrancy. You can tell that he went for maximum vibrancy. Well, that's an act. In fact, he gives us that base note, and then everything that comes after seems like it comes out of that base note; that base vibrancy seems to have enough vibrancy that it would hatch any other note. That's an act. The music there is acting. . . as if the beginning of itself were outside you, or outside itself. It was the base, right? . . . and then that everything that follows can then fall within. You have already heard something of it so it can be within you. And this to me is very much the sense of why that word "act" is important in there. Because actually the beginning is never the first; it's impossible, as Creeley had written me, for people to recognize something that they haven't already seen. So they have to have seen it, and then comes that appropriating it which we call recognition. And when any piece of art pretends, like this is the beginning, and it's prerecognition, it is of course an act. And so, therefore, all three of those films are premised on acts. Whereas *The Art of Vision* is continually beginning anew, so that it's very much more jazzy and very much more acceptable artwise in this century. You can accept it as a work of art much easier than you can something that's premised on document. It was easy for people to pick up on interstices in music, or mathematic progressions, or melody, like Beethoven, like Mozart, but it was more difficult to pick up on a man who was basically premised on timbre.

Grossinger: In what way did you come to the perception of the birth-sex-death relationship in your work, which seems a very accurate take on yourself?
Brakhage: Well, that was just on the phone to you yesterday. I was kind of

being flippant, but, like all flippancy, there was a revelation in it. You remember I wrote years ago, in *Metaphors on Vision*, my subject matter is essentially birth, sex, and death, and the search for God. Of course, I've been involved in all three all along. While I was making *Window Water Baby Moving*, I was photographing *Sirius Remembered*, and I was very shortly thereafter editing *The Dead*. But these had to do with the *ideas* of death. That's just like *The Art of Vision* has to do with an idea, much more than these new films, and that's why critics can write about the *Dog Star Man* or *The Art of Vision*, because it's premised on ideas, which are different than acts. Whereas *Songs* have received very little critical attention because they are, from *Song 1*, as Kelly nailed it, an event, and from *Songs* I become very concerned with event as something totally distinct from drama. And then when you get to the word act, which has been so fucked up in our time, particularly in the movies, I mean that no one can hardly understand what you mean; if you say that they think you mean you've got...actors?, or you treated these policemen as though they were actors? Well, in a way, that was true. In fact, when you see *eyes*, you will see that the scenes are so photographed that you almost can't believe that these aren't actors. And of course that's exactly right, because they're all actors, like we all are. And they are acting their particular role, which is a rather formidable role, and they are acting it...out, to the full. And that's what interests me. Again, Kelly. I get my cues from Kelly here. He said: it's not wrong to act if you really act it out to the full. We've been so disturbed by the word "act," and acting, particularly in art and film, or on stage for that matter, that there's an absolute avoidance of it; and suddenly I embrace the monster. Yes, these are acts. These people are all acting. In fact, the dead on the table are frozen in postures of act, action; that's a nice pun, considering that they're dead. But their last postures are there as solid as a photograph; they're there so solid in fact that... as part of the autopsy they cut the back of the head, and they lift the scalp completely over the face, and bend the face almost in half, in order to cut open the skull, and get the brain out, and in fact what they're, interestingly enough, most after is the pineal gland, that gland that the mystics all say is the door that you push out to get the third eye and so on; that's the gland that contains the most information of any part of the body on most people's deaths, as to the exact cause of it. The dead are so frozen in that last posture that they've done all this, then they pull... they reach over and they pull the scalp back into place, unbend the face, and the face flips absolutely back into that posture it had before they did all this. So that I had the immediate perception that the first masks made in the world must have been the actual faces of the dead, by perhaps the victors, or maybe even the relatives, because this face is so rigid and so rubbery that you can lift it off and clearly wear it. And what's that but the supreme and final act; and it's so whether the people died in their sleep or died violently, or whatever. A man shot in the chest with a shotgun blast carried the whole impact of the horror of that on his face, and it remained there after they had bent the face in half and then put it back, the beautiful young girl who died in her sleep: they both had expressions; their eyes are partly open; the face is lifted almost off the eyes as it's bent over, and yet when it snaps back into place, the pools, the little jellies of the eyes fall into the proper holes...in the case of that girl that almost reduced me to...I mean I almost fainted when I first saw them cutting her open, and she died from having three drinks, came home, was restless, took a few pills, and died in her sleep. Well, that's some of what I have to say about "act." Of course, also, one thing I didn't photograph in the morgue, because it would have actually distracted from what else I was really concentrating on, was that the coroner, and the men who helped him perform, and the med students who perform these autopsies: they act continually...humorous roles...one of them said he always wanted to be Fred Astaire, and he liked to tap-dance around the corpses, and that would, in fact, be another film, or an extension of this one. But of course that's hard to get at too because while they do that they make these outrageous and very bad jokes. Also, they treat the bodies with great tenderness, and, in fact, I had the feeling again and again that many of these poor people probably were more tenderly treated lying on the table being cut apart than in their lives. They refer to the people by name, by first name, very familiarly...oh, well, that's impossible to describe, it's such a...

Grossinger: You referred earlier to the fact that many of your past supporters, even those as central as P. Adams and Jonas, have objected to the recent films, from the police film onwards. Is it, in some ways, as simple as the fact that you made a film about police that didn't criticize them in some obvious way?

Brakhage: That may be part of it. They had already decided what type of films Brakhage made, and they didn't want to be contradicted by anyone like the film-maker himself. I mean, they wanted *Son of Dog Star Man, Dog Star Man Returns, Dog Star Man Meets the Wolf Man,* and I simply wasn't doing that anymore.

Grossinger: Okay, well that's good. I think that's enough.

MANIFEST

16 August 1974

Let me warn once more and then be silent, dark time coming.

(The so-called "dark ages" simply thus/that folk forgot how to dye and thereby came clothed dulled shades gray shags of animal black etcetera, even kings lacking purple —longlivetheking!—till the secret thought was won again and juice of rock wrung and again the fabric of daily life was as flowers.)

Let me then warn that those who would/could restrict our perimeters have drawn lines; and they are these:

that all which is personally perceptible be suspect

(as is immeasurable Color accorded "secondary citizenship" within the hierarchy Science)

that that which is person-privately shareable, trala!, be circumscribed -sized -shaped and weighted by/as commune *all*, Tradit!

(as it is with Sex past tense now taught future participle)

that The Personae, that greek form whereby innerdividual might surface in The Pub. true semblence-of-self, be thought as false as "mask" meaning "screen" to hide or lie behind.

(as The Truth comes to be made to mean the agreed-upon-fact)

that a person, I, be finally unthinkable

(as Art is).

I take it that The Arts afford the last ungoverned public surfacing of Person and constitute thus the greatest threat to those who feel they could/should enslave sensibility,

just as I know Sex to be that first/last move person-to-person beyond governmentality—

truths always, yet!, personally *colored* beyond measurability...

those who rule hate these truths;

this my warning:

: that we not be lulled, as was Garcia Lorca whose last words to his cell-mate were, "Don't worry—they don't shoot poets."

: that we not be fooled by governmental Sup. for Artists

(it's U.S.ence simply this/that:

(1) having made patronage tax deductable, all act of Personal Gen. was subvert to greed.

: (2) having made tax deduct. more and more than difficult Xcept as inst. to inst. shuffles money—see so-called Tax Reform Bill '69—Person was jettisoned in the transact altogether... artists effectively herded into UNIverse Cities or 'left' (UNsupported)out,

: (3) it managed that ONLY bureaucratic Wash. could pick up the rest/"right" cards upon the tabled Arts

so that

: (4) these sacred first/last acts of inner-dependence would be played as if 'twere hobby or per-choice escapist occupation— useful to keep the increasingly leisured discontents from making bombs... (the funds most natch going thus to education, workshops, art fairs, sports-sort competitions and the like).

Anybody for free-verse circumspect finger-only painting homey-movie build-it-yrself archycraft sing-along play act?

Artists!, like they say: let's have *at* it!—all pretense (pre the tendency) we can teach 'em how-to-do-it half-aesthetically...The Muses be made Amuse(govern)ment! "It's a living," say the walking dead. "If you can't beat 'em?"...Fuck 'em.

Most hopeful sign: the *real* young (trapped as I too much am in these schools for *act*ual Youth) those few of them who *really* call my attention (most usually first by the shyness of 'em) do very deliberately shunt publight and all complicity as could be tabbed "a movement" (thus demeaned); and after a good look to and at me, and my contemporaries in The Arts, they sympathetically declare they'll keep it/art absolutely private and/or share theirs only as one would love among one's friends.

Thus I'm coming to believe that as it is in the hopechests and closets of Russ. & China so it will be here for similarity's sake—world's social norm this 20th Cent.

THE SEEN

Remarks following a screening of *The Text of Light* at the San Francisco Art Institute November 18, 1974.
For Robert Duncan and Jess.

I have believed for many years and come to believe more and more the older I get that the art is given as a gift through persons' urgency. And that the responsibility of the artist is to be personal enough. That this gift, this that he or she could not arrive at along a train of logical thought can just come to exist along a line of . . . shaping itself according to the extent of the maker's experience and no more. That is, that it not pitch over into ego or that a maker begins to shape him or herself according to cleverness or whatever. Certainly there is no work that more confirms me in that sense than *The Text of Light*. For me it is most clearly of all things a gift given to me to make. I really have found only two things to say about it that illuminate what I was involved in; one is almost as a prayer bead or a constant reassurance I returned to Johannes Scotus Erigena's "All that is is light." Secondly, William Blake's "To find a world in a grain of sand." These two things were very helpful in actually a very practical sense to help me hold to the promises of this film and fulfill them at least to the best of the ability that I have. So beyond that I really haven't anything, any clarities, and will look forward to some of your questions expanding my thought about this work. I don't in any sense think of it as my own and to an extraordinary sense I never was able to kid myself that it was my own.
Question: How did you make it?
Brakhage: I was trying very hard to make a portrait. I am getting involved in portraits. I have known a man since high school and he subsequently became a multimillionaire. So for years we were separated in that way that millionaires and artists are separated. Finally we overcame that separation, and as this is an art school I think this is a valuable piece of information how we did it. I declared to him that I would never under any circumstances accept any money from him; and in such a firm and full way that he knew I meant it. Then we could be friends. To a man with a great deal of money, a poor man is a bottomless pit. So from that point on it became very interesting, the relationship, because his world was totally distinct fom mine and was quite a mystery. In fact the American business-man is a real bogyman. So along the line of doing the Pittsburgh trilogy on police, hospitals, and at the morgue, I was determined to get a portrait of an American businessman if possible, and that it would be a rare

First issued as a small book by Zephyrus Image, 1976

opportunity, and that here was someone I had known since high school and there was a chance. So I was trying to photograph him in his office and he, terribly embarrassed, was blowing great clouds of Cuban cigar smoke and obscuring everything and I was failing. And it was interesting because I had a macro lens on, which I was using as a kind of distance lens. It has a bellows. And I was failing and the camera slumped forward and the lens bent sort of with the bellows and it seemed hopeless. But I have the habit to always look into the lens before moving the camera. So I looked and saw what seemed to me at first a forest. And I thought, my god, where is this coming from? And looked more close. And I called my friend around and he looked and was astonished and then I looked again and it had changed and a stream was running through it. Then I saw that the lens was pointed at his ash tray. So I began taking single frames of his ash tray. And he is so lovely a man he accommodated this. In fact he's so witty a man that he invited people to go on with conference meetings on business & what not & I went right on photographing this ash tray. His office also is such a location & construction that it has sun all day long. He has windows all round, from dawn to sunset there is wonderful sun pouring into this office. So I just began moving from window to window of this office, and Helen, his secretary, got very excited and brought other pieces of glass; which at first, only not to hurt her feelings, I set kind of around the ash tray. Then I noticed that if I touched the very outer-most piece of glass out here, it very often changed what was in the ash tray. Then someone brought in the grand . . . so proudly, brought in a crystal ball. And this I put in the center of the ash tray. And there was finally a collection of very fine crystal all around the ash tray, and sometimes a little bit in the ash tray, and this way and that way and the crystal ball, and all this was in the sun of course, just shined beautifully and I went on clicking away, most of the film a frame at a time throughout that summer.

Once I remember somebody came to a business conference and they walked through the room and he said to Gordon, kind of very, "What's he doing?" And Gordon without a break in stride just said, "He's photographing our ash trays." This began to help him in business because people became so confused and disturbed at what was this mystery that he had the business edge on them. So it worked out fine for everybody. Except I made one error which I must point out. I became so obsessed with this ash tray that I bent over all summer and ruptured one, possibly two disks. So that's why I have this cane. And anyway it was worth it.

Question: I saw you one of the last times you were here and you were showing *The Act of Seeing with One's Own Eyes.* And before showing it you said it was nothing to be afraid of, it was only about light hitting objects and bouncing back and seeing it with your eyes. And I was interested in why after using light in such a very exquisite, definitive way you wanted to use it in a way that was so unarticulated, that was so abstract.

Brakhage: Well, she is telling me in the form of a question that she thinks my film is unarticulated with respect to light. And I must disagree, that this film is called *The Text of Light* because in that ash tray I found a way to create an equivalent of many behaviors of light that I have observed, that are not recognized by science, and in fact I suppose would be considered mad by some of the less generous scientists of our time. But I will name a few that therefore, that because they are not recognized by science we are not trained to observe; and not very many people have seen these, though some have.

I have seen that before a rainstorm there are light-like streaks that come down through the air that are metaphors of rain though they are not wet. In fact have held my hand and some of them come through that hand with no sense of moisture and of course the fact that the streak goes right through the hand is itself clear that it's not raining. And then rain will follow. And because I live in a place where many clouds pass over and most do not rain, I had a way to check myself. Could I tell within 30 seconds to a minute if it was going to rain or not and invariably I could because always, if that cloud was going to rain, it was preceded by these light-like . . . they would be streaks as if you would see a tiny streak of light or spark in a dark room only they would be bluish. Though they could be yellowish also. Those are interchangeable colors anyway, optically. They could be yellowish.

Then I have seen light-like phosphorescence move horizontally along the ground, as a wind. And I have seen it pool, as if a pool of phosphorescent image. Then I have seen sometimes that streaks shoot up from these pools or from the very ground. Again light-like and ephemeral like a phosphorescence in daylight which makes shapes, shapes of plants. And I have seen this quite a bit in the spring on just dirt and I have seen a similarity of plant grow up in this place. I have seen—as Kirlian photography almost touches on now, and maybe does—I have seen leaves spark or emit a spark-like emanation at their edges that are offshoots directly of the veins within that leaf, and therefore as that leaf then grows, do create a metaphor previous to the actual extension of these veins. These things I have seen, one, because I have been involved with seeing all my life and I'm really open to seeing all there is when I'm well. Two, because somewhere along the line I realized something that was constricting my sight in this pursuit: which was my training in this society in renaissance perspective—in that form of seeing we could call "westward-hoing man's," which is to try to clutch a landscape or the heavens or whatever. That is a form of sight which is aggressive & which seeks to make of any landscape a piece of real estate. In fact the irony that we have so named property our Real Estate demonstrates the western limitation. I would like to see science make a check of the eyes, of the musculature of eastern peoples, let's say as distinct from ours. I believe it would be quite distinct. This search for this form of grasping sight has created a powerful musculature to permit that. And too as is necessary to permit us to drive on these throughways and to move with this mobility among these constructions supportive of that renaissance perspective.

Well, that pursuit is wonderful in itself, and it is of course my native pursuit, but on the other hand it has the problem that it is exclusive of all other kinds of seeing. So what I'm trying to get at, in order to see these things I have to be in an extraordinary relaxed state of seeing. Then all other kinds of seeing become immediately possible and of great involvement with the light of course. And I believe, not only do I believe with Johannes Scotus Erigena that "All that is is light," but I even think that a wonderful thing has happened in our time and passed almost unnoticed. That a dialog beginning with him and reaching a public prominence in the 13th century in the writings of Grosseteste.... Dig that name. The first man whom they tried to put down with the name Bighead. So he picked it right up and made them understand that it was so. And then later Duns Scotus and then of course Francis Bacon who is better known ... who came and tidied up a whole lot of things and therefore is better known. But this brilliance of these Light Philosophies, English philosophers, who because of their feelings stated in words that: *thought was illumination.* I mean the last run down of what they did is in the comic strips when somebody's supposed to have an idea: they make a lightbulb. But they felt their thinking was electrical or light-like. Now hundreds of years have passed and finally an enormous construct of science which would seem to be antagonistic to such thinking has permitted Niels Bohr and Riemann and of course Albert Einstein to prove, within that structure, that matter is still light. Light held in a bind. So what this ash tray permitted me to do was to photograph equivalence of things seen and processes of evolution, of ephemerality of light taking shape and finally taking a very solid seeming shape. Along a line of exactitude. When the film is seen on this level, it's even pedantic.

Question: I was wondering if you actually saw the spectrum through the viewfinder, through the lens?
Brakhage: Yes, I saw very much what you saw on the screen, only it was better of course. Because in the meantime it has passed through...only what Eastman Kodak film would accept has been taken down, only what

the lab didn't botch has been left on the strip. Then it similarly has had to
pass through an interneg, and finally come to a print. So if you enjoyed
this, then go look in an ash tray, or something. Because it's much better.
How it's been able to pass through me so that it can be called a 'text' is that I
have been true to my appreciation & understanding of light operating in
every day life in these fashions, i.e. preceding matter. I even believe it
precedes animal motion. I have not seen that enough to be sure of it. But I
believe that there is a form or at least certain kinds of gestures are preceded
by a flash of light-like emanation. I mean this is very exciting to me, in fact
it's...you see I've been reading Johannes Scotus Erigena and his later
'echo', Duns Scotus, since Ezra Pound gave them to me at 18 or something. But it seems we are so trained in this society to read something and
keep that quite separate from the living experience. So I thought it was
wonderful but I didn't believe it. And then finally I came to see. And now
I have had, through this ash tray, the opportunity to present an equivalent
of it. And if you think about it, this is the most normal film in the world.
Because here I am with a macro lens, which is a piece of glass here, and one
stuck way out here, or several. And they are never more than an inch or
two away from a crystal ash tray which is surrounded by other glass, so
where does the lens end? That *all* could be considered a lens which is
photographing the sun; and that's all that makes these shapes on the screen.
And that's very exciting.

Question: My question has to do with what you said earlier. You said it had
to do with a relaxed way of seeing and I was trying to get back to what you
are now saying about seeing the ash tray. In my mind it seems the relaxed
way of seeing comes about through the high excitement way of seeing.
Brakhage: Well I would agree with you because I don't, by "relaxed,"
mean flaccid. And I avoid the word "meditation" because it has certain
Eastern connotations which in this society are usually misunderstood. So
we need another word. What I'm doing in photographing this ash tray for
instance, I'm sitting for hours to get 30 seconds of film. I'm sitting
watching what's happening and clicking a frame, and sitting and watching, and further than that, I had shot several hundred feet and they seemed
dead. They didn't reflect at all my excitement and emotion and feeling.
They had no anima in them. Except for two or three shots where the lens
which was on a tripod, pressed against the desk, had jerked. Those were
just random, but that gave me the clue. What I began doing was always
holding the camera in hand. For hours. Clicking. Waiting. Seeing what
the sun did to the scene. As I saw what was happening in the frame to these
little particles of light, changing, I would shift the camera very slightly.
If you want to know how slightly you have to realize I was never photo-

graphing in an area bigger than this 4th fingernail. You couldn't tap the camera. It had to be moved by a quivering attention of the hand. That took maybe 13 or 14 moves over a period of ten minutes. Then to get that in mind: what *it* was doing and changing and how I was dancing with it had to be extended in memory; one, how that would come out at 24 frames a second and two, as to, was the dance real?

And all the time I was doing this I had to have a friendly argument in my mind with Jordan Belson who I knew would hate just exactly this. He would say, Oh wonderful what it is, but why is it jerky? Or why not centered? Or, you know . . . and to hold myself together I would say, No, Jordon, it has to be this way. So I, I owe him very much. He sustained me in that way a beautiful argument can, because it was very much in his territory. I mean this film is very much on his side of the street.

Though there is another man. I want to mention that the film is dedicated to Jim Davis. I suddenly one night had this overwhelming feeling . . . I got mad because someone had written an article on many people working with the so-called abstract film, which term I don't believe in anyway. But they had not mentioned Jim Davis, and he has always resisted being mentioned. It is true, he's a very shy man. He had lived all his life, the last 20 years at 44 Wiggins St., in Princeton, N.J., very ill with diabetes and with a lot of back trouble and in bed the last decade. With his great construct before him, so that from his bed he could photograph whenever his constructs created a light pattern that seemed real to him, refracted light. He was literally the first man who had shown me refracted light on film. So I called him up and asked him if I could dedicate the film to him. And I was surprised that he didn't say no; but I'm so glad I did because he was dead a week later. Almost totally ignored. So he is someone to be looked at now that he's dead.

Question: I just want to follow that up . . . I think that most people are part-time film makers. And it's the moment of high excitement in which you realize you've got something there. As I watched this film for example, I have very severe night blindness, as I watched this film I began to realize how important this night blindness is to me.
Brakhage: Oh yes, wonderful.
Question: I was able to see a lot of things I never associated with that. It's the high excitement of the moment of capturing something which is so critically important to pass on to people. It's not to analyse in a philosophical way.
Brakhage: Yes, I appreciate that: only it depends on how you use information. I mean, most people misuse philosophy worse than any other discipline in this time. And yet, I am very deficient in reading philosophy.

Part of that, I was pre-prejudiced that this was the dullest area on earth by a series of very dull teachers. And only a very dear friend, Forrest Williams, who happens to be here tonight, has maybe saved me; and I would like to pass on to you, in philosophy you can find the most practical information in the world. You see, this line, "All that is is light" as translated by Pound & threads its way through the *Cantos* — many thoughts have moved along this line as if it's a very solid string. So it led me to the possibilities of this film. Now you say other people in the room want to make films and what will lead them? I don't know because that is truly a personal matter. And that's what excites me. Because it took me all these years to realize I could never be anything but personal. So then I had to ask myself, What did I think I was being those other times? Well . . . I thought I was being a good boy, and behaving myself, as I had been trained to do, and was continually encouraged for it, in fact threatened by every institute I've passed through. Be it school or job or whatever. And of course constantly by the overwhelming power of the government that is . . . I mean . . . the only contender left in the newspapers for equal space with the government, however stupid it becomes, is the sports field. And both of them move inexorably like a Chinese water torture against any concept of person. Sports move against it by putting the whole emphasis on teamwork to destroy the concept of play. That is the most vicious of all. Because little kids get that first. Play is extensive & absolutely individual until it becomes part of a game and then the game is created to pitch two masses of people against each other in competition. Then the government —I mean I don't need to speak about the government in this year, my god, but . . .

Someone asked me recently, Why have you struggled so hard to see and ended up so different from your neighbors . . . or something . . . who do you think you are? I said quite truly, To save my life! I knew they were trying to kill me and so when I first knew this I developed asthma at one year old. Which gave my mother a lot of other things to do. She was trying to use me because she had adopted me to save the marriage; and I'd failed. So she had for her efforts a child constantly wheezing. Then I moved to protect my skin surface—I was very fat, so I was again buffered against all this use as much as possible. Then I developed sinus trouble which shut off the nose. Earaches, glasses. Get the picture? By the time I was six . . . I escaped sports because I developed a hernia. The problem was that life wasn't worth living with all these tactics. So the next thing to do was get it all together and stop all this disease. In this society I think, for many, illness has been the only way to get through. And it may be one reason I have this back problem at this moment. Because the pressure is very heavy on me at this time. This may be. And if so, that's great because then I'll come to terms with it and find some other way and get rid of that too.

It has been — what I'm trying to say is that is has been a desperate struggle to keep alive. And to keep alive to me meant that I had to be personal, which is all that I could be. But then, having said all that, I want to say also, persons also wish to be social. So then the social inclinations come out. Like, I can understand that persons want to drive on the right side of the road or the left side so they don't run into each other. And I understand also of course, finally came with great difficulty to beginning to understand the miracle of loving, another. And that was very hard with this route that I took. That may have a lot to do with why I am an artist. And by "artist" I mean someone who makes things under/in trance. Things which can be looked at over and over again, or experienced again & again. Will last. Otherwise you can throw out the term 'art' and I don't care. And I think I came to be able to make that because I had, was so locked in, that I was exploding with things. With feelings and thoughts that I wanted to get out. Then the way to get them out was the same as, I mean ... Morton Subotnick visited recently and told me that he thought the birth of music was the scream. Two things: the scream goes to the greatest pitch that it can, but one cannot sustain that scream. So then the tone would drop way down low to provide a bass which can be held forever. Then a scale is established in between. My sense of it was that it began with the heartbeat which was overwhelming. That some man, woman, creature had to beat upon the chest to get it out, and stamp on the ground and then found a hollow log and then stretched skin over it. And you could send it for miles. Let's make love or war or whatever. So it's always that real — the need to get something internal exteriorized; and whatever the exterior is can only be an equivalent. No drum in the world, not even a stethoscope, will actually make the sound of the heart that you hear yourself in your own ears ... and when it's pounding ... it's pounding and it may fly out of your chest and everyone else is going around and they don't *hear* it — you see. But if someone screams, people pay attention. And if they give it a form, they'll pay attention again and again. Then the miracle is, it's wonderful, this which otherwise just would be an ego-centric trick ... then people start listening to their own screams and heartbeats. Then to me, that's the point.

I fear people getting hung up over art. That is, getting excited about art and just looking at art. To me, always an expression made out of such desperation and taking such a form, and leaping beyond what that person himself could arrive at; that is being informed by what you can call the muses, or god, or the angels or the subconscious, whatever you like. But something in the work process comes through, that I am not capable of thinking along the line of thought. It seems as if it comes from elsewhere; it does not seem as if it comes from me. But it only comes, strangely and ironically, when I am being the most personal that I can be. Where I tell a story that's more unique to me, a unique story like something happening to me that nobody ever heard of happening to anybody else. Then I know more that I am a person. And that's a very strong string for the unconscious, the angels or muses to play upon.

It's caused me an awful lot of trouble, and made me very lonely that I see light behaving in ways that not very many other people see. And the ash tray, and this force that moves through such an experience gave me a way to exteriorize that. So I am very grateful.

Question: What about these flashes of light; do you ever see gestures, flashes of light, is that in the film itself?
Brakhage: No, it's not photographable.
Question: Is this in mind?
Brakhage: No, but that is an interesting question. What part of these visions are feedback fantasy, which is always just a mix, or an Irish stew of memories actually? So the mind can project out of the memory pot all kinds of mixes that do not directly reflect a creature you'll see on earth, but . . .
Question: What I'm talking about, is if you were in this last state you are talking about, would you be able to see what kind of mood I was in?
Brakhage: Well, if I were relaxed and in my home, and able to relax to that extent and see, maybe. I do see auras, is that what you mean?
Question: All the time?
Brakhage: Well, no. I have to drive on the freeways and make a living and so on. And I'm subject also to these ordinary pressures . . . the world as it is. Which socially is, in my opinion, awful. I really feel that the human animal is up against the most intensive drive ever, to stamp out any sensibility of animal life. And, ah, people being persons. And I do feel it's so serious that I think the last public surfacing of persons is through the arts. And of course now, having been unable to starve out the artists, now the government is moving to create, ah, institutes to quote help the arts end quote, and which will, to some extent, do that; but I am very fearful of what the intent is in the long run. In fact I'm not fearful at all, I know exactly what the intent is in the long run of this process. So the hope is they will be stupid—like all other forms of government—and will fail. But the intent is really . . . there is a greater fear, among those who rule, of the arts, than there is of any political opposition. Because the opposition can be, even in a revolution, can be honored. They will behave in all respects like those in power. If they get in power and succeed, they will certainly

behave like those in power. And history has shown this again and again, & how anyone can have any hope in a revolution after reading any history at all, I don't know. Hope springs eternal, but, I mean, really.... On the other hand, the extent to which people within a culture primarily recognize themselves as persons, is *not* controllable. That cannot be massed, except under real emergency. That is, except when there really is an attack on that culture which requires everyone to be massed.

Unfortunately, it is not that there are twelve dirty old men in Washington trying to destroy us all; it is that there is in most people, through a cultural inheritance, an automatic wish to be governed and to govern others. And the government...and so that's the problem. That this is a long-going thing that people tend to seem to feel that they need. The government is just the most...they're the last ones to know anything about anything anyway. But they are the symbol. They are the anchor down of this proclivity. And the arts, artists in this century seem to make the only stance against this. They do this not because they are wiser or braver or anything, but simply because no one has ever figured out how to make *a thing that will last* without being desperately personal during the making & throughout. So you just couldn't...it's inconceivable to me that it could be done any other way—though governments will try to have things done that they will try to sell as art...which are done in exactly the opposite way. So that's the struggle. And you could either regard it as very sad that you live in this time or as very interesting. I do one or the other depending on whether I think I'm going to make it or not....

Question: About personal desperation...you were saying you have to get it out. In your earliest stuff it seems like that was reflective of your repression, the things that were supressed in you...why you had those different illnesses or whatever. Now I was wondering...it doesn't seem like you're trying to say personally through yourself, maybe...or mass repressiveness...

Brakhage: No, I'm not. I don't understand mass actually, finally. I think that is just a meaningless word...though I'm confronted by it, meaningless or not. Most of the words we read in the newspapers are meaningless in that context and we are confronted by them, and they can actually cause things which will kill you. So whether they have any meaning any more or not, or especially that they don't, one still has to deal with them.

Question: No, what I mean is, you said, right, you thought your parents were going to kill you—or now you're concerned that the government or the mass will kill you.

Brakhage: No, I'm not concerned with the government killing me. I'm concerned with me killing myself. Because of this proclivity to govern. And therefore being tricked out, or responsive to, anyone else's desire to govern, of which the primary symbol might be a Texas cop some dark night. Or some name in the newspapers. I mean I don't sit and worry about... I don't have nightmares of Gerald Ford trying to kill me...

Really, I mean it's wonderful to live. And what worries me the most is that so much of the time I don't want to live, and so then I try to figure out why. Why not? Or for instance one of the prominent forms is that I go to the movies about twice a week. Now why? That's just an escape. And what could be more ridiculous when life is so short anyway to spend a lot of time and money and effort escaping. Then of course I get clues, like when I'm on a lecture tour and have to go to the faculty cocktail and it goes on and on and on. Then I stumble back to my motel in Poughkeepsie late at night and I'm desperate for the Tonite Show.

Then I know why I go to the escape movies also. Or why... see I set out on almost every trip with about three books. One is usually a poetry book; the second will be history or maybe some book in that area, an instructive book; and the third, a detective novel. Two days into the trip I... I mean, after I've got through being X-rayed and all the cattle herding of the airplane port, I'm already through with the poetry and I'm into the history. And by the time I've had a day on the road, I'm down to the detective novel. But I don't accept that.

Question: Is there any personal reason why you're not signing your films now?

Brakhage: You see when I first signed films it was because I was making the personal statement really, that is, my signature. That was so long ago, you have to understand, and to scratch a signature on film had some very powerful meaning at that time that really distinguished it from the Hollywood film or any other kind of film. So I've done that for years, but now as of the last couple of years, and certainly this year, I had arrived at a place where I felt that that had become ego-centric. For one thing my name unfortunately is not as much, is not... I don't... I'm not enabled to have as personal a sense of my name as I did, because I've seen it too often in print. And people have used it as a symbol in a way that has nothing to do with person too much. And that's robbed me of that signature to some extent. Two, which is perhaps more important, should be in the first place, I came to sense that, as of the last several years, I've become more & more convinced that I don't make them. So it began to seem ego-centric to sign them. I felt I had the right to copyright them. It's interesting that this came up at the same point that I decided to copyright. I won't do that for very many years, but I wanted to leave something to the children. And that's the only way I could do it. Everything else is in public domain. And I don't want to leave them a fortune, but a little edge. So for a few years I will copyright films. Now the interesting thing is it doesn't bother me at all, which surprised me, that it says copyright 1974 by Stan Brakhage. Oddly I seem to have that right now because I'm not so stupid as to think I have the right to sign them.

Now that's all quite special, but there's a lot of thought and tortured feeling and feeling all the line of it for me. That's how I've arrived at that. I've bracketed the film in copyright, which I don't actually have to do, but I did it because I really want to put titles at the end of the film, which is another insistence which finally broke old habits. That I feel the words come gentler & interfere with vision less, if they occur at the end of the film, even though the people maybe know the title of the film they're going to see. So then I thought—that made me unhappy because then I thought oh shit, once again there's nothing for the projectionist to focus on. So therefore I just left the copyright at the beginning of it as a bracket and the real stuff occurs in the middle.

Question: It seems that your films might be short flashes of light, flashes of mind, inspiration, almost a separate personal eye seeing all these things on the ground, and then how do you structure something like that that seems to almost inherently tend to a short film, how do you structure a long film? *Brakhage:* Well, I exhausted everything I know. That's again as to why it's called *The Text of Light.* There are certain number of extensions of light taking place that I have seen. So I exhaust all those I have seen, within a construction that gives me a sense of the whole world. And in fact to me on one level the film really can be seen very much as if exploring an alien planet which is very similar to the one we live on in many respects. Once I had exhausted . . . the ash tray had metaphored for me and I had exhausted all that I had seen elsewhere, then I stopped shooting. And ordered that like a text, you could almost say an alphabet from the simple to the more complex, from the horizontal to the vertical, from meshes of light just come clumping, making triangles of mountain-like shapes through to finally what appears to me as a whole forest of trees. And that's one level of the film. Again, it was to structure it in a whole world sense and so there's also, there's a four season structure to it which cycles again and again. There's day and night. There's all that I know and all that's most familiar to me. Then too, that I was very moved by the symphonic form. I've always believed film is most close to music of all the other arts. It came quite naturally into four movements.

Question: You answered it in a sense in what you just mentioned about the symphonic form and I was wondering whether at the start or somewhere involved in the middle of the film you have any connections to music or sounds per se because you bring up the scream, etc. . . . & whether the editing or the pace at which the chops either increase in rapidity or decrease, give you any kind of musical sense of sound forms.

Brakhage: In terms of the second part of your question, they don't increase or decrease just like that. There are increases or decreases but I can't say that's true as an overall form. But yes I'm very much involved in music, I listen to music and I mean not just as a background, but I sit or lie down and listen to it when I'm home, two-three hours a day. It may be sheerly coincidental because I don't see any direct ties, but I was very involved in Shubert's Ninth Symphony while working on this film.

Question: Have you ever associated sounds with color per se?

Brakhage: Yes, there is a melodic line constantly going through all the work as of the last decade. And I do think of shifting changes and tones, in most films a very cordial melodic development; and I'm very concerned with that. That's how I feel film & music are the closest—they share tone. And they're also that close in that they're primarily dependent upon rhythm and tempo. And they're continuity arts and so on. But tone I take as seriously in film reaching toward music as Messiaen does in music reaching toward color.

Question: Why didn't you use music to add to the contemplation in this film?

Brakhage: Well because it would distract and be redundant and cut back seeing. All sound that does occur in sync, or intentional relationship with music, does diminish sight. So I've always thought of it—that you have to pay a price when you use a sound. And there are very few people that estimate that rightly. One of the greatest, *the* greatest in my opinion, is Peter Kubelka, who really knows how difficult it is to make a sound film. You cannot take for granted that you just have a picture and a sound to go with it. Not at all. And I never felt a need for sound. Though I'm not against sound, as my praise of Kubelka and James (Broughton) ought to make clear. And Kenneth Anger, all three of whom work with sound in absolutely magical and incredible ways. But for myself I have moved along the line of the silent film which has a very special discipline; and I do that because of my own necessities to see certain particularities that tend to get blurred if accompanied by sound. Or, I have found no way to keep from damaging by any relationship to sound. On the other hand, I have just finished a 20 minute sound/sync film, the first sync film I ever made. And I'm very excited about it.

Question: I know that your 8mm works, your *Songs,* were edited in the camera, and later you were very concerned with the energy you received from . . .
Brakhage: Well, no, some were, most weren't. It's always an ideal to edit in the camera, for obvious reasons . . . I think. The more obvious reasons are to me that there is an energy in the moment of shooting which editing again can leak out for you. What's interesting to me is the energy of immediacy. That comes out of my involvement with Charles Olson. The actual breath and physiology of the living person being present at its most, uninterrupted by afterthought. Editing is always afterthought. Though the way to beat that is to get *that* excited at the editing table. And that's very hard.

But in the case of this film it is very highly edited. And I prefer the word "arranged." And again I think we need a better word. "Arranged" is gentler & reminds me of the composer. "Compose" would be another word. We're talking about a composition in time. To make a construct that will fill completely the length of time it runs. I trust more myself what happens in the immediacy of shooting rather than in this afterthought process.

TO LAICA JOURNAL

26 January 1977

Dear David,

Thanks for thinking of me. Truth is, I'd very much like to contribute, but I've just no time whatsoever with which to do it—other than this note, which you're welcome to pass on as you like.

People are just too damn tired (not from work, but from meaningless work) to tolerate more from film than the easy assurances of escapist traditions. These require a seasoning (each season) of novelty (as do novels)—much as badly prepared and undernourishing food requires a variety of spices. There is a clear relation between violence in movies and sugar: the cookie witch still thrives despite Hansel and Gretel—tho' they've now become teenagers and disrobe occasionally: the scene,(and what is seen) remains the same. I suppose the witch climbed out of the oven while H. and G. were playing with each other, having found this nude game happily distracting. Excessive joy to 'em, I say; and I too like to watch 'em shove the witch in the oven again and again, and watch 'em stroke each other (while she climbs out).

My early work was sufficiently infected by this syndrome that advertising agencies, and the Hollywood movie-makers, were enabled to powder their product with shards of my discoveries—the interruptive flash-frame, of previous or forthcoming scenes, is an obvious example among many. Of late, however, my work (and that of most of my contemporaries) has evolved to something more like an integral (or thoroughly balanced) "meal"; therefore, all but visual "health nuts" tend to pass us by. We offer slim pickings for sugar addicts. We offer too MUCH to intrigue the Peeping Toms.

I personally am pleased that the DIFFERENCE between a potential work-of-art in film and an escapist move is now perfectly clear—at least clear to ME: separation of Church and Art, at last!

POETRY AND FILM

Brakhage: The arts, always, when I went through school—and I only went as far as one incompleted semester at college—the arts were always considered secondary. And the arts are an older discipline than any of these upstarts like science, and cooking; yet cooking is an art in terms of its condition as being an old discipline. So today we are gathered about poetry and film. And I want to say some simple things which are always hard to teach because I have to dig thru a lot of pitchblend to get to the radium.

I think that one of the greatest lessons I ever had in poetry was one night I was invited over to Kenneth Rexroth's house in the early 1950's in San Francisco. Rexroth was one of the two centers of poetic activity in San Francisco at that time. He would send out calls to those who came to his house, and those who would be interested gathered informally in his living room. On this particular night a man from India began to read Tagore in Bengali. Now I have read a lot of translated Tagore, and I never liked it very much; but now out came these extraordinarily beautiful sounds. First of all I was learning that poetry was not translatable. Second, because this was such a great experience beyond anything I had ever had before, or usually sense in poetry, I realized how important it was to approach poetry first thru its sounds. And then I learned, later, that was a way for some people to approach film first, just through its vision. People who had found difficulties with films of mine and other contemporaries because of their subject matter, like they say, or the lack of it, as some thought, or their dislocation of things in subject matter, could suddenly recognize a beauty, just in the tailoring of the light. They saw that this was more than decoration—or something like a light show—but that it was a very articulate rhythm, that is, it carried the motion. One could feel something about just the qualities of the lights. So the trick for seeing that was to throw the film absolutely out of focus. This film I am going to show you most of you have not seen in any other form. Then you will have a chance to test the theory. After you have seen it out of focus, I will show it to you in focus.

(Shows film)

Once I threw a film by Sergei Eisenstein, *Ivan the Terrible*, completely out of focus, and didn't tell people what it was, but I asked them to state their emotional feelings about certain passages. I did passage by passage. There was quite an accuracy: 80-90% agreed what was a sad passage or an excited one, and even thematic senses of battle between good and evil, black and white. Certainly very simple things, to be sure, but they at least were in agreement that this film out of focus and with no subtitles to read and no sound

Recorded at the University of North Carolina, Chapel Hill, March 22, 1977. *Credences 5-6, 1978*

track to hear caused accurate, what would have been regarded as accurate emotional responses.

So I know there are people, for instance, that if you think of all the trouble people have with the meaning they take Ezra Pound—for example or Allen Ginsberg—to have, then they are just put off from hearing the music; whereas what they hear in a foreign language doesn't prejudice them against the song. They may indeed later decide that the things that have shaped the poet's life bother them in one way or another, but they aren't predisposed against the song. As I understand it that's terribly important, because what we have in the arts is that you may listen to your worst enemy's song.

Now I'm trying to talk about things that are all the same between poetry and film. That it, it is a meeting ground, as I see it. How many of you have seen Leni Riefenstahl's *Triumph of the Will*? Well, she in my view is a great film artist who, to be sure, made films that Hitler admired, about Hitler that he admired very much, notably *Triumph of the Will*. Jewish organizations, with all their justification, gather and picket the showing of her works. I think that's a mistake, actually; I think it would be far smarter if the Jewish organizations arranged wide distribution of those films for the following reason: because she was an artist, she left us a portrait of that whole time. I wish that the terrifying images which Leni Riefenstahl managed in *Triumph of the Will* of Hitler—which is really about the Nurenberg rally—I wish that that was available for people to see because, as an art, it is not persuasive. The interesting thing about *Triumph of the Will* is that Hitler thought it was marvelous as a portrait of him, and, at the same time, the British Propaganda Ministry used that film to scare Britain into arming. That was the last straw: they didn't change one word, they didn't misrepresent one thing, they took the whole thing just as Hitler liked it and Leni Riefenstahl made it and scared the western world half to death with it. Because it was an art, it changed the capacity for people to see something. And I have no doubt that most of the people most of the time will decide against that, so the wide distribution of Leni Riefenstahl's work would be a benefit in the world; whereas when people don't decide, everything that Hitler was gets distorted by public education. Gradually the menace he represents—and to me a terrible menace—falls into a kind of hero worship, the kind that Napolean would get, who was the same kind of bastard.

So there are grounds that film and poetry and other arts in various ways share. But film and poetry relate rather closely for this reason: poetry is dependent upon a language that is in the air. All poets inherit at scratch a language—I mean they inherit it the first time they start scratching their ears with sound and start to make sense out of it, that is, as babies. And they inherit not only their language, but the possibility of language, which is a concept which is really incredible. It enables them, for one thing, to go on to learn other languages. There's something very solidly there that's not there as an art tradition, but's there as an everyday tradition. Then poets are forever surrounded by other people using this language and using it all the time in a great variety of ways, which shapes each poet's sense of that language. And then — and here's the miracle—they override that constant mundane chit-chat of people that's not actually much different than monkeys. Just chit-chatting and passing clichés, comfort and admonition, back and forth. The five messages of people which aren't much different from what Hollis Frampton defined as the five bird songs. Birds, he says, have about five things to say. As Hollis has it with the birds they say "good morning," "I found a worm," "fuck me," "get out," "good night." Now a great deal could be done with that, which is the ordinary business of the world and a great variety of song can be made of that for those that really listen to the little varieties of generalized bird songs; and therein to the little varieties, if you really get ears that keen, to listen to particular birds of the species. In their own language all those varieties which I love too, all those words, aside from those I just spoke, that fill up the *Oxford English Dictionary,* plus all the words that have been hatched since then. So look at the *OED* and think about what actually has to be said, and see the wonderful variety of possibilities within, particularly, our language, for shades of meaning, or for music. To me, all the rest is noise. That gets quite personal. What's regarded by others as noise your own true love makes as music. Then there is music that overrides just that personal, which is to say, that a noise that some poet makes becomes music to several who care so much about it they will risk their lives to save it for anybody who wants it.

For example, the great moment of this to me in history is when some monks unwrapping paupers' coffins found shards of Greek poetry. For pauper graves they didn't use wood, they took old manuscripts, old books and pulped them, and made little paper coffins for the poor. Some of those were unearthed, and among the papers were found shards of Greek poetry and it was determined from some of the saved poems that these were shards of Sappho, and others. These monks with great excitement sent this news to the Pope. Meanwhile they were slowly pulling apart these coffins to get more and more little shards of poetry. It took a long time, thank God, for news to get around in those days, so by the time the Pope got the message and had determined on it and sent back his determination, these monks were very involved in this poetry and were loving it, loving it enough to keep at this tedious task of slowly unravelling it from a mass of decay. The Pope announced that this was pagan poetry and was to be destroyed. We have to assume for most of the monks that that was the word of God. But they so loved the poetry by that time that they disregarded it, which meant not only that they were willing to die for it, but risk their immortal souls to save the poetry. That's how we have the better part of Sappho that we still have. It doesn't take very many people to save something, but it takes an incredible passion.

Well, I think it starts with a rhythm, it starts with a recognizable rhythm, a rhythm that moves past all the clichés of language. Someone learns to so order these mundane words of chit-chat that they make a rhythm of them which is compelling. One good way to get a sense of what poetry is at its greatest is to get some records of poetry in other languages that you do not understand and listen to the music of them. I don't mean to stop there, I don't mean that poetry is without meaning. That would be sound and fury signifying nothing. But I mean, put the horse before the cart, start with the compelling rhythm that someone lifts from all the chit-chat which is a buzz, a noise or an annoyance to most of us, unless we get our message for the day — do this do that — or hello or I love you, or pass the cereal. Get past that and see that someone was compelled to lift those chunks into a meaningful rhythm. That's what I hope to achieve by showing the film totally out of focus. Now I would like to show you the film in focus and then maybe we can talk about means and meaning.

(Shows film *Two:Creeley/McClure*)

Brakhage: Let me ask if any of you have questions.

Question: Do you have any idea of poetry when you work on films?

Brakhage: Yes, though differently in all cases. I had definitely in mind to get a portrait of Robert Creeley when we visited him in Placitas, N.M., in 1962. With Michael we were leaving San Francisco and I had never taken any images of him. I had, oh, maybe 50 feet in the camera. And I said let me get some pictures of you, and instantly I took the first little bit I suddenly knew that I wanted more than just some pictures of him. That whole section on Michael McClure has no editing—I knew suddenly I had to do something and it took all morning. He very graciously sat down and I got out the image of him with the lion make-up on *Ghost Tantras*—with the hair all over his face—and interspersed images of that with images of him sitting there in the chair, and he meantime was doing certain things as he sat and I was waiting and we were also talking, about Milton, as I recall. Even though that started just to get some pictures of him, very instantly as I started photographing it turned into a portrait. In the case of the film *Hymn to Her* I was just shooting some film, in that case of Jane, as I do around the house, and it fell later into this portraiture.

Question: Do you concentrate in the camera or on the printing?

Brakhage: Both, whatever is necessary. Preferably in the camera because it's cheaper. It also has a higher energy level usually. It's less interferred with—it just has the vibrancy of immediacy that's hard, very much harder to get later, editing or printing.

Question: Was that film *Two:Creeley/McClure* . . .

Brakhage: That was definitely solarized, that is, by having a negative made, and then an A and B roll, and solarizing.

Question: How did you get the shimmering effect on the tree in the film *The Wold Shadow* you showed last night?

Brakhage: Single framing.

Question: It looked like colors running up the tree at one point.

Brakhage: Well, that's painting on glass. The pane of glass sits on an easel between me and the scene. I take a frame and alter what I'm seeing by painting on that glass and taking another frame, etc.

But these things don't happen that way. I don't say, oh, today I'll go and take a piece of glass into the woods and see what hanky-panky I can produce. But quite the reverse. I had an experience at that spot in the woods which did never recur, though I waited for months. A large anthropomorphic shadow appeared over me in the trees; and if I'd been a sensible, so-called primitive person I would have fallen to my knees or run like hell. First, when I saw it, I said, that's interesting how that shadow is made by the light. It gradually dawned on me as I tried to figure out what was throwing that shadow that there wasn't anything, that the light was not so positioned in any way that I could account for that shadow, which then seemed *very* awesome and frightening. I just stood with my mouth open in amazement. Then the shadow faded back into the trees. I presumed that I had seen the god of the forest, or of that place. I went back every day to worship, but that god wasn't up for religion, because he never came again. I did the next best thing to either falling on my knees or running like hell. I went back to that place with the idea in mind to paint the shadow as I had seen it, but better—as I started making the film—I let that go and made an *homage* to that place, an *homage* to that god or goddess, not just out of some kindliness of my heart but so I could sleep easily at night that I had done my bit in the great dance with mystery. And fortunately instead of doing that stupid thing I thought I was going to do, paint the god that no longer reappeared, I made a full exposition of everything of that place that I felt, and I reflected as I sat there painting all those things that Eastman Kodak's film does not usually accommodate. I can't put a camera inside my head to photograph my own optic system as it is seeing, so I have to paint. As I went on painting all day—the day passed slowly—to take a frame and then paint and then take another frame 24 times to make a second of film is a full day's hard labor to get 100 feet thru the camera. And then as I went on painting, all such places came rich in my mind, all such places as the history of painting has brought them to us. The word "wold" is there because if you look in the *OED*, it is a wood. Originally it was a wood and then it came to mean a flat place, and then again a wood. Along hundreds of years of the English language, and directly because of the acts of the poets, the word got shifted to mean these alternative things. We now have "wold" as the source of the word wood. But so all these dreams tumbled thru my head, of language and painting and feeling about that place. The fact is that on one level the film is a whole history of landscape painting right up to an *homage* to someone like Clyfford Still, who is really a landscape painter. And that's how I make films; and that's a very normal process, as far as the arts are concerned.

Question: Your comments on why you use the painting in that film relate to the comments you made last night, and that made me wonder if you ever investigated Kirlian photography.

Brakhage: Yes, Kirlian photography has been very helpful to me because I have seen many of those things, just with my eyes, for years, and when I spoke of them was called quite mad. Many of the reasons I paint on film is to get an approximation of some of the things that are now photographable thru the Kirlian process. So Kirlian photography came along and established that my seeing was not mad. But note the despair of the times in which we live. Because a machine can see it, it's now considered sane. Now I can speak of it as halos that surround plants and fingers and heads, and if people look skeptical I can say I'm into Kirlian photography.

I'm also very grateful for reading some other human's equivalent to something I'm seeing. Much that Wilhelm Reich has seen I had seen before I read him. And in ways sufficiently the same and also different; his writing was a comfort at one point, because it was the only feedback I had. It was a comfort that another human being had also seen some of the things. This is entirely aside from what the orgone box might be. I don't know anything about that. I tend not to be interested in it. But what he wrote about having seen, much of it I have seen in various ways.

We're now talking about means, but not about meaning. Let me tell you this story. When I was going through school I was always carrying a poetry book—I was very interested in poetry and still am—and so I got a bad reputation as a kid carrying books when he didn't have to. When I had my sixteenth birthday party, a bunch of my friends as a joke got together—well first of all they were going to buy me a birthday present—and what else but a book. While they were downtown looking for a present, they found something that would be a hilarious joke. They found a book that was so absurd and ridiculous and impossible that even I would be defeated at trying to read it. They were doubling over with laughter at the thought of giving me *this book* that would truly defeat me. And sure enough came this book all wrapped in tissue paper, and I was delighted because I loved books and they were sensible enough to give me a book; and I opened the paper and there was a very strange book indeed. First of all it seemed to be in English, but at least a third of it was in other languages; and it made references to the gods. Just to get thru some of the courses at school I can remember writing on my arm in indelible ink, Mercury, Zeus, Jupiter and having little definitions of what all these were. It annoyed me to have references to a whole pack of gods from elsewhere; the final incredible thing was that this gift book was filled with Chinese. This of course was Ezra Pound's *Cantos,* which is, if I must choose one book, the single most important book in my life. Indeed I couldn't read it and they had their good laugh. I could only put together three words in a row and then stumble over a lot I couldn't understand and then three more words that I could understand. But right off the bat, because I was too desperate not to be defeated in the teeth of my friends who were getting too much of a laugh out of this, I started the book and it starts "And then went down to the ship." Right there (writes on board) I noticed something: "And." To start off a book like this with "and!" I am very concerned with the beginning and endings of books—"and"—that was thrilling. And immediately it moved all the emotions this way (writes on board→)—so powerful. I remember it brought tears to my eyes, which no doubt increased the laughter of my friends. And the next word which hit me was "down," "and then went *down*." "Set forth" was there too. And within those lines you also get "up." In those first two lines the mind splits, the mind moving, going in two directions and very powerfully and very reinforced. That kind of thing is where the relationship between my sense of poetry and what film can do begins, and that is like the first level set of meaning: direction! The poem has the capacity beyond just its rhythm to make reference to the process of thinking itself. If you set that in a model—that's forward and back. Poetry is having to do with the actual process of thought, as absolutely distinct from what I don't regard as poetry at all, the writer telling you his mind, or something of that sort. It certainly *seems* like Ezra Pound is primarily involved with telling his mind; you know, he's telling what he thinks is good and what he thinks is bad, but I hear his song, and I heard it even when I was utterly baffled by a book that obviously had been given to me as a joke. It wasn't just my stubbornness, and I had certainly encountered other books that were tough and tougher to read than that; but after comprehending something of them I threw them out. Here was one that the more I understood the more yield came to me. So here became the great book for going over and over and over. Now I would say that I can read six to ten, in some places twenty words in a row, which isn't very much still, but it's good progress in a life time's worth of reading. I'm working on it. I've got some of the major slogans that were to sustain me all of my life, prayers, like "All that is is light." That is enough to return me to that kind of person Pound is who would know how important it is to say and give Erigena a translation—"All that is is light." It's so powerful in that context. That's something of what I mean by meaning. And I'M TOUGH ABOUT IT.

I'd like to talk about direction as circle, as in

That's the way Gertrude Stein originally wrote in a child's book called *The World Is Round*. It's first written this way because Rose, the little heroine, carves it in a tree. I think it arose that simply in Gertrude's life, because very shortly she was using it on her stationery. But suddenly Gertrude had the sense that she had been given a great gift. First of all it's a wonderful centerpiece of arguments for her great teacher, William James, about the nature of being and nothingness before it got obfuscated into that, in my opinion, by the existentialists. It looks like a silly thing—ok, we got it—a rose is a rose is a rose. It means it is only and ever a rose. That's something to brood on, and we could say that's kind of a silly poem. After it sprang from her subconscious mind into this child's book, she must have come to realize the incredible puns that move through it. There is a reference that she was aware of those, though she wouldn't be as academic as I am to lay it all out here. Someone was once attacking the poem in Chicago, and she said 'all I have to say is that the rose has not bloomed so sweetly in English poetry in 200 years.' Which meant that she had come to recognize what that whole tradition of English poetry is; so poetry always has a tradition, a whole lattice of meaning. So the rose, if having looked at the whole history of English poetry as a history, is used in three basic symbol places: birth, sex, death. (AROSE) Here we have a nice pun for birth, for something coming up; here we have his Eros, sex; and with a slight slur, we can get sorrows; with another slight slur we can get the connective, the thing that relates symbolically, arrows. What springs magically if you start feeling it with the tongue, as distinct from just taking it along with the clichés of everyday language, birth, sex, death is represented back thru the Greek, and perhaps earlier, by the three sisters. The three sisters are in there. She glorified that sense of the forest by laying it out in a line, not always putting it in a circle. So it's a meditation piece as a poem which has to do certainly with the whole history of English toying with these particular words, and these qualities of meaning. There are other kinds of spring-off from it, like for an English garden, that is planted in *rows*. But some of this begins to stretch; but those stretches are important too. To read a poem to its outer limits, or a single line, to take the stretches and know they are stretches of meaning but let the stretches go until they snap at you.

Speaking of the sense of meaning that is sometimes in the air around, in the film that you've seen, *Two: Creeley/McClure*, the rhythmic song of being out of focus, as if it were in another language, and then seen again straight thru, and having talked a great deal about the means of how such things are made, I'd like to emphasize that just like Gertrude stumbled into means so I stumbled into those means or am forced to them. I didn't certainly go out of my way to do A and B rolls, because it's just hell. So, I'm driven to it.

Well, then you say this film is a portrait; what does it have to do with Robert Creeley or Michael McClure? Michael McClure when he reads his poetry, he often reads especially softly the capitalized letters. Now he may have changed his act these days, but in the past that was a shock to people because Michael uses a lot of capitalized whole lines. Everyone expects when you see capitalized, that means headlines, that means *WAR IS DECLARED!* No—he reads them softer than the rest. He reads slowly, and he moves slowly. But his section in the film is the flashy one with a lot of single framing and quick movements, and there is quite a variety of rhythms in there. Unless you're really up to looking at rhythms fast right off, it just looks like all flickering and burning, whereas Michael tends to move very stately. But I saw him as a man containing an electricity that is just terrifying. It can be deceptive. Everyone says he is so in control, but really he *has* to be, because he is so nervous. He is such a bag of nerves that if he lets himself go he might just go up in smoke. And this manifests itself to the careful looker thru the slightest of ticks or ripples along his skin or in his voice. To the slightest shift of means and meaning. And it is all there in his poetry.

Also you come to who's doing the viewing. Marvell's view of a coy mistress is not going to satisfy a women's libber of then or now. So when someone writes a poem about someone, the primary thing one is learning about is the poet and what he or she thinks, and the rhythm of the self it carries. And the other thing becomes the lumen. Well, people call me subjective because I insist that I am I. There is this argument against my work which says that the film is all me, it's enclosed but it doesn't communicate, doesn't have anything to do with social values, other people can't understand it, and so on. And I make my case as the following. If they are right, if a documentary indeed has to be made as if I have in mind an audience of six-year-old adults being spoonfed the right idea—if that's documentary, or represents the truth, or any kind of a full circle, well then the newspapers do best represent truth, because that's their bright idea. How many of you have had any kind of newspaper write about you? Did you think the article represented truth? It's the most available source of such undercurrent parlance that we have. A color-blind reporter at an art show would obviously do better than an editor writing the story in the office, particularly if he knew his credentials. He could say, this is what I saw. This is the first level of truth; but the other is, if it goes into the lattice which the arts represent, if it's in relationship to a history or a tradition, then we have the possibility that the tradition can be learned sufficiently to read that thing, be it in paint or along the line of notes in the air or poetry or film—to have a world that passed thru one another human-being that's up there spinning, so to speak. That's obviously a world as when Michelangelo saw people beginning to worship the Pieta, what did he do?—a beautiful artist's thing kicking in the teeth of the whole Renaissance as he did so—he carved across the breast band of the Virgin: "made by Michelangelo." It was more outrageous than a factory worker writing "made in Tokyo" across his work.

The anecdote comes from Charles Olson—"There is no such many as mass." Which is an incontrovertable truth, or a simpler way to get it is to go out on the street and ask people "are you the average man or woman," and some will say yes, because they've been taught to do so, and then ask them how they've come to think they are. Poets know this, film makers know this, and it isn't a case of my using the "I" egocentrically, as so much as Robert Duncan, another poet, puts it: "I" must never arise in the poem except as the communal "I," That's where we come to means and meaning. I know *Two: Creeley/ McClure* is a film and I wish to make a world which is built out of what has

passed thru my experience of those two fine men. And to approach each of
them with all that I have of my experience of each of them. In both cases it
happened to involve much more time spent reading their poetry than sitting
around talking with them. I know it's me reading poetry — it isn't a great books
compendium survey of how people read Michael McClure or Robert Creeley,
it's my reading of them that's informed my life. Who else can I speak for. And
that shapes the rhythm of which these films are compounded; along with, and
in a dance with each of them, which in many ways is contradictory, the poetry
rhythms actually on the page, unless you look closer. In Michael's case it
would appear to be very stately and very composed. But right under the skin
surface ripple constantly impulses that are visible if you choose to look for
them, however hard he builds his muscles at Vic Tanney's gym and holds
himself in, firm. All the firmness, as of my being a film maker as distinct from a
poet, has to do with centered weakness. He must be strong, he must be
composed, he must be almost statuesque at times to contain this fire that moves
thru him. He expressed it in one statement he gave me in the 60's — as we used
to call to each other in desparation across the yawning void — "Be a solid
moving thru an Inferno." That has to do with the flickering side of him. In
relationship to Creeley — those who know Creeley — well, he's a man who
didn't come to full sentences until he was 11 or 12 years old, and he stumbles
into speech with great hesitancy and enormous power and fantastic delicacy.
He's New Englandish; shy, he's incredibly shy. Bob seems like one of those
people born old — an old soul you could say. And I saw him that way. Also he
commands a kind of attention where the eyes can become saturated, so
engaged and reaching out to help him to come to speech that you get a reverse
action. I'm sure all of you are aware if you watch a light bulb that actually at
some point, if you're relaxed, that light bulb can be impressing the optic nerve
so much that it turns black. Closing the eyes will leave a blue light bulb,
usually, drifting off into the void, which is a reversal color of yellow. In the will
to give out, it has to be relaxed, at least in my experience; a person can shift
from positive to negative. That is, the values can reverse, the eyes are
saturated and go to the opposite. So I'm always in that sense after equivalents
of things I've seen. My experience isn't exactly like it appears on film, but it's
an equivalent. And this reversal of light-value vision happens very often to me
when I'm with Robert Creeley. So it seems necessary in the film to seem true to
my experience of him.

Question: What you've said about the film has already helped my appreciation
of it. Have you ever done program notes, or does that go against your purpose?
Brakhage: I think there are ways to talk about all the arts. I'm here talking but,
finally, the world is really *attacking* its contemporary arts with language,

largely. I think one of the signs of the greatness of Dante's *Divine Comedy* is that it has survived hundreds and hundreds of years of footnotes. All that attack against the essential ingredient, which is a celebration of mystery! That doesn't mean a lack of mystery. Celebration of mystery allows the maker to acknowledge, by the way he or she has done something, that he or she knows something. But this knowledge also acknowledges mysteries. And the work reverberates. And the mysteries open up further knowing. Now, Robert Frost is a perfect example of someone who just writes a mystery. He writes poems which do celebrate mystery and in the second stage, when you see that he understands something of the mystery, it still can reverberate a little further. But for me it didn't reverberate any further than that. So he is a kind of a nostalgia. I deeply appreciate what he gave me. He's a simple-minded poet, which is OK. It isn't that he lacks intellect. A real simple-minded poet is Christopher Smart, but "My Cat Jeffrey" keeps yielding more and more as I read it across the years as distinct from "The Road Not Taken." At some point the road not taken is completely taken. There are nursery rhymes that have lasted better. That's what I've called a weak impulse, but there are people one outgrows, or moves away from. It would be nice to think there will be a senile old age when Robert Frost will be just the thing. That is not a put-down. It will be an enormous relief to think that when I get older and get simple-minded I and Frost and nursery rhymes can survive all the same. But in the meantime Ezra Pound is the sustaining one, the one I still can't understand. But at every stage of gained knowledge *The Cantos* reveal more and more to me. They may be rummaged for further understanding he is opening up to me: the Chinese dictionary, which I have now been studying for several years, *The Egyptian Book of the Dead*. Pound probably wouldn't have approved of the *Egyptian Book of the Dead,* but that Dover edition with the way to study the ideograms came along, and I've been studying it. Pound goads me on because at each turn in the reading of him I come to new mysteries which he has set significantly within learned reach.

Question: Again, your appreciation of Pound has come from reading the poems again and again, as well as the materials around the poems. For us to appreciate films more, have you ever thought of writing program notes?
Brakhage: I've written several books. *Metaphors on Vision* which is considered *the* most difficult book on film to read. I also consider it as such. I think it's worthily difficult, but I wish it could have been simpler, like *The Brakhage Lectures*. One of the nicest books I wrote is *The Moving Picture Giving and Taking Book,* or *Seen*. I've written a lot and I make a living talking about films, and I'm also aware and would warn you, that the only value in this lecturing to make a living decently, is that we see how works withstand this honest verbal

outpouring. We see that despite all this talk they still stand there, withstand the investigation. I don't really trust doctors, certainly not surgeons. I think the great thing about going to the hospital and having surgery is to survive it. To survive this probing, the operation called education, is really my sense of it. Then I see the colleges as a vast salmon run with most students flopping on the rocks at the side and some few despite the downpour making it up stream to spawn. I think it is a more severe survival testing grounds than the US Marines.

What would be the point to all these lectures. Finally I hope to take a silly little poem like "A Rose is a rose is a rose" and ask that question in Grand Forks, North Dakota and in New York City, where almost anyone's heard it, and chuckled over it and then dismissed it. But at least for whatever it's worth, it's one poem that's in the language and known by more people probably than any other poem in the world. And there is a lesson in that. If you start breaking it down, you see that that little tiny bit contains, from my view point, an infinite amount of meditative possibilities. It keeps being alive and rolling around and round in my head and yielding more and more. All of which is to say that film does not have a chance equal to a poem in our time, because there is no way I can pass out to those of you who are interested *Two: Creeley/McClure* to take it home and run it to death or into a lifetime's viewing. I've written a lot, I've spoken a lot, I've tried to make talk into as much integrity as possible.

TO HENRY HILLS

13 January 1978

Dear Henry Hills,

I want to thank you for one of the best reviews I've yet read. You presented your opinions just exactly as that—opinions—leaving the reader free to find out for him or her self; and yet you did give enough personal orientation (re: jazz, Coltrane, Mark Twain, earlier films of mine, "THE TRANCE FILM," etc.) that we know where you're coming from, have lines of perspective on yourself. It is clearly a human being writing (a rare clarity); and you do treat me most humanly. I, of course, don't always agree with you, but I ALWAYS respect your opinion and even wonder if perhaps you might be (might prove in the long run to be) correct. Which of any of us KNOWS the signification of new creative work?: only a fool would claim absolute surety... certainly not the maker. I think and very much feel that 'The Governor" IS one of the greatest works ever given to me to do; and it more than fulfills (so far) every expectation I had of it while working on it: but only Time will tell, like they say.... One clarity from me which you do deserve: "The Gov." was NOT commissioned. In fact, it was emphatically stated to Governor Lamm that there could be NO interference with my making. The deal, as is my usual in cases of portraiture or similarity of Doc., WAS that I would pay for the film myself (so there be no strings attached) and that I would complete it the same as any other film of my making AND that then he would be allowed to decide whether or not it could be released. No changes were permitted him, nor were requested. If he hadn't accepted ALL of the film as is, then I would have stuck it

away in the vault until one of us was dead... (preferably, had that been the case, him). The work could never have been made if he hadn't accepted these terms; and happily he does very much like it. Another point of fact: it was absolutely NOT made with T.V. in mind; and there are not, nor ever have been, any hopes of it being shown on television. Its length, and those 'blanks' you think were designed for "commercials," is/are integral parts of the form. It is important to me that those misapprehensions of yours be corrected because I think they may have biased your viewing, will certainly bias the viewing of some people, and DO suggest that I work under commission... something I've been at great pains to discourage other artists from doing... and something I've suffered a great deal to avoid doing myself: (for instance, during the making of "The Gov.," at a time I very much needed money, I turned down a commission to make a film on the President of Mexico). All this is NOT to suggest your opinion of "The Governor" is wrong. It is the most generally dis-liked film I've made since "Anticipation of the Night"; and that also is NOT to suggest your opinion is wrong. We'll both have to wait and see... if we live so long. Another fact I'd like to correct: I do continue photographing Jane. Much of this footage will, if as usual, come to something in the future—most not (tho' I shouldn't really try to out-guess that, as I've been unable in the past to ever know what will finally turn up in a completed film): BUT it should at least be noted that the face of the sleeping woman in the first of "Short Films: 1976" is that of Jane, AND it is her childhood photos which start "Short Films: 1975," her vagina which touches off the 'trip' in the second film of that series... other parts of her anatomy weaving throughout that series, AND her face and figure which dominate much of the super 8mm films. I hasten to correct this assumption of yours that "since 'Hymn to Her' Brakhage has apparently ceased to exploit her image" because it seems similar to that assumption YOU so carefully contradicted in your review—i.e. that I'm "over the hill" or somesuch... put in perspective by your witty "he didn't die as expected." Every couple years some reviewer suggests that I don't photograph Jane enough; and about once a year a number of our friends call to make sure we haven't separated or divorced, prompted by some recurring rumor. I can only guess at what prompts these rumors, this particularity of gossip; but I am naturally quick to correct it. I commiserate with Jane's fans wishing more image of her, and I bow to their (and her) criticism of her image in the films; but it is precisely beCAUSE I do NOT "exploit her image" that The Muse (or the subconscious, if you like) has the last vis-a-vis. in the matter. A couple other points, just 'for the record': it is not "a fuck scene," nor ever visibly such, which puzzled you (perhaps thus?) in "Short Films: 1975," but rather something more resistant to naming... but which, had it been named, might have been called "Dalliance"—tho' I hadn't wished to be so Elizabethan as that either; AND it is "Doc Holliday's/ Jimmy Ryan Morris's daughter who appears in that scene with him... Pagan Morris her name. Had you seen her as a little girl it might have made the scene less (or possibly more) "incomprehensible" for you: and I DO realize how difficult it IS to comprehend all these particularities of detail in one, or even several, viewings of these films—and do thank and praise you for the extent to which you HAVE been accurate in your

review... this letter in homage of the worthiness of your review rather than any criticism of it.

I don't know if you are one of the editors of Cinemanews, but I did want to comment that I found this issue of it unusually interesting: the interview with/of Hollis Frampton was excellent... Hollis is at his best, which is (in my opinion) the VERY best.

P.S. Jane says I'm too "picky" about "a fuck scene" and Jimmy's daughter AND that you deserve MORE praise— it being the very BEST review we've seen in some time. And I think she's right, as usual. A film must survive its suggestions—i.e. if the suggestion is fucking, then the film's particularities OUGHT counter-balance that for some full measure of meaning which contains place for tangential interpretation or counteracts them altogether; and I don't think that film successfully does that... and the little girl DOES pun on woman (a shade of that scene I'd not thought of before). Okay, so, and PRAISE PRAISE PRAISE!

1 February 1978

Dear Henry Hills,

I looked at "Porter Springs: 2" last night (I was unable to view "3" because it started slipping in the gate—probably not broken-in sufficiently yet for the careful tolerances of my RCA... very easy on film but commensurately finicky; and I didn't want to risk damaging it, so am returning it unseen), and I keep thinking of conversations recently with Donald Sutherland (the REAL D.S., not the actor) wherein he suggested that The Arts are still too much enthralled by "the small true fact." Donald says the earliest example he can find of that interest, stated as such, is in Stendahl (sp?), and at that time it was thought of as something to be occasionally introduced into literature 'to anchor' the ordinary cosmic considerations of The Arts. Thence we come finally to William Carlos Williams' "red wheel barrow" upon which "it" (the poem?) "depends." Donald's point is WHAT depends upon the wheel barrow? His rhetorical question haunts me. EVERYTHING depends on it, that's Williams' echoing answer in my head; BUT...everything CAN be very close to NOTHING. I keep thinking that perhaps it is a specifically modern drive to find that ONE stable spot in the universe that is SOLID wherefrom (with lever, or even fulcrum of language, music, paint, carved stone, photo or film), *and thus whereWITH* we might MOVE that "universe." I don't think "Porter Springs 2" is that spot. Its facts/phots seem too much a collection simply along a line of 'liking'—likenesses, then...along a line of your pleasure; and tho I very much like the cut from house to cow, and even the cut from feet to barn, and sense clear end as cow ambles down the hill, I do NOT know why much of the rest of the film need be between these cuts at all... except, again, as it is your pleasure—a pleasure in the small true facts of your experience of this place? There is, yes, a quality of terror that moves thru this work; and that interested me the most (tho' it didn't seem dependent upon the length, or dotage upon certain images, you've given it—a half dozen shots of those kids, ditto house, ditto barns with those intervening cuts mentioned and the end SHOULD, or could, have done it...I think; but then I'm often wrong.)

So many people ask to see the films, in the sense you have, that if we obliged there'd soon be no prints left to rent and no money wherewith more could be made. It pains me to turn you down because it is such a reasonable request you've made. I don't know the solution except perhaps that someone apply for a grant to buy prints of my work so that they'd be available for people to study in the way you propose—i.e. non-theatrical private screenings...very personal screenings (which certainly mean the most to me: I just can't afford to support it). We make very little profit off ALL the rentals of all these films. If Jane and I were to be paid the minimum wage for checking all these prints, mailing 'em, etc. plus their cost, our whole "distribution business" would probably be "in the red." Thus, each showing of each print MUST contribute financially to maintaining the very availability of those films. Another possible way out of this sadness: why not get your local libraries, or S.F. library, to purchase the films you and your friends want to study? Enough concentrated demand should accomplish that. Most libraries buy film trash—book trash too—by the cartload. Who, of late, has tried to shift that stupidity?

There was a time when I had a standing offer to look at ANYone's film sent me and to write whatever I honestly could in return to them. It was my desire to help all unknown film-makers in whatever way I could—to give them at least a few words they might use to get their works up into the light of public projector or somesuch. I was finally deluged with films and found myself unable even to check my own prints because of the mass of other's works to be looked upon, let alone proceed with making new films myself. Thus, I took back the offer. Now, it is okay that you sent these films without asking me BUT I am in some terror (considering your position) that your mailing may be followed by those of your friends or others in general. So, for that reason ONLY (and my inability to any longer cope with that) I ask you to make CLEAR I DO NOT accept films mailed to me without my specifically asking for 'em anymore. I usually just have them turned back at the post office so I don't have to pay return postage (for that had become a very heavy expense every week also). I am severely overloaded with *work that must be done* before I can even begin to think of CREATIVE work. I am still the only patron of my creative activity, the only patron also of the preservation of my films. I must wear all these silly money-making hats in order to continue making films at all... in order, also, to preserve what has been made (an increasingly nightmarish cost as the years roll on, roll heavily over the delicacy of films). And I did NOT, by the way, take "lightly" your "lack of interest in the early work"... but, rather, did appreciate the interest you were enabled to take. I presume anyway that part of that "problem" (as I see it) IS the lack of availability of film for study: which puts this dragon's tail in the mouth of the last paragraph.

In *Metaphors on Vision* I wrote: "I'm thru writing thru writing." That finally begins to be true. Except for letters, I just don't write anymore (haven't for about 6 years), thus don't have anything to contribute to "Cinemanews" other than these letters which you are very welcome to publish. (I especially wish you would publish at least the previous letter, or those parts of it sufficient to

correct those *few* mis-impressions I felt you had: subsequent to writing you I realized that the longest portrait of Jane occurs midst those Super 8mm films: *Rembrandt, Etc., And, Jane.*) I am now also trying to stop public speaking. That'll be very difficult, as it is the only means I have for making anything like a steady living; but it is exhausting my health and creative potential. I feel that it was essential I speak OUT an alternative aesthetic and absolutely BATTER away at it until I'd stamped upon the public scene SOME space for a more traditionally normal acceptance of film as an art... more "normal" than those attitudes toward film I'd confronted younger—such as Film-as-a-trick-of-Dada, Film-as-an-(Underground)-tangent-of-revolutionary-unrest, Film-as-Vox-Populi, Film-as-Psychoanalytical-substitute, Film-as-everybody's-play-pen, Film-as-illustration-to-Rock, etc... including (of late) Film-as-(Structural)-Teaching-aid, or Film-as-stepping-stone-to-Video, or even Film-as-propaganda-tool-for-Woman's Lib. I feel that there are now enough tapes, and transcripts of tapes AND written books, for me to "rest my case" and get back more steadily and continually to my work... at least I hope this is so, and that I can find some other way to support myself.

Good luck to you; and thanks again, for your interest.

AN OPEN LETTER

10 July 1980

I've said often to Diana Barrie, Gary Doberman, Jim Otis, Willie Varela, and others whose work I've loved of late, that I will most probably do more social harm by championing their films than I would by writing or speaking against them. Every younger filmmaker I've publicly praised as "discovery" in the last decade I've heard characterized as "disciple of mine" or "imitator" or somesuch (except those whose reputation was well established before I came to their work: Ernie Gehr, Andrew Noren, for example). My opinion has been regarded as self-serving egotism. Some have, more gently, suggested that I'm "blind" to those who are perceived as "following in my path." How it is possible for a living American independent filmmaker NOT to share kinship with me? By DELIBER-ATELY not! And this would be the council of the arbitrary arbiters of taste of our Time. Film Academism splits two ways (BOTH ignorant of the mid-ground where most work of lasting value is being accomplished): (1) structural aesthetics nuf said) and (2) the thoughts of those who credit ONLY the-techne-new . . . and then too those who seek the NEWS-new whereby we get American Academized Dada.

I've long maintained that current public critical standards are creating an American Samizdat. The most creative younger artists I've known, in ALL the arts, are tending to such privacy as will void publication or public presentation altogether. As Gary Doberman put it to me once: "The public scene is so disgusting I don't want to be associated with it at all." When I asked Diana Barrie if I couldn't write something on her films *The Annunciation* and *Sarah's Room* for distribution or program notes, she said (speaking of her sense of her contemporaries): "No, we've taken a good look at you and your generation—and the public hassle you're having—and want to find some way to keep out of that altogether." (Edith Kramer finally asked me for statements on her work, which is how I came to write what I did.) Day before yesterday I found myself (almost surreptitiously) slipping Jim Otis a note in homage of his accomplishments, but warning him he'd already have trouble with my "shadow" just because he's from Boulder, Colorado. He acknowledged his awareness of "the problem." Barrie Archer, from Leavenworth, Kansas, doesn't have such a problem because he doesn't even make prints (gives his originals away — the one I have can only be seen at my house) and thus escapes this syndrome. I've felt more able to praise his work without political worry . . . or to praise Dean Stockwell's films because he, with his OWN reputation as a movie star overshadowing his films, has never felt free to make any public presentation of them.

What IS this? WHAT circumstance has so stifled the natural human relationship of known artists to sponsor the work of younger or unknown artists, the traditional means of recognition, etc. It is, if I hear these recalcitrant friends correctly, fear of art politics and/or their fear of specious and ABSTRACT usage. One would shun being aesthetically associated with me beCAUSE that could only, ever, be some partial recognition—if true at all. Yet the LIBRARIAN tendency these days IS to catalogue art works by these partial recognitions—i.e., along a line of past tendencies — thereby obfuscating the glorious uniqueness of any given work, the absolute difference each maker makes. Then there's structural aesthetics, where the JOB of investigating film-as-film molds itself after scientific enquiry, social studies, etc., regardless of individuality... (nuff).

I think that in this century the three greatest traditional possibilities for the English language, from James Joyce, Gertrude Stein and Ezra Pound, have been stifled by just such superficial attitudes as those which crimp film appreciation these days. Writers attempting to work the large "fields" of consideration created by their main mentors were immediately characterized as Joycian, Steinian, Poundian and summarily dismissed. In the meantime, those still working over the largely dead linguistics of the 19th century novel were praised to the skies for every simplistic trick whereby they could keep "this old hoss" kicking a while longer; and further, the study of dead linguistics itself, the structure of dead language, has elicited snobbish critical and institutional approval to the expense of ANY, even, personae of person. Do we have here a mini-example of feudal court- and church-fostered continuance of dead Latin across centuries during which the populace (not understanding the language at all) didn't have to think about what it was hearing in the slightest?... what a heaven for the sophisticated, and what a haven-hole for those who wish to BE enslaved by overlordliness — well, things aren't that bad, YET. All the same, we must recognize that the language discoveries of the early part of this century seem, now, islands—proudly defended, from any possibly influential "poaching," by exactly the same kind of aesthetician who rejected Joyce, Stein, Pound in the first place. Even as obviously unique a poet as Charles Olson is continuously tabbed "Poundian." Only Robert Creeley and Robert Duncan have dared mine Stein with regularity (though Duncan felt the need to characterize his first investigations as "Stein-like imitations"). Is there any living writer other than Marguerite Young who seeks to "extend the realm" of the Joyce novel? Beckett?... ANYthing (even nothing) but.

Just as it is competitive writers who mostly point the accusative finger and shout "imitator" at their literary fellows, so too is it usually filmmakers who gossip-forth judgement at each other... filmmakers and, occasionally, media center programmers (and the like) on the lookout for the obviously new or the OBVIOUSLY old. Professional film critics have almost ceased to exist, except as reporters of event. Like their literary counterpart, they will do their "librarian" damage classifying-by-"school" or announcing "movements" but rarely take time to note any extensive similarities-in-depth and/or the passage of a tradition from one filmmaker to another. (I wish to distinguish Ken Kelman's article "Portrait of the Young Man as Artist: From the Notebook of Robert Beavers," *Film Culture*, 1979, as a remarkable exception to the above.)

When I was young, the then director of the MOMA film department, Richard Griffith, said my films were "imitative of Maya Deren." I had, at the time, only seen *Meshes of the Afternoon*... once; but he was picking up on the tilt-wall sequence (a conscious "steal") and dismissing not only *In Between* BUT *Desistfilm* (made before any knowledge of Deren), *The Way to Shadow Garden*, and even *Interim*... and me... because that slight use of Deren's effect gave him the excuse to do so. At the same time Ian Hugo, closer to the mark, saw *The Way to Shadow Garden* as "in the tradition of Jean Cocteau," and prized the continuance of that tradition. He, however, put too much emphasis upon the use of motion picture negative and thus overlooked the more direct influence of Kenneth Anger's *Fireworks* on *Desistfilm*. My first film, *Interim*, was most directly inspired by Cocteau, specifically his *Orpheus*... (usually only Rossellini's influence on it is detected).

To my surprise, NObody ever questioned my most conscious and continuous "theft" — the use of sun's rays, or other back-light beams, directed into camera lens, such illumination shattering rhythmically and reflecting psychological mood, refraction creating symbolic shape... source?: Kurosawa's *Rashomon*. (The two, very opposite, film masters most carefully furthering the "psych-symbol" aspect of this tradition are John Luther and Francis Ford Copolla: it is no accident that in the wake of *Apocalypse Now* Coppola seeks to help the old Kurosawa to make another film... it is an unusual blessing of recognition.)

My most brazen whole "takes" of others' films passed without notice: Sidney Peterson's *Mr. Frenhofer and the Minotaur/Reflections on Black* (this oversight despite the fact that I've credited him as my "teacher" clearly; and it is interesting to note that I didn't use the anamorphic lens he'd passed on to me until making *Dog Star Man*, far removed from his aesthetics albeit benefitting much from his wisdom); Ian Hugo's *Jazz of Lights/Anticipation of the Night* (also many more generalized influences and a number of specific tricks of multiple superimposition "filched" from his *Melodic Inversion* for *Dog Star Man, Scenes From Under Childhood,* and even *Duplicity* in-the-making; the whole developing world view of Jim Davis/*The Text of Light* (this influence ignored even though the work was dedicated to Jim, in memoriam). And so it has been that while people have latches, meanly or favorably, upon effects as memorable characteristics in my films they have often missed the traditional basis I was actually building upon. (I think Annette Michelson was the first, 20-some years later, to fully recognize my debt to Sergei Eisenstein, for example.) What is all this "likeness" fuss anyway, some aesthetician equivalent to Simon-says?

Yesterday I took another look at the three film prints I own by Gary Doberman, *Fisheries, The Rhyme* and *The Moieties,* and satisfied myself that, yes, the last several years his work has been THE most persistent influence on my films—almost all of the Super-8mm-to-16mm "blow-up" films: *Thot Fal'n, Burial Path, Purity and After* (especially *After* and @ most particularly)...though not so much influence, interestingly enough, on either film in which Gary partially appears: *Centre* and the 16mm *Nightmare Series* (which, coupled with my delay in using Peterson's trick lens, suggests a need of the maker to "cover tracks" of source, a psychological hesitancy no doubt caused by the public attitudes I'm questioning in this essay...for, surely, shyness always operates as hindrance in the creative process, calls down the deadly lance of The Muse upon the maker, as Cocteau has vividly pictured in *The Testament of Orpheus).*

Gary Doberman and I, from the first, shared some obvious aesthetic affinities; and as I WAS first, he could be said to be "inheritor" of some of the "grounds" of these affinities filmwise; but wouldn't that be placing undue emphasis upon what he and I share "in the dark" of the movies to the expense of our light-lives in general? Perhaps not—I'm remembering Jean Cocteau's description of his first visit to The Theatre and how his creative life began then, as he found usual: art answering art, not life. And yet "Ars longa, vita breva:" the sources of aesthetic affinity stretch back centuries and mostly infuse us by the oblique means of everyday living. Dante gathers what he needs for *The Divine Comedy* from his poet friends (some of whom he places in hell, for thanks) and takes as his guide the Latin poet Virgil (perhaps less influential upon his language than others not mentioned)...(what influences am I, right now, concealing?—Gregory Markopoulos, whose work I attacked for years!...or possibly Michael Snow?)

What CAN be said is that Gary and I have inspired each other. What MUST be said (as how else would this society know it?—his films being unavailable) is that his work has directly influenced not only the "shaky" (camera hand-held) "grounds" of rhythmic vision in those films of mine already mentioned, but also *Creation* and my work-in-progress, *Made Manifest*. *Fisheries* and *The Rhyme* have affected my whole "slippery" relationship with The Sea. I've cared for (and always been very scared by) Ocean-as-subject. My vision of it in (1) *Song 8*, (2) *eyes*, and (3) *Rembrandt, Etc., And, Jane*, for instance, has (1) twisted and turned to seek its subjectivity UNDER Hokusai wave, and (2) taken it as extreme metaphorical object, and (3) cut it to "ribbons"/rhythms of visual music so beautiful as to remove that (note, unNAMED) section from the rest of the film's context.

Doberman's *Fisheries* and *The Rhyme*, albeit taking some few tricks from me, HAVE managed Sea-sight in the service of his beloved Ellen (always center of his work) but of such a balance as to avoid any subservient Ocean, as metaphor or other. The Ocean becomes OCCASION (especially in *The Rhyme* where it is, after all, only the visual "echo" of the rhythm structure at the beginning ... which itself is, anyway, an oblique metaphor of seascape)—occasion, then, as are the fishermen, the boat, OF Ellen's being there ... the whole film, after all, a rhyme of *Fisheries*. Ellen is only slightly pictured in these films, but each film turns within the fulcrum of colors, shapes, and rhythms of those pictured moments. (Some of his films, such as *The Moieties*, seem to picture Ellen constantly; but a length-count of imagery will show her picture to be more pervasive—by such tactics of color/shape/rhythm carry-over — than constant.) Gary Doberman has made it possible for me to subjectify The Sea (in *Creation* and, now, *Made Manifest*) without subverting surface, symbolizing depth, or diminishing it as object moving. I am eternally grateful — Sea being my first intended instrument-of-suicide when I was 17 ... that temporal diminishment and psychological haunt finally put to rest ... infinite possibilities opening up.

I recently had the chance to re-see Gustave Machaty's 1933 film *Ecstasy* which created an international scandal and some enduring popularity because of some brief nude scenes of the beautiful Hedy Kieslerova (later Hedy Lamarr). I have, since my first view of the film in my teens, thought it very much more interesting AS A FILM than its antique sexploited reputation would lead one to believe, and I have wondered why Machaty wasn't better known (I haven't been able to see ANother film by him or heard him discussed in over 20 years). The film opens on one of the favorite themes of bawdy balladry: an aged man carries his young bride over the theshold of their rooms, she glowing white with bridal veils, he darkened by his formality and tottering under her light weight. The first 15 minutes of the film their relationship is explored thru vignettes of lights and darks — her silhouette profile emerging into hard bars of backlighting, his polished shoes gleaming fitfully in a corner of the frame, etc. These often almost abstract scenes wherein the viewer's eye is entirely dependent upon slight rhythmic shifts, subtle framings, and shaped symbols of narrative emotion, are predecessors in the development of some of my work and, even more clearly, of that whole "field" of Gary Doberman's envisionment of male/female tension wherein he presents similar scenes in the service of his love — almost as if to transform the neurotic opposite of Machaty. Gary has never mentioned *Ecstasy*. He might well have seen it during his school days at Berkeley or even as part of his L.A. youth; but does it really matter? An impulse of sexual nuance arises thru human shadow play variously: what is exciting, at least to me, are the light-sparks trembling music-like themes of related longing midst and against black.

I've written this essay because I cannot live ALONE with the irony that the few times Gary Doberman can be persuaded to show *Fisheries*, *The Rhyme*, or *The Moieties*, he's likely to have them related to *Creation*, *Made Manifest* or my Super-8 "blow-ups" as imitations of Brakhage. Even were his work well known and often shown, he'd still suffer the same fate: (who, for instance, has tabbed me for the interruptive black leader effects of *23rd Psalm Branch* filched from Bruce Conner's *A Movie* and *Cosmic Ray*?: Ken Kelman, in the article mentioned above, is clear about what passed on "from Brakhage to Conner no matter how disparate their materials and themes may be," but he's not been clear about what passed BACK midst closeness of materials and themes: and "ex-pupil Bruce Conner" very wrongly characterizes our relationship).

The Greeks didn't see these "flatteries" between artist friends as a problem — but, rather, saw Mercury as patron god of both artists and thieves.

Ah well, let the "carping mentality" in current aesthetics HAVE at ME then, too, as imitator: they'll find me finally "disciple" of so many predecessors and contemporaries as'll keep them busy cataloging for years. As for the rest? Come! Let's join together in appreciating each other as well as what we happily share AND, as Pound says, "gather a live tradition from the air."

APPENDIX

SELECTED CATALOGUE DESCRIPTIONS OF THE FILMS

FILMOGRAPHY

SELECTED BIBLIOGRAPHY

INDEX

SELECTED CATALOGUE DESCRIPTIONS
OF THE FILMS

For distribution catalogues Stan Brakhage has commented on a number of his films; the following is a selection to outline the range of his conscious concerns. A complete filmography follows on page 255. — R.A.H.

Aftermath (1981)

The raw meat of the mind's imagination, the pounding blood of it, attempting to erase (rather than assimilate) a televised movie of ferocious popular appeal...a life versus death struggle played out in the purely visual (anti-numerical) area of thought.

@ (1979)

The first film of mine which is so very much there where it's *at* THAT it deserves visual symbol as title and no further explanation from me at/et? all.

Angels' (1971)

This then the property of many angels.

Anticipation of the Night (1958)

The daylight shadow of a man in its movement evokes lights in the night. A rose bowl held in hand reflects both sun and moon like illumination. The opening of a doorway onto trees anticipates the twilight into the night. A child is born on the lawn, born of water with its promissory rainbow, and the wild rose. It becomes the moon and the source of all light. Lights of the night become young children playing a circular game. The moon moves over a pillared temple to which all lights return. There is seen the sleep of innocents in their animal dreams, becoming the amusement, their circular game, becoming the morning. The trees change color and lose their leaves for the morn, they become the complexity of branches in which the shadow man hangs himself.

Aquarien (1974)

"EN"?—as the dictionary has it: "made of, of or belonging to" (as I have it) Aquarious/an(d) so forth: Latin water carrier in the sky, etc. This is my first fully conscious "tone poem" film.

Arabic One (1981)

The beginning of a new series. In the tradition of the Roman Numerals, yet entirely unique, this shift-of-vision takes its cues from consideration of the mind itself as jewel.

Arabic Two (1981)

Echoing an earlier mode of film (*Roman Numeral IX*) this could be seen as an equivalent of vis.a.vis./transference — this film as "key" to the difference between the two series...a metamorphosis "at the border" of differing levels of thought.

Arabic Three (1981)

It begins to be clear that the Arabic Numeral Series is (as thought process) more purely envisioned music than any previous film-making given to me to do.

The Art of Vision (1961-1965)

Includes the complete *Dog Star Man* and is a full extension of the singular visible themes of it. Inspired by that period of music in which the word *symphonia* was created and by the thought that the term, as then, was created to name the overlap and enmeshing of suites, this film presents the visual symphony that *Dog Star Man can be seen as* and also all the suites of which it is composed. But as it is a film, not work of music, the above suggests only *one* of the possible approaches to it. For instance as "cinematographer," at source, means "writer of movement," certain poetic analogies might serve as well. The form is conditioned by the works of arts which have inspired *Dog Star Man,* its growth of form by the physiology and experiences (including experiences of art) of the man who made it. Finally it must be seen for what it is.

Bird (1978)

This the first clear vision I've had of the hot-blooded dinosaurs still living among us.

Black Vision (1965)

...is inspired by the only passage in Jean Paul Sartre's writings which has ever specifically concerned me —the passage from *Nausea* wherein the protagonist sits in a park and imagines his suicide.

Burial Path (1978)

The film begins with the image of a dead bird.

The mind moves to forget, as well as to remember: this film, in the tradition of *Thot-Fal'n,* graphs the process of forgetfulness against all oddities of remembered bird-shape. The film might best be seen along with *Sirius Remembered* and *The Dead* as the third part of a trilogy. In Memoriam: Donald Sutherland.

Centre (1978)

A series of narrative events, stories if you like, but so clustered visually as to

have a center, so to speak, slightly off centre.

Clancy (1974)

This is a portrait of the man I choose to call "the greatest I've known": Clancy, whom the fates surnamed Sheehy, personifies for me that which is simply human beyond condition and all conditioning.

The Dead (1960)

Europe weighted down so much with that past, was *The Dead.* I was always Tourist there; I couldn't live in it. The graveyard could stand for all my view of Europe, for all the concerns with past art, for involvement with symbol. *The Dead* became my first work in which things that might very easily be taken as symbols were so photographed as to destroy all their symbolic potential. The action of making *The Dead* kept me alive.

Deus Ex (1971)

I have been many times very ill in hospitals; and I drew on all that experience while making *Deus Ex* in West Penn. Hospital of Pittsburgh: but I was especially inspired by the memory of one incident in an Emergency Room of S.F.'s Mission District: while waiting for medical help, I had held myself together by reading an April-May, 1965 issue of *Poetry Magazine;* and the following lines from Charles Olson's "Cole's Island" had especially centered the experience, "touchstone" of *Deus Ex,* for me: Charles begins the poem with the statement, "I met Death—" and then: "He didn't bother me, or say anything. Which is/ not surprising, a person might not, in the circumstances;/ or at most a nod or something. Or they would. But they wouldn't,/ or you wouldn't think to either, if it was Death. And/ He certainly was, the moment I saw him." The film begins with this sense of such an experience and goes on to envision the whole battle of hospital on these grounds, thru the heart surgery seen as equivalent to Aztec ritual sacrifice...the lengths men go to avoid so simple and straight a relationship with Death as Charles Olson managed on/in "Cole's Island."

Door (1971)

This is the only all-inclusive autobiography I've yet managed; and as I'm still alive, it is to be understood as a metaphor which defines the limits of expectation.

Duplicity (1978)

A friend of many year's acquaintance showed me the duplicity of myself. And, midst guilt and anxiety, I came to see that duplicity often shows itself forth in semblance of sincerity. Then a dream informed me that *Sincerity IV*, which I had just completed, was such a semblance. The dream ended with the word "Duplicity" scratched white across the closed eyelid (as the title *The Weir-Falcon Saga* had been given to me). I saw that the film in question demonstrated a duplicity of relationship between the Brakhages and animals (Totemism) and environs (especially trees), visiting friends (Robert Creeley, Ed Dorn, Donald Sutherland, Angelo DiBenedetto and Jerome Hill among them) and people-at-large. I saw that the film shifted its compositions equally along a line of dark shapes as well as light, and that it did not progress (as did earlier Sincerities) but was rather a correlative of *Sincerity III*. Accordingly I changed the title to *Duplicity*.

Duplicity II (1978)

This, the second film of the continuing autobiographical Duplicity series, is composed of superimpositions much as the mind 'dupes' remembered experience into some semblance of, say, composed surety rather than imbalanced accuracy—as thought may even warp 'scene' into symmetry, or 'face' into multitudinous mask. What will have been becomes what will *be be*ing. I've tried to 'give the lie' to this genesis of all white-lying.

Duplicity III (1980)

The final Duplicity in this series does seem a resolve with the term. All previous visual manifestations have been extended (thru 4-roll superimpositions) to their limit. Obvious costumes and masks, Drama as an ultimate play-for-truth, and totemic recognition of human *animal* life-on-earth dominate all the evasions duplicity otherwise affords.

Eye Myth (1972, 1981)

190 frames, begun in 1968 as sketch for *The Horseman, The Woman, and The Moth*.

eyes (1971)

After wishing for years to be given-the-opportunity of filming some of the more "mystical" occupations of our Times—some of the more obscure Public Figures which the average imagination turns into "bogeymen"...viz.: Policemen, Doctors, Soldiers, Politicians, etc.:—I was at last permitted to ride in a Pittsburgh Policecar, camera in hand, the final several days of Sept. 1970—this opportunity largely due to the efforts of a Pittsburgh newspaper photographer, Mike Chikiris...who was sympathetic to my film show at The Carnegie Institute and responded to my wish as stated on that occasion—therefore pleaded my "cause" eloquently with Police Inspectors of his acquaintance: my thanks to him, to Sally Dixon of The Carnegie Institute and to the Policemen who created the situation that made this film possible.

As to the film itself: "Polis is eyes," said Charles Olson, having found the archeological root of the word-end (thus beginning) of, say, "metropolis," etc. 'Police is a clear etymological derivative of 'polis'."

The more currently popular fix on these terms comes from, say, Dashiel Hammet's "private eye," & the sense of response-ability which Raymond Chandler and even Ross MacDonald give to their detective heros under that term.

The Police, then, are the public eyes; and they are, thus, expected to be Specialists of that ability-to respond which most of the rest of the society has lost all Metro sense-of.

The experience of making this film prompted that clarity of terms: "Polis is eyes" was my constant prayer, to make that experience clear, the last entire day of photographing.

The film mostly assembled, rather than edited, is thus the surest track I could make of what it was given to me to see.

It is "framed" by clouds and the ocean for the simplest reasons of "perspective."

Fifteen Song Traits (1965, 1980)

A series of individual portraits of friends and family, all inter-related in what might be called a branch growng directly from the trunk of *Songs 1 thru 14*. In order of appearance: Robert Kelly, Jane and our dog Durin, our boys Bearthm and Rarc, daughter Crystal and the canary Cheep Donkey, Robert Creeley and Michael McClure, the rest of our girls Myrrena and Neowyn, Angelo DiBenedetto, Ed Dorn and his family, and Jonas Mekas (to whom the whole of the *Fifteen Song Traits* is dedicated), as well as some few strangers, were the source of these *Traits* coming into being—my thanks to all...and to all who see them clearly.

Films By Stan Brakhage (1961)

I had a camera with which I could make multiple superimpositions spontaneously. It had been lent to me for a week. I was also given a couple of rolls of color film which had been through an intensive fire. The chance that the film would not record any image at all left me free to experiment and to try to create the sense of the daily world in which we live, and what it meant to me. I wanted to record our home, and yet deal with it as being that area from which the films by Stan Brakhage arise, and to try to make one arise at the same time....

Fire of Waters (1965)

Inspired by a statement in a letter from poet Robert Kelly: "The truth of the matter is this that: man lives in a fire of waters and will live eternally in the first taste"—this film is a play of light and sounds upon that theme.

Flight (1974)

Pun on "light" intended—that short preceeding expellation of breath perhaps the "subject matter" of this film which centers in consideration of death. It is the third tone poem film and did much surprise me by thus completing a trilogy of the "4 classical Elements."

Foxfire Childwatch (1971)

Ken, Flo, and Nisi Jacobs in the Syracuse Airport: this is what you might call baby-sitting in the swamp.

The Governor (1971)

On July 4th, 1976, I and my camera toured the state of Colorado with Governor Richard D. Lamm, as he traveled in parades with his children, appeared at dinners, lectured, etc. On July 20th, I spent the morning in his office in the state capitol and the afternoon with himself and his wife in a television studio, then with Mrs. Lamm greeting guests to the governor's mansion and finally with Governor Lamm in his office again. These two days of photography took me exactly one year to edit into a film which wove itself thru multiple superimpositions into a study of light and power.

"he was born, he suffered, he died" (1974)

The quote is Joseph Conrad answering a critic who found his books too long. Conrad replied that he could write a novel on the inside of a matchbook-cover, thus (as above), but that he "preferred to elaborate." The "Life" of the film is scratched on black leader. The "elaboration" of color tonalities is as the mind's eye responds to hieroglyph.

The Horseman, The Woman, and The Moth (1968)

A long myth drawn directly onto the film's surface, which is painted, dyed, treated so that it will grow controlled crystals and mold—as textures of the figures and forms of the drama—, some images stamped thru melted wax crayon techniques, some images actual objects (such as moth wings) collaged directly on the celluloid...so that the protagonists of this myth (as listed in the title) weave thru crystalline structures and organic jungles of the colorful world of hypnogogic vision—edited into "themes and variations" that tell "a thousand and one" stories while, at the same time, evoking Baroque music... the primary musical inspiration being the harpsichord sonatas of Domenico Scarlatti.

Hymn To Her (1974)

"Her" to me is always Jane, in the first place, but also Hera: "goddess of women and marriage," naturally enough. Then too, as it is a hymn of light, and as he/me feels the self that way, it sings of and to itself.

Oh Life—A Woe Story—The A Test News (1963)

Three TV "concretes."

Lovemaking (1966)

An American Kama Sutra—Love's answer to filmic pornography...four visions of sexual loving which exist in an aesthetic balance of feeling the very opposite of the strip-tease as usually encountered in both Hollywood movies and the foreign, so-called "Art Film": a totally new experience.

Made Manifest (1980)

"Every man's work shall be made manifest, for the day shall declare it, because it shall be revealed by fire and the fire shall try every man's work of what sort it is."—1 Corinthians 111-113

Mothlight (1963)

What a moth might see from birth to death if black were white and white were black.

Murder Psalm (1981)

"...unparalleled debauchery, when man turns into a filthy, cowardly, cruel, vicious reptile. That's what we need! And what's more, a little 'fresh blood' that we may grow accustomed to it..." (Dostoyevsky, *The Devils*, Part II, Chapter VIII). "In my novel *The Devils* I attempted to depict the complex and heterogeneous motives which may prompt even the purest of heart and the most naive people to take part in an absolutely monstrous crime" (Dostoyevsky, *The Diary of a Writer*).

Nightmare Series (1978)

Four films so related to each other as to

be an equivalent of that frightful dreaming which makes Wake of the following day, so that it be spent mourning the events of the night. A decade and a half ago, poet Robert Kelly told me that the "crucial work" of our Time might be what he calls "the dream work": I hope, with this *Series*, to have entertained his challenge more thoughtfully than with any previous "dream" filmmaking. In homage to Sigmund Freud and Surrealism, this film proposes clear visible alternatives to the consideration of both "The Interpretation of . . ." and all previous representation of . . . dreaming.

Other (1980)

A film photographed in Amsterdam but dedicated to capturing a quality of mind engendered there—not, certainly, alienation (as often in travel) but rather some heightened sense of being other. Dedicated to Virgil Grillo.

Pasht (1965)

In honor of the cat, so named, and the goddess of all cats which she was named after (that taking shape in the Egyptian mind of the spirit of cats), and of birth (as she was then giving kittens when the pictures were taken), of sex as source, and finally of death (as this making was the salvage therefrom and in memoriam).

The Peaceable Kingdom (1971)

This film, one of the most perfect it has ever been given to me to make, was inspired by the series of paintings of the same title by Edward Hicks.

The Presence (1972)

The Presence reflects some sight of Insect as Being. The imagined aura and environment of a beetle creates a "world" wherein this solitary insect may simply be seen.

The Process (1972)

LIGHT was primary in my consideration. All senses of "process" are (to me) based primarily on "thought-process"; and "thought-process" is based primarily on "memory re-call"; and that, as any memory process (all process finally) is electrical (firing of nerve connection) and expresses itself most clearly as a "back-firing" of nerve endings in the eye which DO become visible to us (usually eyes closed) as "brain movies"—as Michael McClure calls them. When we are not re-constructing "a scene" (recalling something once seen), then we are watching (on the "screen" of closed eye-lids) the very PROCESS itself . . .

Purity And After (1978)

Two short films, the first NOT about purity itself, whatever that might be, but rather an equivalent of the process of searching for purity in the mind . . . the second film, then, thought's rebound from that.

The Riddle Of Lumen (1972)

The classical riddle was meant to be heard, of course. Its answers are contained within its questions; and on the smallest piece of itself this possibility depends: upon SOUND — "utterly," like they say . . . the pun its pivot. Therefore, my *Riddle Of Lumen* depends upon qualities of LIGHT. All films do, of course. But with *The Riddle Of Lumen,* "the hero" of the film is light/itself. It is a film I'd long wanted to make—inspired by the sense, and specific formal possibilities, of the classical Eng.-lang. riddle . . . only one appropriate to film and, thus, as distinct from language as I could make it.

Roman Numeral Series

The Roman Numeral Series is dedicated to Don Yannacito.

I (1979)

This begins a new series of films which would ordinarily be called "abstract," "non-objective," "non-representational," etc. I cannot tolerate any of those terms and, in fact, had to struggle against all such historical concepts to proceed with my work. Midst creative process, the sound "imagnostic" kept ringing in my ears. It seems to be an enjambment of Latin and Greek; but Charlton T. Lewis' "Elementary Latin Dictionary" gives me (via Guy Davenport) "image"...Sanscrit = AIC = "like," GNOSIS "knowledge," GNOSTIC AGNOSCO = "to recognize"/"to know" and the happier IMAGINOSUS "full of fancies"/"fantasies," illustrated by Catullus' singular use (perhaps creation of the term?) in the line "His mind solidly filled with fancies of a girl." Even though exhausted by this etymological pursuit, and despite my prejudice against taking on "foreign airs" of tongue, "Imagnostic," keeps singing in my head and escaping my lips in conversation. I'm not sure if this work is titled "I" for "Imagnostic," or "I" as designating first person singular, or "I" Roman Numeral One.

II (1979)

Now that *II* has been completed, one would suppose that the above film *I* is "One"...unless, of course, this film's spoken title is "aye-aye" or even, perhaps, slyly referring to the two "eyes" which made it, as distinct from the singularity of vision which flattens space in the making of its predecessor.

III (1980)

The third in this series of Imagnostic Films seems particularly magic to me inasmuch as I cannot even remember the photographic source of these images or, thus, of having taken them.

IV (1980)

The term "deja vu" comes to mind each time I view this film—this, then, somehow the "echoing" of the birth of imagery.

It was while studying this film that I decided to group these "romans" under the title *Roman Numeral Series* and to give up the term "imagnostic" altogether...also to dedicate the series to Don Yannacito who had seen something "concrete" and even narratively dramatic in this work.

V (1980)

An imagery sharp as stars and hard as the thought-universe (turning back upon itself) absorbed in gentle patterns of contemplation.

VI (1980)

What shall one say?

VII (1980)

What CAN one say?—that won't limit, by language, the complexity of moving visual thinking?...the skein of pattern that seeks to make its own language.

VIII (1980)

This the most formal of all these works.

IX (1980)

This the most absolute.

Salome (1980)

Portrait of the great chess master, aesthetician, human being Eugene Salome.

Scenes From Under Childhood: Sections 1-4 (1967-1970)

A visualization of the inner world of foetal beginnings, the infant, the baby, the child—a shattering of the "myths of childhood" through revelation of the extremes of violent terror and over-whelming joy of that world darkened to most adults by their sentimental remembering of it...a "tone poem" for the eye—very inspired by the music of Olivier Messiaen.

Sexual Meditation No. 1: Motel (1970,1980)

This film was originally photographed in 1970 in regular 8mm. It has now (a decade later) been blown-up to 16mm so that it can join the rest of the Sexual Meditation Series.

Sexual Meditation: Room with View (1971)

Directly in the tradition of *Sexual Meditiation No. 1: Motel* (first available *only* in 8mm), this "sequel" does explore further the possibilities of nudes in a room; and as it was made in 16mm, it is available in both 16 and 8mm.

Sexual Meditation: Faun's Room, Yale (1972)

This, the third, of the Sexual Meditation Series might also be seen as a triangular portrait of Julia and P. Adams Sitney and Jane Brakhage.

Sexual Meditation: Office Suite (1972)

This film evolves from several years' observation of the sexual energy which charges the world of business and the qualities of palatial environ which this energy often creates. It is one of the most perfect films it has been given to me to make.

Sexual Meditation: Hotel (1972)

This film takes its cues from that ultimate situation of Sex Med./ masturbation—the loft-and-lonely hotel room. It is thus easily twice the length and complexity of any previous film in this series.

Sexual Meditation: Open Field (1973)

This film takes all the masturbatory themes of previous Sexual Mediations back to source in pre-adolescent dreams. *Open Field* is in the mind, of course, and exists as a weave of trees, grasses, waters and bodies poised and fleeting at childhood's end. The scene is lit as by sun and moon alike and haunted by the pursuant adult.

The Shores of Phos: A Fable (1972)

Phos = Light, but then I did also want that word within the title which would designate *place*, as within the nationalities of "the fabulous"—a specific country of the imagination with tangible shores, etc. The film adheres strictly to the ordinary Form of the classical fable.

Short Films 1975: 1-10

This is a series of ten deliberately untitled films, each separated on the reel by several feet of black leader.

Short Films: 1976

Four films verging on portraiture, converging to make a drama for all seasons, starring: Jane Brakhage as The Dreamer; Bob Benson as the Magnificent Stranger; Omar Beagle as The Snow Plow Man; Jimmy Ryan Morris as The Poet, and as Doc Holliday.

Sincerity (1973)

This, the first completed reel of work-in-progress, draws on autobiographical energies and images which reflect the first 20 years of my living. I have three definitions of the word "sincerity" to sustain my working along these lines of thought with this autobiographical material: (1) Ezra Pound's marvelous mistranslation of a Chinese ideogram—"Sincerity..the sun's lance coming to rest on the precise spot verbally"...(of which I would change, for my purposes, the last word to "visually"), (2) Robert Creeley's trace-of-the-word for me on the back of a Buffalo restaurant menu—"Sym-keros...same-growth   (Ceres) *create*...of the same growth," and (3) Hollis Frampton's track-of-it to "the greek," viz—'a glazed pot (i.e. one which will hold water)." This film might best be seen, then, as a graph of light equivalent to autobiographical thought process.

Sincerity II (1975)

This continuation of my autobiography is composed of film photographed by many people: Bruce Baillie, Jane Brakhage, Larry Jordan and Stan Phillips, among others. Most of the footage is drawn from 20,000 feet of "home movies," "out-takes" and the like, I've salvaged of my photography over the years.

It is of the Brakhage family's coming into being.

It is composed in the light of those electrical traces we call "memory"; and it is as true to that "thought process" as I was enabled to make it. This project was supported by a grant from the National Endowment for the Arts.

Sincerity III (1978)

In the autobiographical tradition of earlier Sincerities, this film takes up the light-threads of our living 14 years ago when the Brakhage family found Home and "settled," like they say, into some sense of permanence. This quality of living in one place tends to destroy most senses of chronology: thus, along lines-of-thought of growing and shifting physicality, events *can* seem to be occuring simultaneously (a thot-process 'kin to that of *The Domain of the Moment*), and the memory of such a time IS prompted and sustained by details of living usually overlooked or taken-for-granted (such as Proust's cookie

which prompted *Remembrance of Things Past*). Michael McClure's *Fleas* and Andrew Noren's *The Exquisite Corpse III* were additional sources of inspiration for the making of this work.

Sincerity IV (1980)

This, the 6th film of the Sincerity/ Duplicity series, seems rooted in the earliest tradition of my work, Psycho-Drama, as well as in the most recent, Imagnostic, directions taken. It is remembrance as thought fashions it in lonely hotel rooms, sincere return of the mind to that which is loved, ephemeral faces of children growing older, familiar objects interwoven with easy alien familiarity, the images of strangers in UNeasy identification, sexual posture and the lure of The Beloved as irreducible image.

Sincerity V (1980)

This, then, finishes eleven years of editing drawing on 30-some years of photography. I will surely work autobiographically again, but the modes of "Sincerity and Duplicity" seem completed with this film which, on the one hand, is as simple in its integrity-of-light as those follow-the-ball "sing along" early silent movies and as complicated as teen-age metamorphosis. Childhood dissolves in flame, struck from the hearth.

Sirius Remembered (1959)

I was coming to terms with decay of a dead thing and the decay of the memories of a loved being that had died and it was undermining all abstract concepts of death. The form was being cast out of probably the same physical need that makes dogs dance and howl in rhythm around a corpse. I was taking song as my source of inspiration for the rhythm structure, just as dogs dancing, prancing around a corpse, and howling in   rhythm-structures   or   rhythm-intervals might be considered like the birth of some kind of song.

Skein (1974)

"A loosely coiled length of yarn (story)... wound on a reel" — my parenthesis! This is a painted film (inspired by Nolde's "unpainted pictures"): "skins" of paint hung in a weave of light.

Sluice (1978)

It is a wooden silver-retrieving sluice, thus light-catch, awash with something like "cheek and jowl clippings of Argentine bulls" (as Hollis Frampton reminds us) and many chemical residues of earth. My mind has grown TREE out of the forest of all of it.

Sol (1974)

"1: SUN 2 *not cap:* GOLD—used in alchemy 3: the sun-god of the ancient Romans"; but then also, as I understand it, a french word for "earth," wherefrom we get our "soil"; and then (puns always intended, as I hear them): soul...this also, then, a tone poem film.

Soldiers and Other Cosmic Objects (1977)

This begins the 4th chapter of "The Book of The Film" and entertains directly the considerations of Chapter 2 (*The Weir Falcon Saga, The Machine of Eden,* and *The Animals of Eden and After*). *Person* begins to be defined by what it is *not*. It might be said that Chapter 1 (*Scenes From Under Childhood*) set forth birth and being, Chapter 2—consciousness, Chapter 3 (*Sincerity*)— *self*-consciousness; thus *Soldiers and Other Cosmic Objects* begins that strictly philosophical task of distinguishment (from, in this case, the rituals and trials of public school). I like to think of it as a work that Ludwig Wittgenstein might have found more than enjoyable.

Songs 1-7 (1964,1980)

Songs 8-14 (1965,1980)

After much technical difficulty and elaborate color RE-creation, and thanks to economic assistance from Anthology Film Archives, I've managed to enlarge the REGULAR 8mm *Songs 1-14* into 16mm films, which saves them from extinction (due to rough-&-tumble of Reg. 8mm lab. work these days) AND permits them a larger public life. My thanks to all those who helped make this possible, especially Jonas Mekas and Mike Phillips.

Song 1

Portrait of a lady.

Songs 2 & 3

Fire and a mind's movement in remembering.

Song 4

Three girls playing with a ball. Hand painted.

Song 5

A childbirth song.

Songs 6 & 7

6—The painted veil via moth-death; 7—San Francisco.

Song 8

Sea creatures.

Songs 9 & 10

9—Wedding source and substance; 10—Sitting around.

Song 11

Fires, windows, an insect, a lyre of rain scratches.

Song 12

Verticals and shadows caught in glass traps.

Song 13

A travel song of scenes and horizontals.

Song 14

Molds, paints and crystals.

Star Garden (1974)

The "STAR," as it is singular, is the sun; and it is metaphored, at the beginning of this film, by the projector anyone uses to show it forth. Then the imaginary sun begins its course throughout whatever darkened room this film is seen within. At "high noon" (of the narrative) it can be imagined as if in back of the screen. Then it can be seen to shift its thought-light gradually back thru aftertones and imaginings of the "stars" of the film till it achieves a one-to-one relationship with moon again. This "sun" of the mind's eye of every viewer does only occasionally correspond with the off-screen "pictured sun" of the film; and anyone who cares to play this game of multiple illumination will surely see the film in its most completely conscious light. Otherwise it simply depicts (as Brancusi put it): "One of those days I would not trade for anything under heaven."

The Stars Are Beautiful (1975)

This is the first sound film I've completed since 1962 — the first sync sound ever. It is a philosophical film... extending the realm of *Blue Moses*. Its finest viewer, so far, has written:
   "The sun, — moon — and stars, really are the footprints of God. — and the broken fragments of the mirror that reflects reality. — and they are quite beautiful. I had not seen them before." (John Newell)

Super 8mm Films in 16mm (1976, 1978)

(*Airs; Window; Trio; Desert; Absence; The Dream, N.Y.C., The Return, The Flower; Gadflies; Sketches; Rembrandt, Etc. and Jane; Highs*)

The Super 8mm films listed above have been optically enlarged to 16mm. Some have "translated" better than others (*The Dream, N.Y.C., The Return, The Flower,* for instance, seems to me much greater in its 16mm composition than in the original Super 8mm), but all of them have benefited color-wise from this process due to the careful supervision of the transfer; and it was my enthusiasm about the possibilities of color-control during optical "blow-up" which inspired the series of films shot in Super 8mm ONLY to be shown in 16mm (all those 16mms listed to be shown "at 18 f.p.s."): thus the entire procedure of making these enlargements has provided a crucial turning-point in my work. The films listed above should, perhaps, be regarded as translations from Super 8mm work; and it would be interesting, in that context, to show Super 8mm and 16mm versions of the same films in conjunction. Then, also, this procedure has made it possible to show this very important series of films in auditoriums which cannot accommodate 8mm.

The Text of Light (1974)

"All that is is light" — Duns Scotus Erigena. "To see a world in a grain of sand" — William Blake. These the primary impulses while working on this film. It is dedicated to Jim Davis who showed me the "first spark" of refracted film light.

Thigh Line Lyre Triangular (1961)

Only at a crisis do I see both the scene as I've been trained to see it (that is, with Renaissance perspective, three-dimensional logic—colors as we've been trained to call a color a color, and so forth) and patterns that move straight out from the inside of the mind through the optic nerves . . . spots before my eyes, so to speak . . . and it's a very intensive, disturbing, but joyful experience. I've seen that every time a child was born. . . . Now none of that was in *Window Water Baby Moving;* and I wanted a childbirth film which expressed all of my seeing at such a time.

Thot-Fal'n (1978)

This film describes a psychological state 'kin to "moon-struck," its images emblems (not quite symbols) of suspension-of-self within consciousness and then that feeling of "falling away" from conscious thought. The film can only be said to "describe" or be emblematic of this state because I cannot imagine symbolizing or otherwise representing an equivalent of thoughtlessness itself. Thus the "actors" in the film, Jane Brakhage, Tom and Gloria Bartek, William Burroughs, Allen Ginsberg, Peter Orlovsky and Phillip Whalen are figments of this Thought-Fallen PROCESS, as are their images in the film to themselves being photographed.

Three Films (1965)

Includes three short films: *Blue White,* "an intonation of child birth"; *Blood's Tone,* "a golden nursing film"; *Vein,* "a film of baby Buddha masturbation."

Tragoedia (1976)

This film was conceived about 10 years ago when I heard Norman O. Brown define "Tragedy" as "goat-song" (or as Webster's has it: "Greek *tragoidia* fr. *tragos* goat + *aiedein* to sing; prob. fr. the satyrs represented by the original chorus"). I disagree with the last part of the Webster explanation and tend to think that the quality of sound of goats

crying did prompt the greeks to choose this term for their drama. In any case, the film *Tragoedia* is also ironic (thus, perhaps, the Latin of its title) as, often, is goat "lamentation"; and finally I should quote this from the O.E.D.: "As to the reason of the name many theories have been offered, some even disputing the connexion with 'goat'."

The Trip To Door (1971)

Directly in the tradition of *Scenes From Under Childhood,* this film may indeed constitute a third chapter to "The Book of The Film."

23rd Psalm Branch: Part 1 (1966, 1978)

This work, created in Reg. 8mm a decade ago, optically enlarged to 16mm, was in great danger (as all the *Songs*) of being lost forever due to deterioration of the Original and all Lab Masters. Despite great expense, I've managed to enlarge the Original (step-printed) into a 16mm Master. I chose this film (above all other *Songs*) FIRST because the multiple splices and hand-painted sections of it endangered it the most AND because I fear the war-inclination of this society at this time once again. P. Adams Sitney writes (in *Visionary Film*): "The furthest that Brakhage came in extending the language of 8mm cinema was his editing of the *23rd Psalm Branch.* . . . The phenomenal and painstaking craftsmanship of this film reflects the intensity of the obsession with which its theme grasped his mind. In 1966, out of confusion about the Vietnam war and the American reaction to it, Brakhage began to meditate on the nature of war. . . . The fruit of his studies and thoughts was the longest and most important of the *Songs* . . . it is an apocalypse of the imagination."

Two: Creeley/McClure (1965)

Two portraits in relation to each other,

the first of Robert Creeley, the second of Michael McClure. (These companion films were reduced to 8mm for necessary inclusion in *Fifteen Song Traits* —see *Songs* —but may also be rented in their original form.)

The Weir-Falcon Saga

The Weir-Falcon Saga (1970)
The Machine of Eden (1970)
The Animals of Eden and After (1970)

The term *The Weir-Falcon Saga* appeared to me, night after night, at the end of each of a series of dreams: I was "true" to the feeling, tho' not the images, of those dreams in the editing of this and the following two films. The three films "go" very directly together, in the (above) order of their making: yet each seems to be a clear film in itself. At this time, I tend to think they constitute Chapter No. 2 of "The Book of The Film" I've had in mind these last five years (considering *Scenes From Under Childhood* as Chapter No. 1): and yet these "Weir-Falcon" films occur to me as distinct from any film-making I have done before. They engender, in me, entirely "new" considerations. I cannot describe them: but there is an excerpt from "The Spoils," by Basil Bunting, which raises hair on the back of my neck similarly:

> Have you seen a falcon stoop/ accurate, unforseen/ and absolute, between/ wind-ripples over harvest? Dead/ of what's to be, is and has been—/ were we not better dead?/ His wings churn air/ to flight./ Feathers alight/ with sun, he rises where/ dazzle rebuts our stare,/ wonder our fright.

I might add that, *The Machine (of Eden) operates* via "spots" —from sun's disks (of the camera lens) thru emulsion grains (within which, each, a universe might be found) and snow's flakes (echoing technical aberrations on film's surface) blots (upon the lens itself) and the circles of sun and moon, etcetera; these "mis-takes" give birth to "shape" (which, in this work, is "matter," subject and otherwise) amidst a weave of thought: (I add these technicalities, here, to help viewers defeat the habits of classical symbolism so that this work may be *immediately* seen, in its own light): the "dream" of Eden will speak for itself.

Western History (1971)

This is a comedy, tho' few will know the subject well enough to laugh; for it meticulously represents the whole personal story of Westward Ho and Hoeing Man as He might attempt to remember it while watching a Pittsburgh basketball game.

The Wold Shadow (1972)

"Wold" because the word refers to 'forests' which poets later made "plains," and because the word also contains the rustic sense "to kill" —this then my laboriously painted vision of the god of the forest.

The Women (1973)

A psychodrama. A being-without-clothes (as inspired by the painter Paul Delvaux). A film which searches thru two women its definitive "The."

FILMOGRAPHY

All films are silent unless otherwise noted. This filmography uses one assembled by Joyce Rheuban in 1973 for *Artforum* as its basis and includes corrections to that listing as well as post-1973 films.

The listings for "blow-ups" and "reductions" are more than technical notations. Brakhage has noted that their "transference was creative (often taking more energy than to make a new film), i.e., where the new millimeter (film) is *at least* a translation of an earlier work."

1952
Interim (16mm) 25 min B/W; music by James
     Tenney

1953
Unglassed Windows Cast A Terrible Reflection
     (16mm) 35 min B/W
The Boy and the Sea (16mm) 2 min B/W (lost)

1954
Desistfilm (16mm) 7 min B/W; sound by
     Brakhage
The Extraordinary Child (16mm) 10 min B/W
The Way To Shadow Garden (16mm) 10 min B/
     W; sound by Brakhage

1955
Untitled color film of Geoffrey Holder's wed-
     ding (16mm), made with Larry
     Jordan in response to an invitation by
     Maya Deren
In Between (16mm) 10 min color; music by John
     Cage
Reflections on Black (16mm) 12 min B/W; sound
     by Brakhage
The Wonder Ring (16mm) 4 min color
     (suggested by Joseph Cornell, who used
     the footage to make his own *Gnir Rednow*)
Footage for an incomplete film, *Tower House*,
     that Joseph Cornell (who suggested that
     Brakhage shoot the film) made into his own
     Centuries of June

1956
Zone Moment (16mm) 3 min color (lost)
Flesh of Morning (16mm) 25 min B/W; sound
Nightcats (16mm) 8 min color

1957
Daybreak and *Whiteye* (16 mm) 8 min B/W;
     sound
Loving (16 mm) 6 min color
1958
Anticipation of the Night (16mm) 42 min color

1959
Wedlock House: An Intercourse (16mm) 11 min
     B/W
Window Water Baby Moving (16mm) 12 min
     color
Cat's Cradle (16mm) 5 min color
Sirius Remembered (16mm) 12 min color

1960
The Dead (16mm) 11 min color

1961
Thigh Line Lyre Triangular (16mm) 5 min color
Films By Stan Brakhage (16mm) 5 min color

1962
Blue Moses (16mm) 11 min B/W; sound
Silent Sound Sense Stars Subotnick and Sender
     (16mm) 2 min B/W (lost)

1963
Oh Life —A Woe Story —The A Test News
     (16mm) 5 min B/W
Footage for the film *Meat Jewel* (16mm) color,
     which was incorporated into *Dog Star Man:
     Part II*
Mothlight (16mm) 4 min color

1961-1964
Dog Star Man
     1961
Prelude: Dog Star Man (16mm) 25 min color
     1962
Dog Star Man: Part I (16mm) 35 min color
     1963
Dog Star Man: Part II (16mm) 7 min color
     1964
Dog Star Man: Part III (16mm) 11 min color
     1964
Dog Star Man: Part IV (16mm) 5 min color

1961-1965
The Art of Vision (16mm) 270 min color (derived
     from the film *Dog Star Man*)

1965

Three Films [consists of *Blue White, Blood's Tone,* and *Vein*] (16mm) 10 min color
Fire of Waters (16mm) 10 min B/W; sound
Pasht (16mm) 5 min color
Two: Creeley/McClure (16mm) 5 min color
Black Vision (16mm) 3 min B/W

1967

Eye Myth (35mm) 9 seconds color (not shown in 35mm until 1981, at the Telluride Film Festival; released in 1972 in 16mm)

1968

The Horseman, The Woman and The Moth (16mm) 19 min color
Lovemaking (16mm) 36 min color (film consists of Parts I-IV)

1964-1969
Songs
1964
Song 1 (8mm) 4 min color
Songs 2 and 3 (8mm) 7 min color
Song 4 (8mm) 5 min color
Song 5 (8mm) 6 min color
Songs 6 and 7 (8mm) 6 min color
Song 8 (8mm) 5 min color
1965
Songs 9 and 10 (8mm) 9 min color
Song 11 (8mm) 5 min color
Song 12 (8mm) 5 min B/W
Song 13 (8mm) 5 min color
Song 14 (8mm) 5 min color
15 Song Traits (8mm) 47 min color
Song 16 (8mm) 7 min color
Songs 17 and 18 (8mm) 8 min color
Songs 19 and 20 (8mm) 14 min color
Songs 21 and 22 (8mm) 10 min color
1966-1967
23rd Psalm Branch (8mm) 100 min color; Part I is dated 1966; Part II and the Coda are dated 1967
1967
Songs 24 and 25 (8mm) 10 min color
1968
Song 26 (8mm) 8 min color
My Mountain Song 27 (8mm) 26 min color
1969
Song 27 (Part II) Rivers (8mm) 36 min color
Song 28 (8mm) 4 min color
Song 29 (8mm) 4 min color
American 30's Song (8mm) 30 min color

Window Suite of Children's Songs (8mm) 24 min color (films made by the five Brakhage children; Brakhage arranged them in this form but did not edit them)

1969

Nuptiae (16mm) 14 min color; photographed by Brakhage for James Broughton; music by Lou Harrison

1967-1970
Scenes From Under Childhood
1967
Scenes From Under Childhood: Section No. 1 (16mm) 30 min color; until the late 1970s a sound version of this section of the film was in distribution—now only a silent version is available
1969
Scenes From Under Childhood: Section No. 2 (16mm) 40 min color
Scenes From Under Childhood: Section No. 3 (16mm) 27½ min color
1970
Scenes From Under Childhood: Section No. 4 (16mm) 46 min color

1970

The Weir-Falcon Saga (16mm) 29 min color
The Machine of Eden (16mm) 11 min color
The Animals of Eden and After (16mm) 35 min color

1970-1972
Sexual Meditations
1970
Sexual Meditation No. 1: Motel (8mm) 6 min color
1971
Sexual Meditation: Room With View (16mm) 3 min color
1972
Sexual Meditation: Faun's Room Yale (16mm) 2 min color
Sexual Meditation: Office Suite (16mm) 3 min color
Sexual Meditation: Open Field (16mm) 8 min color
Sexual Meditation: Hotel (16mm) 5 min color

1971
"The Pittsburgh Documents"

eyes (16mm) 35½ min color
Deus Ex (16mm) 33¼ min color
The Act of Seeing with one's own eyes (16mm)
    32 min color

1971
Foxfire Childwatch (16mm) 3 min color
Angels' (16mm) 2 min color
Door (16mm) 1¾ min color
Western History (16mm) 8¼ min color
The Trip to Door (16mm) 12¼ min color
The Peaceable Kingdom (16mm) 7¾ min color

1972
Eye Myth (16mm) 190 frames color
The Process (16mm) 8 min color
The Riddle of Lumen (16mm) 13½ min color
The Shores of Phos: a fable (16mm) 10 min color
The Presence (16mm) 2½ min color
The Wold Shadow (16mm) 2½ min color

1973
Sincerity (16mm) 25 min color
Gift (S8mm) 6½ min color
The Women (16mm) 3 min color

1974
Skein (16mm) 5 min color
Aquarien (16mm) 3 min color
Sol (16mm) 5 min color
Flight (16mm) 5½ min color
Dominion (16mm) 5 min color
Hymn to Her (16mm) 2½ min color
Clancy (16mm) 4½ min color
Star Garden (16mm) 22 min color
The Stars Are Beautiful (16mm) 19 min color;
    sound by Brakhage
The Text of Light (16mm) 71 min color
he was born, he suffered, he died (16mm) 7½ min
    color

1975
Sincerity II (16mm) 40 min color
Short Films: 1975 (16mm) 44 min color (divided
    into Parts I-X)

1976
Short Films: 1976 (16mm) 20 min color
Tragoedia (16mm) 35 min color
Gadflies (S8mm) 13½ min color
Sketches (S8mm) 10 min color
Airs (S8mm) 21 min color
Window (S8mm) 10 min color

Trio (S8mm) 8 min color
Desert (S8mm) 12½ min color
Rembrandt, Etc. and Jane (S8mm) 16 min color
Highs (S8mm) 7 min color
Absence (S8mm) 8 min color
The Dream, NYC, The Return, The Flower
    (S8mm) 21 min color

1977
Soldiers and Other Cosmic Objects (16mm) 22
    min color
The Governor (16mm) 58 min color
The Domain of the Moment (16mm) 14 min color

1978
Sincerity III (16mm) 38 min color
Duplicity (16mm) 23 min color
Duplicity II (16mm) 15 min color
Nightmare Series (16mm) 21 min color
Airs (16mm) 21 min color (first issued in 1976
    in S8mm)
Window (16mm) 10 min color (first issued in
    1976 in S8mm)
Trio (16mm) 8 min color (first issued in 1976 in
    S8mm)
Desert (16mm) 12½ min color (first issued in
    1976 in S8mm)
Rembrandt, Etc. and Jane (16mm) 16 min color
    (first issued in 1976 in S8mm)
Highs (16mm) 7 min color (first issued in 1976
    in S8mm)
Absence (16mm) 8 min color (first issued in
    1976 in S8mm)
The Dream, NYC, The Return, The Flower (16mm)
    21 min color (first issued in 1976 in S8mm)
Purity and After (16mm) 5½ min color
Centre (16mm) 9 min color
Bird (16mm) 4 min color
Thot Fal'n (16mm) 11½ min color
Burial Path (16mm) 9 min color
Sluice (16mm) 4 min color

1979
@ (16mm) 6 min color
Creation (16mm) 17½ min color
23rd Psalm Branch: Part I (16mm) 30 min color
    (first issued in 1966 in 8mm)

1980
23rd Psalm Branch: Part II (16mm) 70 min color
    (first issued in 1967 in 8mm)
Sincerity IV (16mm) 37 min color
Sincerity V (16mm) 40 min color

Duplicity III (16mm) 23 min color
Salome (16mm) 3 min color
Other (16mm) 4 min color
Made Manifest (16mm) 12 min color
Aftermath (16mm) 10 min color
Murder Psalm (16mm) 18 min color
Sexual Meditation No. 1: Motel (16mm)
     6 min color (first issued in 1970 in 8mm)
Songs 1-7 (16mm) 28 min color (first issued in
     1964 in 8mm)
Songs 8-14 (16mm) 34 min color (first issued in
     1964-1965 in 8mm)

1979-1981
Roman Numeral Series
     1979
I (16mm) 6 min color
II (16mm) 7½ min color
     1980
III (16mm) 3 min color
IV (16mm) 4½ min color
V (16mm) 4½ min color
VI (16mm) 12 min color
VII (16mm) 4½ min color
     1981
VIII (16mm) 4½ min color
IX (16mm) 3 min color

1981
Nodes (16mm) 4 min color
15 Song Traits (16mm) 47 min color (first issued
     in 1965 in 8mm)
RR (16mm) 15 min color
The Garden of Earthly Delights (35mm and
     16mm) 2¼ min color

1980-1982
Arabics
     1980
1 (16mm) 4 min color
2 (16mm) 4 min color
3 (16mm) 9 min color
     1981
4 (16mm) 7 min color
5 (16mm) 7 min color
6 (16mm) 11 min color
7 (16mm) 11 min color
8 (16mm) 7 min color
9 (16mm)
0 + 10 (16mm)
11   13   15   17   19
12   14   16   18

Brakhage films are available from:

Filmmakers' Cooperative
175 Lexington Ave.
New York, NY 10016

Canyon Cinema Cooperative
2325 Third St., Suite 338
San Francisco, CA 94107

London Film-makers' Cooperative
42, Gloucester Ave.
London NW 1, England

Some films are also available from:

Freunde der Deutschen Kinemathek eV
1 Berlin 30
Welserstrasse 25
West Germany

Cine Pro
Obere Waldstrasse 13
D 4500 Osnabruck
West Germany

Cooperative Des Cineastes
   Independants
3684 Boulevard St. Laurent
Montreal, Que H2X 2V4
Canada

MacMillan Films, Inc.
34 MacQuesten Pkwy., S
Mount Vernon, NY 10550

A three-program retrospective is available from:

The American Federation of Arts
41 E. 65th St.
New York, NY 10021

SELECTED BIBLIOGRAPHY

Arthur, Paul S. "Stan Brakhage: Four Films," *Artforum, 11*(5), Jan. 1973, pp. 41-45 [on *The Wonder Ring, Sirius Remembered, Song 13,* and *Fire of Waters*].

Barr, William R. "Brakhage: Artistic Development in Two Childbirth Films," *Film Quarterly, 29*(3), Spring 1976, pp. 30-34 [on *Window Water Baby Moving* and *Thigh Line Lyre Triangular*].

Bershen, Wanda. "Autobiography in Stan Brakhage's *23rd Psalm Branch," Field of Vision,* 2, 1977, pp. 1-5.

Blank, Ed. "On Shelf 22 Years, *Pittsburgh* Premieres: Festival Screens $150,000 Curiosity," *Pittsburgh Press,* June 10, 1979, E-1 [about the 1957 city-symphony Brakhage worked on and then was removed from].

Boultenhouse, Charles. "Pioneer of the Abstract Expressionist Film," *Filmwise,* 1, 1961, pp. 26-27 [on the new style of the "flying camera"].

Brakhage, Jane. "The Birth Film," *Film Culture,* 31, Winter 1963-64, pp. 35-36 [on *Window Water Baby Moving;* also in *Film Culture Reader,* 1970].

Callenbach, Ernest. "Films of Stan Brakhage," *Film Quarterly, 14*(3), Spring 1961, pp. 47-48 [on *Anticipation of the Night, Sirius Remembered, Wedlock House: An Intercourse, Cat's Cradle,* and *Window Water Baby Moving*].

Camhi, Gail. "Notes on Brakhage's *23rd Psalm Branch," Film Culture,* 67-68-69, 1979, pp. 97-108.

Camper, Fred. "*The Art of Vision:* A Film by Stan Brakhage," *Film Culture,* 46, Autumn 1967, pp. 40-44.

_____. "*23rd Psalm Branch* (Song XXIII) A Film by Stan Brakhage," *Film Culture,* 46, Autumn 1967, pp. 15-18.

_____. "*My Mtn. Song 27," Film Culture,* 47, Summer 1969, pp. 23-26.

_____. "*Sexual Meditation #1: Motel,* A Film by Stan Brakhage," *Film Culture,* 53-55, Spring 1972, pp. 101-104.

_____. "*Western History* and *The Riddle of Lumen," Artforum, 11*(5), Jan. 1973, pp. 66-71 [also on *Anticipation of the Night*].

_____. "The Super-8 Stan Brakhage," *Soho Weekly News,* Dec. 23, 1976 (p. 32) and Dec. 30 (p. 28) [on *Gadflies, Sketches, Airs, Window, Trio, Rembrandt, Etc.* and *Jane, Desert, Highs, Absence,* and *The Dream —N.Y.C. —The Return — The Flower*].

_____. *Stan Brakhage: A Retrospective.* Filmex '76. Los Angeles, 1976 [23 page catalog].

_____. *By Brakhage: Three Decades of Personal Cinema.* New York: American Federation of Arts, 1981 [8 page catalog].

Carroll, Noel. "The Other Cinema," *Soho Weekly News,* Feb. 22, 1979, pp. 50, 54 [on *Sincerity 1-3, Duplicity, Sluice, Thot-Fal'n,* and *Burial Path*].

Clark, Dan. *Brakhage.* New York: Film-Makers Cinematheque, 1966, 82 pages.

Cohen, Phoebe. "*Scenes From Under Childhood," Artforum, 11*(5), Jan. 1973, pp. 51-55.

_____. "Brakhage's *Sincerity III," Millennium Film Journal,* 4-5, 1979, pp. 153-156.

_____. "Brakhage's *I, II, III," Millennium Film Journal,* 7-8-9, 1980-81, pp. 234-237.

Creeley, Robert. "Mehr Licht..." *Film Culture,* 47, Summer 1969, pp. 22-23 [on *Anticipation of the Night* and light].

Curtis, David. Section of book *Experimental Cinema.* New York: Universe, 1971, pp. 130-33.

Davenport, Guy. "Two Essays on Brakhage and His Songs," *Film Culture,* 40, Spring 1966, pp. 9-12 [on *Songs 1-22*].

Delancey, Clinton. "A Varied Burst of Brakhage," *Village Voice,* June 21, 1973, p. 88 [on *Eye Myth, The Process, Riddle of Lumen, The Shores of Phos: A Fable, The Act of Seeing With One's Own Eyes, The Wold Shadow, The Presence, Room With a View, Faun's Room: Yale, Office Suite, Hotel, Open Field, Sincerity*].

Dunbar, Jennifer. "Stan Brakhage: Life behind the camera," *Boulder Monthly,* Sept. 1979, pp. 24-29, 74-75.

Dwoskin, Stephen. *Film Is: The International Free Cinema.* Woodstock: Overlook, 1975, pp. 145-52 [brief survey in this book].

Field, Simon. "Stan Brakhage: An Introduction," pp. 4-27 in the catalog *Stan Brakhage* published by the Arts Council of Great Britain in 1980 or 1981.

"Fourth Independent Film Award," *Film Culture*, 24, Spring 1962, p. 5 [awarded for *The Dead* and *Prelude*].

Gallo, William. "Filmmaker Stan Brakhage: 'Movies Weaken Your Mind'," *Denver*, Jan. 1976, pp. 48-51, 70-74.

Gordon, Eric Arthur. "Stan Brakhage's Critics," *Filmwise*, 1, 1961, pp. 16-18 [notes on opinions of Mekas, Parker Tyler, Raymond Borde, Arthur Knight, Ernest Callenbach].

Grossman, Manuel L. "Surrealism in *Dog Star Man*," *Dada/Surrealism*, 1972, pp. 71-77.

Haller, Robert A. "Stan Brakhage in Pittsburgh," *Field of Vision*, 9-10, 1980, pp. 8-11.
_____. "Stan Brakhage: Recent Directions," *Downtown Review*, 2(2), Spring 1980, pp. 18-19 [on *Creation*, and "abstract" cinema].

Hill, Jerome. "Brakhage and Rilke," *Film Culture*, 37, Summer 1965, pp. 13-14 [on first ten *Songs*].
_____. "Two Essays on Brakhage and His *Songs*," *Film Culture*, 40, Spring 1966, pp. 8-12 [on *Songs* 11-22].
_____. "*23rd Psalm Branch* (Song XXIII) A Film By Stan Brakhage," *Film Culture*, 46, Autumn 1967, pp. 14-15.
_____. "Brakhage's eyes," *Film Culture*, 52, Spring 1971, pp. 43-47.

Hills, Henry. "Hyperkinetic Stan/dards," *Cinemanews*, 77(6), Nov.-Dec. 1977, pp. 4-5 [on *Sincerity 2*, *Short Films 1975*, *Tragoedia*, and *The Governor*].

Hoberman, J. "Duplicitously Ours: Brakhage in New York," *Village Voice*, April 8, 1981, pp. 45-46.
_____. "Formal Documents of Power," *Village Voice*, Nov. 21, 1977, p. 43 [on *The Governor*].

Jenkins, Bruce and Carroll, Noel. "*Text of Light*," *Film Culture*, 67-68-69, 1979, pp. 135-138.

Johnson, Paul. "Brakhage: A Learned Language," *Village Voice*, Jan. 20, 1972.

Kelly, Robert. "Robert Kelly on *The Art of Vision*," *Film Culture*, 37, Summer 1965, pp. 14-15 [framed by letter to Jonas Mekas from Brakhage].

Kelman, Ken. "Perspective Reperceived: Brakhage's *Anticipation of The Night*" in P. Adams Sitney, ed., *The Essential Cinema, Essays on the Films in the Collection of Anthology Film Archives*, Vol. 1. N.Y.U. Press, 1975. pp. 234-239.
_____. "Animal Cinema: Four Frames," *Film Culture*, 63-64, 1977, pp. 25-27 [on *Mothlight*].

Kroll, J. "Up From the Underground," *Newsweek*, Feb. 13, 1967, pp. 117-119 [capsule summary of career].

Lamberton, Bob. "*23rd Psalm Branch* (Song XXIII) A Film by Stan Brakhage," *Film Culture*, 46, Autumn 1967, p. 15.

Landow, George. "*Flesh of Morning*," *Filmwise*, 1, 1961, pp. 20-21.

Lee, Douglas. "Discovering Stan Brakhage," *Film Library Quarterly*, 4(3), Summer 1971, pp. 23-32 [review of MoMA 1952-1970 Retrospective].

Levine, Charles. "Comments on Stan Brakhage and His Work," *Filmwise*, 1, 1961, pp. 3-4 [on *Anticipation of the Night* and *Window Water Baby Moving*].

Levoff, Daniel H. "Brakhage's *The Act of Seeing With One's Own Eyes*," *Film Culture*, 56-57, Spring 1973, pp. 73-81.

Maas, Willard. "A Love Affair: I talk to Myself about Stan Brakhage," *Filmwise*, 1, 1961, pp. 32-36.

Mapp, Thomas. "Comment," *Filmwise*, 1, 1961, pp. 22-23 [very brief survey of career to date].

Markopoulos, Gregory J. "Stille Nacht," *Filmwise*, 1, 1961, pp. 4-5 [two paragraph tribute].

McClure, Michael. "*Dog Star Man*," *Film Culture*, 29, Summer 1963, pp. 12-13.

Mekas, Jonas. *Movie Journal, The Rise of a New American Cinema, 1959-1971*. New York: Collier, 1972 [Extensive mention throughout this selection of commentary].
_____. "Movie Journal," *Village Voice*, March 30, 1972, p. 65 [on the "Pittsburgh documents"].
_____. "Movie Journal," *Village Voice*, Nov. 14, 1974, p. 96 [on *The Text of Light*].
_____. "Notes on Films of Joseph Cornell," *Castelli Gallery Catalog*, 1976 [Background on films Brakhage shot for Cornell].
_____. "Brakhage and the Structuralists," *Soho Weekly News*, Nov. 24, 1977, pp. 25, 38 [see also Brakhage's reply to Mekas in the letters column of the *Soho News* of Dec. 8, 1977].

Michelson, Annette. "Camera Lucida/Camera Obscura," _Artforum, 11_(5), Jan. 1973, pp. 30-37 [the Brakhage section, "Camera Obscura," is reprinted in _New Forms in Film_ (Montreaux, 1974)].

Nesthus, Marie. "The Influence of Olivier Messiaen on the Visual Art of Stan Brakhage in _Scenes From Under Childhood,_ Part One," _Film Culture,_ 63-64, 1977, pp. 39-51, 179-181.

_____. _Stan Brakhage._ Minneapolis/St. Paul: Film in the Cities and the Walker Art Center, 1979 [23 page monograph].

Pike, Robert. "A Letter From the West Coast," _Film Culture,_ 14, Nov. 1957, pp. 9-10 [has fragment from Brakhage letter explaining his new direction in the late 1950s].

Pruitt, John. "Stan Brakhage's _Sincerity,_ Reels One, Two, and Three," _Downtown Review, 1_(2), April 1979, pp. 9-11.

Renan, Sheldon. _An Introduction to the American Underground Film._ New York: Dutton, 1967 [biographical entry, pp. 118-127].

Richie, Donald. _Stan Brakhage: A Retrospective, 1952-1970._ Program notes the author once intended to reprint as a book. Assembled for the Museum of Modern Art, 36 pages.

Sainer, Arthur. "Stan Brakhage, 'the courage of perception'," _Vogue,_ Sept. 1, 1970 [on _Horseman, Woman and the Moth_ and _Sirius Remembered_].

Schultz, Victoria. "Independent Film," _Changes,_ May 1, 1972 [on _The Act of Seeing with one's own eyes_].

_____. "Stan Brakhage: Reflections on a Patriarchal Eye," _Changes,_ July 1972 [survey of films and aspirations].

Sharrett, Christopher. "Brakhage's Dreamscape," _Millennium Film Journal,_ 6, Spring 1980, pp. 43-49 [on the _Nightmare Series_].

Simon, Bill. "New Forms in Film," _Artforum,_ Oct. 1972, pp. 78-84 [on Pittsburgh trilogy].

Sitney, P. Adams. "Introductions to Stan Brakhage," _Filmwise,_ 1, 1961, pp. 28-31 [on _Anticipation of the Night, Flesh of Morning, Daybreak,_ and _The Dead_].

_____. "_Anticipation of the Night_ and _Prelude,_" _Film Culture,_ 26, Winter 1962, pp. 54-57.

_____. "Imagism in Four Avant-Garde Films," _Film Culture,_ 31, Winter 1963-64, pp. 15-21 [on _Dog Star Man,_ Part I; reprinted in _Film Culture Reader,_ 1970].

_____. "Avant Garde Film," _Afterimage,_ 2, Autumn 1970, pp. 8-13 [on _Lovemaking, Scenes from Under Childhood, 23rd Psalm Branch_].

_____. "The Idea of Morphology," _Film Culture,_ 53-55, Spring 1972, pp. 1-24 [on _Reflections on Black, Thigh Line Lyre Triangular, Way to Shadow Garden, Dog Star Man, My Mountain, Song 27, Anticipation of the Night_].

_____. _Visionary Film: The American Avant-Garde 1943-1978,_ New York: Oxford, 1979, chapters 6, 7, and 12.

Smith, Katherine. "Stan Brakhage: Transforming Personal Vision into a Rhythmic Structure," _Film Library Quarterly,_ 4(3), Summer 1971, pp. 43-47 [survey of 20 years of work].

Stoller, James. "Cinema 16: A Criticism and a Challenge," _New York Film Bulletin, 1_(20), Oct. 1960, pp. 1, 4-5 [request that Cinema 16 show Brakhage program, not haphazardly show single films].

Sutherland, Donald. "A Note on Stan Brakhage," _Film Culture,_ 24, Spring 1962, pp. 84-85 [on _The Dead_ and _Prelude_].

Talley, Dan. "Aspects of Defamiliarization in the Films of Stan Brakhage," _Substitute,_ May 1975, pp. 14-16 [on _Cat's Cradle_ and _Sirius Remembered_].

Taubin, Amy. "Packaging Brakhage," _Soho Weekly News,_ April 15, 1981, page unknown [mostly on _Murder Psalm_ and philosophical assumptions].

Tyler, Parker. "Stan Brakhage," _Film Culture,_ 18, April 1958, pp. 23-25 [on all films through _Loving_].

_____. "New Images: _Loving,_" _Film Quarterly,_ Spring 1959, pp. 50-53.

_____. "An Open Letter to Stan Brakhage from Parker Tyler," _Filmwise,_ 1, 1961, pp. 18-19 [expression of disenchantment over new direction of Brakhage's film-making].

Varela, Willie. "Fire of Vision," _Southwest Media Review,_ Spring 1981, pp. 35-37.

Youngblood, Gene. _Expanded Cinema._ New York: Dutton, 1970, pp. 87-91 [on _Dog Star Man_].

INDEX